Alone Across America on Horseback

LADY
LONG RIDER

BERNICE ENDE

FARCOUNTRY
PRESS

DEDICATION

To Linda James Benitt, my "Great Aunt Linda," the first woman to graduate from the Harvard T.H. Chan School (then the Harvard-MIT School for Health Officers), who stirred my imagination, and her sister, my grandmother Francis James Hoy, whose love of the horse I share.

ISBN: 978-1-56037-722-1

Front cover photograph © 2012 Emily McKee Morioka.
Back cover inset photograph by Sam Kaufman, © 2010 *Andrews County News.*

For more information about our books, write Farcountry Press, P.O. Box 5630, Helena, MT 59604; call (800) 821-3874; or visit www.farcountrypress.com.

Library of Congress Cataloging-in-Publication Data

Names: Ende, Bernice, author.
Title: Lady long rider : alone across America on horseback / Bernice Ende.
Description: Helena, MT : Farcountry Press, [2018] | Includes bibliographical references.
Identifiers: LCCN 2018014989 | ISBN 9781560377221 (paperback : alk. paper)
Subjects: LCSH: Ende, Bernice. | Horsemen and horsewomen--Travel--Biography.
Classification: LCC SF284.52.E53 A3 2018 | DDC 636.10092 [B] --dc23
LC record available at https://lccn.loc.gov/2018014989

 Produced and printed in the United States of America.

Printed on 100% Postconsumer Waste.

23   22   21   20   19   2   3   4   5   6

TABLE OF CONTENTS

This book took longer to write than all of my rides took to ride. I kept insisting, "I am a rider, not a writer." I owe much to many for their support.

For encouraging me through the ten years it took writing this book, I thank Larry Ziak and Jim Hammond who edited my early writings, and Constance See who devoted many hours gently pushing and suggesting. I owe many thanks and appreciation to Nina Lockwood and Gary Stine who pulled honest narrative from my lips, and to Rita Collins who continually prodded with "are you writing?" Thanks are also due Theodora Brennan who offered enormous support in every way and to Janna Pekaar who visited me on every ride. Special thanks to CuChullaine O'Reilly of the Long Riders' Guild for all that he does for the guild and for his continuing support and long-riding advice to me over the years.

Thank you Kathy Springmeyer, Will Harmon, and the team at Farcountry Press for your encouragement and confidence and for publishing this work. Also my thanks to C. W. Guthrie, author of eight books, including Glacier National Park's anniversary edition *The First 100 Years* and most recently a co-author of *Death and Survival in Glacier National Park*, who painstakingly filled in the gaps and smoothed out the rough edges of my manuscript and finally for putting the book into a presentable form. She has become a mentor and friend.

Long rides are long but they surely are not lone rides. I could not have made this many trips and traveled these many miles without the enormous support from the thousands of people who over the years extended their help—providing hot showers, food, water, and shelter—and who gave directions, encouragement, and interest. My thanks to all of you who so graciously helped me along the way.

And to my other sponsors who, by their generous support, transformed me from a vagabond to a respectful looking Long Rider I extend my deep appreciation and heartfelt thanks:

To Outfitters Supply, who have been with me since the beginning and provided the durable saddle packs, lightweight and sturdy hobbles, snaps, feed bags, water buckets, and the pack saddle. It is one thing to expect packs and saddles to hold up for a weekend or the occasional two-week trip into the wilderness, but it's quite another thing to expect packs and saddle to hold up to daily use for months and months and years and years. These do!

To Tucker Saddles. I write Tucker often to let them know how it feels to ride thousands of miles with their saddles. The saddle also doubles as a chair or a back rest at the end of a long day. I have ridden Tucker High Plains, Black Mountain, Gen 11, and Endurance Trail saddles for more than 30,000 miles of problem-free comfort for me and the horses. "Nothing comes between me and my horse but a Tucker Saddle."

To Skito Saddle Pads. I use Skito saddle pads that are custom fitted for the horses. It has not always been so. I have used all sorts of padding. The padding and the way I pad for long riding is very different than what a roping horse, endurance horse, or trail horse might have under its saddle. It took trial and error, but the advice from the folks at Skito was a leap forward for me in providing the ideal saddle pad fit for the horses I ride.

To SunBody Hats. Then there is the gear that I wear. Jimmy Pryor, owner of SunBody Hats, sent me the hat I presently wear to replace the one he had sent me previously. Hart was trying to eat that hat when the wind caught it and carried it away never to be seen again. When that happened I contacted Jimmy to tell him I didn't feel like a Long Rider without the SunBody hat. He sent me a new one right away. This hat protects me from the sun, shades my eyes, cools my shoulders, and looks great.

To Ariat Boots. When I first began these adventures, I picked up shoes—anything from tennis shoes to ill-fitting work boots—at second-hand stores as I went. Now I walk seven to ten miles in my Ariat Ropers every day without getting sore feet. I use steel, horseshoe-like cleats that prevent wear and tear on the heels.

To Mountain Vista Veterinary Services' DVM Nancy Haugan of Eureka, Montana. Nancy generously donated time and costs to vet check, vaccinate, and recommend treatment for health problems concerning the horses and Claire while we were in other parts of the country.

To Montana Mountain Horse Ranch and Swede Granstrom and Dottie Smith for many enjoyable hours of horse talk and for providing Montana Spirit, a great mountain and long-riding horse.

The Blacksmith Shop's Roger Robinson has brought a new level of hoof care for me. He provides me his special one-of-a-kind horse-shoes that are pre-shaped and ready for me to put on. They last many, many more miles than a regular shoe and allow me to ride safely on wet pavement and ice. I would not even think of riding without these horseshoes.

A special hat tip to Bridger Deville of Benchmark Maps for supply-ing me with maps to help me get there, wherever there happened to be.

And my thanks and appreciation to my other gracious sponsors who make it possible for me to long ride:

- Dream Catchers Therapeutics, who graciously donated Liska Pearl to my rides.
- Cashel Company, which provides me with fly and mosquito pro-tection.
- Source Micronutrients for providing healthy, effective nutritional supplements for *all* of us, horses, dog, and human.
- Climb-On Intensive Skin Repair has been providing great skin care products for years.
- Equine Veterinary Services who came to my aid when I lost Honor.
- Tangleo's Custom Handmade Cinches, the finest cinches I have ever used.
- Find-A-Ranch Realty who donated Hart when I stood hopelessly without a horse in Texas.

I also owe a special thank you to the Shoshone-Bannock Tribes of Fort Hall, Idaho, and to the Blackfeet Nation and Confederated Salish and Kootenai Tribes of the Flathead Nation in Montana. Thank you also to the Ganadonegro families of the Alamo Navajo Tribe west of Albuquerque, New Mexico. They rescued me on my 5,000 mile ride in 2007. Caught in a snowstorm, I stayed for nearly a week. And finally, thank you to the Margret and Charles (now deceased) Gwinn families, members of the Confederated Tribes of the Yakima Nation in Washington. The tribe not only allowed me to cross private tribal forest land, twice, but the Gwinn family took in a very tired, footsore long rider and let me rest long enough to ride on. Thank you, to all our culturally rich Native American tribes for opening your doors to me.

To the Ende of the Trail website hostesses Lisa Eades, Marlane Quade, Eileen Kelly, Emily McKee, and Linda Vigil who have all done a terrific job handling the website over the years—a sincere thank you for all that you have done.

Thank you, all of you everywhere, who have made my long rides possible. We are now friends, though many of us were strangers then, and you graciously bestowed kindness upon a band of rovers you had never met. You are all a testimony to the generosity of our country and a reflection of the goodness that fills our land.

Date: 07-12-15
To: Melissa Anderson – *Cavalier County Republican Newspaper*
From: CuChullaine O'Reilly – The Long Riders' Guild
Subject: Lady Long Rider
CC: North American Long Rider Bernice Ende

Dear Ms. Anderson,

CuChullaine O'Reilly of the Long Riders' Guild here, replying to your questions regarding North American Long Rider Bernice Ende.

Before I comment on your questions regarding Bernice, allow me to explain the mission of the Long Riders' Guild, the world's first international association of equestrian explorers and long-distance travelers. With members in forty-five countries, every major equestrian explorer alive today belongs to The Guild.

More than a hundred of these extraordinary Long Riders are also Fellows of the Royal Geographical Society. The Guild also oversees the Long Riders' Guild Academic Foundation. It's mission is to provide an open-source academic forum where scientists, poets, authors, and equestrian experts can share their wisdom with the public.

The LRG accepts no advertising of any kind, and is therefore a trusted resource for thousands of regular visitors.

I have provided this information to you so as to place Bernice's equestrian accomplishments into their proper perspective—moreover, because of my work as a researcher, author, and publisher (and co-founder of LRG), in their proper *historical* perspective.

What is ironic about the timing of your questions is that the Long Riders' Guild is about to publish news regarding the fact that Bernice has passed the 25,000-mile mark during her many journeys.

While she quietly describes herself as a simple "Lady Long Rider," Bernice is far more than that. No other living female equestrian traveler

x

has done as many journeys or ridden as many miles as Bernice. Nor has any other living female equestrian traveler spent as many consistent years in the saddle as Bernice has. And though you didn't ask, let me explain that the result of those journeys resulted in Bernice becoming what the Japanese describe as a Ningen Kokuhô. This is a popular term for those rare individuals who have been declared to be "Preservers of Important Intangible Cultural Properties." Bernice is a living treasure trove of endangered Long Rider knowledge. That is another way in which you can detect her importance, i.e. by the willingness with which Bernice shares the hard-won lessons of the road, which she gained from years in the saddle.

What you also did not ask was if the journey Bernice is currently on is of historical significance [2014–2016, 8,000 miles]. Perhaps no one has explained that riding "ocean to ocean" across North America is incredibly difficult on a logistical, emotional, and physical level.

Few people have ever completed an equestrian journey between the two oceans in either direction. But no one in history has ever attempted to ride ocean to ocean in both directions on one journey! Thus the fact that Bernice is not only undertaking that difficult journey, but is doing so well, demonstrates the depth of her expertise.

Instead of drawing attention to herself, Bernice has used the ride to recognize the hard-won political liberties gained by the suffragettes. As you may already know, because of the historical importance of this journey, Bernice has been honored by carrying the Guild's flag to both oceans. However, that is a collective honor. When a person is admitted into the Guild, they are not awarded a silver trophy, a blue ribbon, or a shiny big belt buckle. All they receive is the respect accorded to them by their fellow equestrian explorers, a respect earned by an elite group of men and women scattered around the globe, all of whom, like Bernice, chose to saddle up their horse and set out on a life-changing equestrian journey.

In closing, there are millions of people who ride horses. In stark contrast, there are only a handful of Long Riders scattered around the world.

And even among the Long Riders there are only a rare few, like Bernice Ende, whose journeys transcend miles and instead resonate in countless lives for years to come.

Kind regards,
CuChullaine O'Reilly FRGS

PHOTO COURTESY OF JOHN CRANDELL.

AN INTRODUCTION
TO LONG RIDING

In the midst of space-age, high-speed technologies, a band
of humans has slowed down the earth and sky sweeping
past them by seeing the world from the back of a horse.
They are called Long Riders.
—QUOTED FROM THE LONG RIDERS GUILD

The equestrian long ride was never a once-in-a-lifetime dream for me, but somehow it has become my life. As early as my first ride, I felt like I'd climbed into my own skin, but it took years learning to wear it well.

I'm not sure when the name for me—Lady Long Rider—got started. It seemed to have happened when I first began my long rides. Whenever a man or a woman approached me, they were startled to see that the stranger riding a horse following a dog was not a man as they expected. Since that first long ride, I have heard many times "Oh, I thought you were a guy!" and just as often I hear "It takes a lot of balls to do what you are doing." But I have no balls.

Nevertheless I take it as an intended compliment and proudly ride as the woman I am.

As a lady long rider I try to appear tidy, pleasant, and willing to stop and share my adventure. No one is a stranger. I enjoy visiting with people and sharing stories, and to my delight I receive invitations to speak at schools, churches, and private homes.

Whether it's a male or female in the saddle, the essential element in a long ride is the rider's relationship with the horses. There are exhausting hardships and numerous life-threatening risks on a long ride. The only way to endure the hardships and survive the risks is to infuse absolute trust between rider and horse. The rider plans and plots the route, sees to it there is food and water for herself and the horses along the way, shoes the horses and doctors them when they need it, and guides the horses through all kinds of country, weather, and threatening situations. Always alert and often wary of new surroundings, the gallant, trusting horses carry the rider and the packs of supplies the thousands of miles that make up a long ride. If well cared for, the horses will enjoy the journey.

I am not the first lady long rider by any means. In 1910, sharpshooter Nan Aspinwall was a headline act in Buffalo Bill's Wild West Show. The showmen argued about whether a woman could ride from the Pacific to the Atlantic alone. Nan set off in September to prove it was possible. Mounted on her thoroughbred, Lady Ellen, this first Lady Long Rider carried a letter from San Francisco Mayor P. H. McCarthy addressed to his colleague Mayor William Gaynor in New York. During Nan's journey, she refused to allow anyone else to care for Lady Ellen, even to the point of shoeing the horse herself fourteen times. After months on the road, Nan arrived in New York astride Lady Ellen on July 13, 1911, becoming the first woman to ride alone across the United States.

A year later, in 1912, Alberta Claire made one of the most remarkable rides of the early twentieth century. The daughter of an English sea captain who settled in frontier Wyoming, young Alberta rode off on an 8,000-mile journey that took her from Wyoming to Oregon, south to California, across the deserts of Arizona, and on to a triumphant arrival in New York City. Alberta Claire undertook her long ride for two reasons. Though few people now recall, in 1912, the Suffragette Movement was in full swing. But women were still denied the right to vote, and polite society expected women to ride in a side saddle. Alberta made her ride to promote the then revolutionary ideas of a woman's right to vote and her right to ride astride!

Lady long rider, Nan Aspinwall.

After former president and 1912 Bull Moose Party candidate Theodore Roosevelt endorsed women's suffrage during his campaign in the presidential election of that year, the side saddle, which had been used since antiquity, disappeared from use almost overnight thanks to Alberta Claire and women like her. Eight years later, in 1920, women got to vote.

I did not discover Ana Beker until many years into my own long riding. I remember thinking her ride makes mine look like a cakewalk. In 1950 at age thirty, Ana rode 17,000 miles from Argentina to Canada, alone. Ana began planning her long ride after hearing a lecture in the 1940s by the world-famous Swiss-born Argentine professor, writer, and horseman Aimé Tschiffely, who had ridden 10,000 miles from Argentina to Washington, D.C. in the 1920s. Ana challenged Tschiffely's scoffing statement that she, a woman, could not make such a ride. Ana set out to prove she could. Furthermore, she intended to go farther than Tschiffely. And she did!

The International Long Riders Guild defines an *equestrian long ride* as one thousand continuous miles. Most of the long riders ride a thousand miles or more once. In 2008, as I neared 10,000 miles of equestrian travel in three long rides, I remember thinking enthusiastically, "Now I'll really be a long rider." But it didn't happen. I didn't feel like a truly bona fide long rider. It wasn't until my eleventh year of long riding, with six rides and 25,000 hard miles strung out behind me, having just ridden from the northwest corner of Montana to the Atlantic Ocean, that I felt, for the first time in my life, a real sense of accomplishment.

As of this writing, I have been long riding for thirteen years and ridden 29,000 miles in seven rides. I never imagined I would fill this many years with so many miles in the saddle, or that I would come to love such a life as I now know.

Bernice Ende. PHOTO COURTESY OF LYDIA HOPPER.

CHAPTER ONE

MY MONTANA

Living is a form of not being sure,
not knowing what's next or how.
—AGNES DE MILLE

I came to Montana's remote northwest corner in 1993 on the heels of divorce and illness. Several years earlier, my husband and I had purchased property with a log cabin as a vacation home. I went there and stayed; it was the ending of one of my *long rides* of life and the beginning of another. I know now and was beginning to know then that there are many kinds of long rides. There are the long rides of school, job, military, marriage, and motherhood. Life is a long ride, "a journey of transition and transformation, of discovery marked with points of passage," as William Bridges so eloquently wrote in his book *The Way of Transition*. It is a time of learning, marked with deep-felt, often painful endings and wonderful, never-imagined beginnings.

I think I began long riding as a child on my parents' dairy farm in central Minnesota. After watching black-and-white reruns of Roy Rogers, Hopalong Cassidy, and the Lone Ranger, I would sprint to the kitchen to announce, "Mom, I need a sandwich, I'm riding to the pasture." In my five-year-old mind it was a great distance and I would need nourishment. I would bridle Spot, our family's aging Welsh pony, lead him over to our Chevy car, and climb up on the hood so I was high enough to straddle Spot's back. We'd hobble along (a child's version

of Don Quixote), facing the greatest of adventures—a long ride in my child's mind. But the calling to ride and the call to Montana goes back long before me.

My grandmother, Francis Linda James, is described in family records as "an artist, an intellectual stimulant, a gentle aristocrat, who had flower gardens and bird sanctuaries, and executive ability, fearless, a student of science, philosophy and astronomy." She was all those things, but it was her love of horses and her passion for adventure that in 1912 stirred her to leave St. Paul, Minnesota, for a vacation in Montana. She stayed to teach in a country school and married a cowboy, Charlie Hoy. Charlie was the son of Abraham Lincoln "Link" Hoy who settled in the Bynum-Choteau area in 1886-1887. (Hoy Coulee, west of Bynum up against the Rocky Mountain Front, is named for Link Hoy.)

My grandmother's Minnesota upbringing was a sharp contrast to my grandfather's life as a cowboy and the life she would have in Montana. Her parents were Easterners from a world of books, art, and travel. I can't help but imagine that eyebrows rose and murmurings were heard throughout stately Minnesota homes when Francis Linda James boarded the Great Northern Railway train headed for the wild un-knowns of Montana. She went for the adventure and she stayed for Charlie, their "home on the range," and the freedom women enjoyed in the West that was not socially acceptable in the East.

Francis and Charlie homesteaded on the Rocky Mountain Front. The black-and-white photographs of my grandfather on a bucking horse that my grandmother sent to her parents in Minnesota show the land the horse bucked against was like no other. There were no trees, no lawn, just a rough log cabin plopped on bare earth and a horizon that stretched on forever. She later compiled letters and illustrated a book about her years in Montana. It was titled *A Little Grey Home in the West*. Her colored pencil sketches show a tidy, sparse, but comfortable interior of two small rooms, rugs, a round oak table, and even a mirror.

In 1916, a long drought drove my grandparents from their Montana home to Minnesota. My mother, Cornelia Francis Hoy, was born in Montana six months before they left for Minnesota.

I did not actually know my grandmother. I only know of her. While she was in Montana, she was dragged by a horse and later developed epilepsy. She died at the young age of fifty-three. But I imagined my grandmother's Montana years were happy ones, and it was her yellowed black-and-white photographs and *A Little Grey Home in the West* sketches that would all these years later lure me to follow her path to Montana.

ON MY TOES

During the twenty years before I moved to Montana, I taught classical ballet and related dance exercise programs in Minneapolis, Portland, Seattle, and San Francisco. My beginnings in ballet started when my mother took me and my sisters to see the Lipizzaners when they were performing in Minneapolis. I was intrigued by the strength and graceful movements of the horses and the masterful elegance of the riders in bringing out the natural athletic ability and willingness of the horse to perform. The training and performance is known by the French term for training: dressage. Later on there were other influences. I saw Walt Disney's 1963 film *Miracle of the White Stallions* about the 1945 U.S. evacuation of the famous Lipizzaner stallions from the Spanish Riding School in Vienna, Austria, to save them from the bombing raids. Then, sometime later, while sitting in a laundromat waiting for my clothes to dry, I read a *Time* magazine article about the American prima ballerina Cynthia Gregory and became even more captivated by ballet. As a rider, dance was good body and mental training for dressage. As a woman, ballet provided graceful body discipline and self-confidence, and the movements—done well—were both challenging and satisfying. I started taking ballet lessons, but I never imagined I would take it as far as I did.

As a seventeen-year-old high school graduate, I hungered to know more than my Minnesota surroundings. While waitressing at a café, I was lured west by a young man working construction for the summer. I followed him to Washington. A short time later, he went back to

Minnesota, but I stayed. I supported myself by waitressing, washing logging trucks for Weyerhaeuser, training horses, giving riding lessons, and working at a gas station. Eventually, I bought a house in Long Beach, Washington. I married.

In the 1990s, my husband and I drifted apart and then divorced. The divorce affected me more than I thought it would or could. My long brown hair began to fall out. The name given for this unsightly condition is alopecia, a fancy name from Latin for "hair loss." I had alopecia universalis, a severe form, leaving me with no eyebrows or eyelashes. The embarrassment of my baldness doomed me to always wear a bandanna over my head, and of course it affected my personal life in many ways. I managed to complete the classes I was leading as a dance and fitness instructor, but then I left Washington and hunkered down in the "getaway" cabin my ex-husband and I had bought in Trego, Montana. Within a year, he was killed in a car accident.

For many months I walked around in my log cabin, very alone, very sorry for myself, and very broke. Then, with the help of newfound friends, I pulled myself together and established a very unorthodox ballet studio. These times were the beginning of memorable chapters in my life, a time of growth and transformation, a successful and rewarding time of community support and new friends.

BACK ON MY TOES

My one-room dance studio, complete with woodstove and outhouse, reminded me of photographs I had seen of the one-room schoolhouse where my grandmother taught school. In 1997, the Trego Hall became the home of the Community Dance Studio. The year 1947 is etched in the building's old cement foundation and it has long provided a central gathering place for local residents.

Recounted stories tell of Saturday night dances—parents and friends, young and old, dancing to lively fiddle and accordion music, their children dozing on wooden benches wrapped in dreams, while a cold, white winter moved through its season. The sounds of dancing feet were

The community hall in Trego, Montana.

embedded in the walls of this old building long before my young students worked out complicated ballet movements in point shoes.

No child's dream of dancing was turned away; I would always encourage, "Come anyway, we'll work something out." Such an unorthodox studio would have been hard to find, and yet we had traditional year-end recitals and a small performing group who entertained at local schools, nursing homes, the county fair, or any local event welcoming our creative efforts. Support came from parents, grandparents, friends, and the Sunburst Community Services Foundation, a non-profit organization in nearby Eureka.

Montana has a rich and colorful blend of tradition and liberalism—of roughness and culture. In this tiny unassuming community, young students, often from bare-bone, dirt-floor homes, learned the art of classical ballet. I was never under the illusion that I was preparing students for a professional dance life, but I did have thorough training, which provided these students with quality Royal Academy of Dance (RAD) classes. I emphasized correct upright posture, balance, coordination, confidence, the ability to express themselves within a group, focus, and presentation—skills that might adhere to their bones and complement whatever life they would grow into.

The Trego Hall was heated by a double-barrel woodstove made from two fifty-five-gallon oil drums stacked one on top of the other. Parents who couldn't afford classes for their children would instead trade me firewood, morning "fire duty," or food. To banish winter's cold, someone had to fire up the stove at least five hours before afternoon classes began.

Most of my students walked from the tiny Trego School up the road to my studio. Many homeschoolers participated in the program and were driven to classes by parents who often waited in the hall on long wooden benches made by a local handyman over fifty years ago.

When temperatures dropped below zero and the big stove's heat was insufficient for the large open hall, young dancers clutched hand-made portable wooden ballet barres wearing mittens and a cap. "Ms. Ende, I have to go pee" meant stopping class, bundling the young four- and five-year-olds in boots, coats, and mittens, and then sending them trudging through snow to the outhouse accompanied by an older student. I watched them all the time through the window as I continued on with the class. I purchased used tights, slippers, and leotards from secondhand stores in nearby towns, acquiring enough ballet attire for every student even if parents were unable to provide such extravagances. Thanks to the community arts and education support from western Montana's Sunburst Foundation, we mounted the dazzling, if not legendary, "Not Quite the Nutcracker" production each year.

This period of my life was a new beginning for me. A beginning far beyond anything I could have imagined when I first arrived in such a despairing state of mind. The success I met within this isolated rural community was not all my doing. It really took parents, grandparents, private sponsors, and community members that cared about their tiny spot on the map and the children that grew from it.

Today the Trego Hall is called the Trego Civic Center, and it's fitted with modern indoor plumbing, but the historic outhouse remains. The hardwood floor continues to support dancing feet with energetic square dancers and wedding dances. A new roof and siding has brought a neat, maintained look to the community hall where, depending upon the time of year, you will find an Easter egg hunt in progress, a community Thanksgiving dinner, or the local Trego Christmas Bazaar taking place.

Forty miles south of Trego is the prosperous ski resort town of Whitefish. I opened the Whitefish School of Classical Ballet two years after opening the Trego Studio. I ran this program through the Whitefish Parks and Recreation Department, and it supported me for six years. Classes were held in a small log cabin fitted with ballet barres and mirrors the city owned. Students came from more affluent professional families with children preparing for further education and professional lives. This became another successful program of parents and students—a gathering of wonderful people that I came to know and love.

The drive from my cabin to Whitefish took an hour and a half on a good day. At home, I had to park my 1967 turquoise Ford Falcon on the main road and walk an eighth of a mile through deep snow to the car, often carrying the car battery I had taken out the night before and brought inside my cabin to keep warm. On terribly cold days, I took red coals from my log cabin's woodstove, placed them on a metal garbage can lid, pulled it to the road with a sled, and placed them under the oil pan to warm the engine. Otherwise the old car would never have started as the oil had nearly frozen.

Horses had re-entered my life shortly after arriving in Montana. First came a little wild, neglected white pony I called "Little Pony." Then came Sarah, an enormous Belgian draft horse. Then Babe, a horse I had owned when I lived in Long Beach, Washington, was returned to me. I began offering dressage lessons and training horses in the summer. For nearly ten years, many students from my ballet program also participated in the riding program held at my picturesque cabin.

SOMEHOW NOT ENOUGH

Times were good. I had made many friends and I felt the warm glow of having contributed something worthwhile to the youths of the communities where I lived and worked. I was pleased with what I was doing and it was very satisfying, but somehow it was not enough. My alopecia plagued me. I was embarrassed by my baldness and always wore a scarf on my head. It had been years since long brown hair hung down the middle of my back. Much has grown back now, but at that time in my life I still looked sickly even though I remained strong in every other way. Perhaps not emotionally, but physically I remained strong as a horse, no pun intended. Day after day, I taught children and visited with families and friends, and enjoyed every minute of it. But I always returned home alone.

The truth was, I was lonely. For years after coming to Montana I'd been drawn toward, or maybe it was infatuated with, someone I had known since I was a teenager, but I refused to believe he could possibly ever love me. I don't think I loved myself enough to think anyone could or would love me. My baldness kept me from even entertaining the thought of an intimate relationship. I deeply wanted to be with this man, yet nothing within me would let me reach out to him or let him get close to me. I drove myself crazy thinking about it. I can only explain it as emptiness, a deficiency in my life that gnawed at me.

CHAPTER TWO

SOMETHING PRETTY
INTERESTING TO DO

Why did I leave on my first long ride? Where did I get such an idea? Some said it must have been a calling of sorts. But the idea of riding long and slow came in the summer of 2004. I clearly remember the day and circumstances.

I'd been training a couple of three-year-olds for the McCurry Ranch in Trego where they raise Tenneessee Walking Horses. I was riding one horse and leading the other. We were stopped on a steep mountain grade overlooking the Whitefish Range of the Kootenai National Forest. The two horses grazed on sweet mountain clover. At my side was my dog Claire.

Claire had come into my life a few years earlier. One sunny March day, I was out riding on a countryside road when I caught a glimpse of two puppies lying in the snow in the ditch on the side of the road. One was lifeless, the other growled out a warning. I slid off my horse Babe's bare back and struggled over the snowbank and through the deep snow in the ditch. All the while, the tiny puppy, barely alive, growled with fear. I was wearing heavy gloves and reached down and picked up the pitiful, still growling puppy, then climbed back up on Babe, putting the puppy in my lap. As we rode, her growling stopped and the clear thump, thump, thump of her wagging tail beat against my thigh.

Her shabby coat was calico and she had a black mask, with one blue eye and one half brown and half blue eye. I called her a rare breed of unknown origin and named her Claire. I didn't know it at the time,

Claire, a rare breed of unknown origin.

but Claire was a remarkable dog and stands out in my life as a faithful, benevolent companion. We would walk and ride 20,000 adventurous miles together.

Now on this summer day in 2004, Claire stood stock-still, keenly aware of something in the air between us. I know it sounds crazy, but as I sat in the saddle looking out over the impressive Whitefish Range, I saw what I can only describe as a "vision." I don't know what else I could call it. What flashed before me in a moment of instantaneous imagery, like a black-and-white movie, was myself, grubby and haggard, packed and traveling across a desert, mounted upon a horse I did not recognize. Even more powerful than the image was what filled my whole being, the idea was so complete in its message.

In this vision, the summer sun pressed down on me as I sat absorbing this wild, inconceivable idea. "What had just happened? Where did *that* come from?" Was it a dreamer's wish, or a thinly veiled taste of hope mesmerizing me? Whatever it was, this thought or vision, like a sprouting seed in its first moments reaching toward the sun, had life. Please, believe me—I am sensible enough to have reasoned with this fanciful notion of my destiny. My mind quickly replied, "I don't have enough money," I resisted. "I need horses." "I don't know, maybe next year, maybe," I said to myself in purposeful doubt. But the idea burrowed in, plopped itself on my couch, and screamed in my face as I went about my daily chores. It haunted my dreams and would not leave. I could not for the life of me stop this idea from possessing me.

When I could no longer stand the depth of this secret idea that was manifesting in me, I confided in two friends, Theresa Vermeulen and her husband Oscar Pride. Theresa and Oscar were the set designer and costume designer extraordinaire for the Trego Community Dance Studio. Oscar had spent most of his life managing a cattle ranch in Colorado, and he continued to live and breathe "cowboy" even into his retirement years. I felt confident he wouldn't laugh at this wacko idea. And what does Oscar say? He said what would turn out to be the mantra I would hear over and over and over again in the years to come from people all over the nation. "I have always wanted to take a long horseback ride like that—just get on my horse and ride." He then handed me his old .44 revolver and added, "Go for it." Yes, I would "go for it," but I needed horses.

O. V. and Evelyn McCurry were already iconic figures in Trego when I first met them. In the late 1960s, they had helped bring Trego's tiny public school together, and they owned several businesses in the community, including the Trego Trailer Park. "Mac," as he was known to most people in the community, was eighty-seven, squarely built, and nearly blind. He wore a variety of hats atop his balding head that overflowed with stories. In contrast, his wife Evelyn, a young ninety-one-year-old, stood tall and slender. After sixty years together, they both moved with canes as one. Rarely were they apart. Both had served in World War II: Evelyn Fahlgren was a lieutenant commander in the Navy, and Mac served as a boatswain's "bosun's" mate and chief warrant officer (CW04). They met in China in 1948. Imagine the stories they could tell! They married in 1949. Evelyn resigned her commission and became a Navy wife. They lived in California and then Washington. Mac retired from the Navy in 1957 and in 1958 purchased the Fahlgren

Ranch in Trego from Evelyn's mother. The ranch had been in the family since 1917. Mac and Evelyn moved to the ranch in 1960.

Evelyn and Mac had been raising foundation line Tennessee Walking Horses for over thirty years. I had been admiring their herd of twenty or so horses for years before meeting them. Mac knew I rode and asked me if I might want to ride some of his horses. That's how we met. I had been training the McCurry horses during my summer months for five years when the urge to long ride came upon me. With an uncommitted question, I asked Mac, "What do you think about me taking a couple of your horses for a ride, a long ride?"

"Well, how long is long?" Mac wanted to know. By this time I had conceived of where I would ride. "From Trego, Montana, to Albuquerque, New Mexico," I told him. Mac had an ancient, adventurous soul. He sort of sat back in his chair and gave it some thought. Finally he replied in a slow, hesitant voice. "Well," he said, "that is a long ride isn't it, might just be something pretty interesting to do." A grin came over his face, his mind setting out on the adventure.

Originally, I started training a couple of four-year-old Walking Horses from Mac's herd, but I quickly realized the skill of taking two horses was more than I was ready for. In the end, I took only one, a strong, big-boned, 16-hand Tennessee Walking Horse named Pride. I had handled him on and off for two years at the McCurry Ranch. He was a spirited, flashy sorrel containing not an ounce of trust when I first began working with him.

Throughout the fall of 2004 when I spoke to others of my projected ride, I spoke with absolute conviction. "I am riding to New Mexico on a horse next summer," I would assert. I heard my voice saying the impossible. I told a few other people until I had no way of backing out. I had convinced myself I could do it and the idea had such a firm grip on me that I stopped thinking about anything except how I would ride— this ride.

A few friends besides Theresa and Oscar and the McCurry's offered support, but I was unprepared for the bombardment of resistance I encountered. People declared, "You'll get yourself killed." "There's so damn many goofballs out there, are you nuts?" "What the hell do ya wanna do something like that, it's crazy." "Good grief, you're fifty years old, you'll never make it."

After a while, single-mindedness set in. I refused to listen to both the friends who supported my madness and the naysayers who punctured me with doubt. I had enough of my own insecurities racing through my head without hearing discouraging remarks from others.

I hesitated calling my sister Mary Ann. I so wanted my big sister's approval. She and I were the horse girls in the family. Mary Ann was a serious rider who'd considered a career in the equine industry before becoming a schoolteacher. I looked up to her. I wanted her sharing in the excitement of this adventure. I would surprise her.

Five months into my planning, I was still struggling with a route. Maps covered the walls and were spread out over the floors. It was then that I finally picked up the phone and called my sister, who still had no idea of my gigantic plan of riding 2,000 miles to see her. My sister is by nature more conservative in her actions and more cautious than I am. I'd been the daredevil-reckless rider as a child, not her. I suppose it was naive of me to think her reaction would be anything but what it was. It horrified her to think I'd be attempting such an absurd ride. After an hour struggling back and forth with why, how, and when, I got off the phone, sprawled on the floor, and shed tears of disappointment. My sister adamantly opposed my riding from Montana to New Mexico!

In my enthusiasm about the long ride, I had selfishly neglected the fact that those who loved me—my sisters most assuredly—would be put under constant worry for my safety. But for me, the window of opportunity was open and I had one leg dangling out. I was single, had no children, and both my parents had passed away years before. My siblings and their families were doing fine; no one needed my help. No one needed me. I was fifty, I was restless, and I needed change. I had to go. And Mac might be right. It might be "something pretty interesting to do."

MONTANA TO
NEW MEXICO
1ST LONG RIDE

MAY TO SEPTEMBER 2005
2,000 MILES

CHAPTER THREE

LIONS AND TIGERS AND BEARS, OH MY!

I long to rapture among the sounds of rustling evergreens,
dancing creeks and birds abound . . .
I long to lose my self under silent moons, eternal stars,
worlds not yet found.
—BERNICE ENDE

B etween my legs is a mass of jittery horseflesh. What is it that agitates Pride like this: a bear, a cougar, wolves? Something a horse can smell but a human cannot? No, it wasn't bear, cougar, or wolf, although in Montana it surely could have been! Somehow Pride had sensed what we were about to do. We were taking the first steps of a very long journey into strange lands and unknown adventures. Pride felt the same nervousness that I felt. He wanted to go back home, and, truthfully, so did I. If I turn north I go back to the safety of home. If I turn south I keep moving on a journey I had scarcely begun and for which I was already riddled with doubts about the wisdom or madness of riding 2,000 miles from the northwest corner of Montana to Albuquerque, New Mexico, to see my older sister. Faced with the immediacy of my first night out and Pride's unexpected nervousness, which barely exceeded my own, I wanted to forget the whole damn thing, go back and try it at another time, and yet . . . I could not. The only thing to do was keep moving south until the edginess wore off.

It wasn't easy letting go of my life when the time finally came to set forth. I cried as I packed my final bags, trepidation dripping from

my tan cheeks. This journey began as all journeys do, with an ending. I didn't know it at the time, but I packed away part of me, leaving behind someone I once had been and would never be again.

Earlier in the day, friends gathered in Trego to bid "safe journey." They brought parting gifts—a charm, a book, a journal, oatmeal cookies—possibly thinking they'd never see me again. I tried creating a clean, confident image of myself as I set out on my journey. I wore a white, long-sleeve cotton shirt tucked into blue jeans, a black vest, riding boots, and a straw hat with a pretty but, I would find out later, completely worthless broad brim. An assortment of secondhand bags in varying colors and shapes hung from the saddle horn in front of my legs. The bags were filled with food, vet supplies, a gun, an extra pair of socks and underwear, toiletry items, a portable fence, and a tent. I was obviously a "greenhorn," and I surely wouldn't have acted so bravely, so foolishly sure of myself, had I foreseen the storm I was casting myself toward.

MAY 5, 2005, FIRST NIGHT ON THE TRAIL

I bid farewells to my friends and the McCurry's shortly after two o'clock in the afternoon and officially began my first long ride. It was typical northwest Montana weather for May, cool and overcast. I traveled twelve anxious miles then chose a spot near a small creek with grass enough to satisfy Pride. I strung a portable electric fence wire from tree to tree, creating a small pen, then began assembling my tent. My watch read six o'clock when I took another bite of an oatmeal cookie and gave Claire the rest. I felt a mixture of apprehensiveness and lightheartedness. Everything seemed idyllic; after months of laborious preparations I had arrived at my first campsite.

Suddenly, Pride began recklessly moving around inside the wire fence. The flimsy portable fence would never hold him if he bolted. I put hobbles on him, holding his front two legs together. He hopped like a rabbit in the confines of his small pen. He'd stop short, blow a loud snort out his nose, and fix his gaze to the south, clearly troubled by something I could not see or hear. I took the hobbles off and tied him to a sturdy tree near the tent. Less than half an hour of light remained, and it began to drizzle.

Pride began pawing with his front hoof. He tore at the dirt around the tree, thrusting himself, pitching his weight at the tree, lunging from side to side. I unsuccessfully tried calming him with apple treats. Like a mad dog, he began pawing with both front feet, biting at the rope. Pride would hurt me, not meaning to, but in this state of mind he'd easily hurt me if I wasn't careful. I managed, with great difficulty, to put the saddle on his back. He must have thought he was going home, as this did calm him. But the calm lasted only minutes. He swung around, knocking me to my hands and knees, barely missing me with his steel horseshoes.

"He's either going to break his halter or his neck or mine," I thought, watching him while on my knees, rolling the bedroll, tent, and bags haphazardly together. It would be the first and last time I used a tent on this ride. Whatever was out there, I would have to deal with it in blackness. I stepped into the stirrup and swung myself up and onto a horse that was determined to go home. The unbalanced packs and saddle I'd managed to get on Pride with difficulty and haste were not securely on, not with Pride's nervous dance, which pitched me right and left, but if I got off now to balance the packs I'd have a heck of a time getting back on him.

A distant train whistle beckoned. I looked to the north, once again seeing the safety of home. Then I looked south, hearing the lonesome wail of the distant train whistle as I looked down a tunnel of towering tamaracks at the dark narrow strip of paved road that offered me miles and months of uncertainty. I was riding a hysterical horse with steel horseshoes on slick, slippery pavement with imbalanced packs. What a way to begin a journey of 2,000 miles!

ON OUR WAY

"Lions and Tigers and Bears, oh my!" the silly line from the *Wizard of Oz* that summoned Dorothy's cheerful optimism to go on kept running through my head. It was a trick of the mind to crowd out my doubts. Then I heard the crisp, clear sound of steel horseshoes striking the paved surface of Fortine Creek Road heading south. The rhythm of Pride's steady clip-clop filled my head with the comforting sense that, whether I had made the right decision or not, we were on our way.

I pulled the blue nylon rain poncho from my front pack. Claire Dog led the procession. Pride and I followed close behind. Lions and tigers and bears, oh my . . . the refrain kept playing in my head.

We traveled a little less than three miles when the blast of an on-coming train whistle exploded into the night. Seconds later we were stopped statue still by the attack of blinding light from the oncoming train as it gobbled up the darkness. We appeared to be directly in its path. My eyes squinted, searching for Claire. "Get over here!" I screamed. I knew we couldn't possibly be in its path but it appeared to be rapidly heading straight for us. The fierce beam of light plowed over us, close and getting closer, and my body said, "You're on the verge of getting run over by a train." My mind knew it couldn't be possible, that it was an illusion, but that didn't slow my heart rate. We appeared to be doomed by a collision. I held my breath in disbelief until the very last second when the light pulled away following a long, slow curve. The train roared past not more than forty feet away, instantly leaving us wrapped in darksome night. The violent click, cling, clang of rolling steel on narrow steel tracks shook the earth with the sway and commotion of railroad cars. I couldn't see the monstrous metal snake raging through the night. I could only feel the air resisting the intruder. And then it was gone, just like that—gone. The sound lulled off behind me until we stood in silence. I shook with relief.

The rain persisted, sometimes steady, sometimes a light drizzle, but at least there was no cold wind. It was so dark I could not read the forest service road signs unless I rode close enough to touch the sign. Even then I had to use my headlamp to make out the numbers. In the absence of light, timelessness attached itself to every perilously long mile. I could not see to measure my passage. I could only feel time in the movement of Pride's long stride. What I thought had been a long time and many miles were but a short time and only one or two miles.

Another train whistle rent the air. A mile ahead, an intense beam of light awaited us, but it appeared stationary. We'd reached the east portal of the Flathead Tunnel where the Burlington Northern Santa Fe Railway channeled through—a seven-mile passage, the second longest in the United States.

A brilliant blinding light followed by a train poured out of the tunnel entrance as a second train waited under powerful spotlights, occasionally shrieking out blasts of high-pressure air from its brakes. In contrast to the surrounding sleepy green forest, it seemed I'd ridden into a surrealistic nightmare of lights, action, steel, and concrete. It felt chaotic and dangerous, and I wasn't even twenty miles from home.

It was my first night out, and with each step my daring odyssey was unraveling. My rain gear was inadequate, my leather gloves and jeans were wet, my boots were wet, but thankfully my feet were still warm. Pride was on the verge of exploding. "Easy," I said, reassuring Pride, but mostly to reassure myself. "Easy boy, it's okay. Just walk, walk easy." The bone-chilling night twisted my thoughts, eroded my enthusiasm, and poked me with doubt. I had never been down this road at night. The faint image of a sign appeared; I flashed my headlamp on it. "Slow. Sharp curve ahead." How ironic, slow down! What I needed was a sign reading "just keep moving."

I passed mile marker 26, then mile marker 25. My watch read two o'clock in the morning. I'd been back in the saddle since 9:30 P.M. With my headlamp I could make out a clearing just off the road. I hoped Pride might stand quietly and we could all rest. I dismounted and sat on my heels inhaling the scent of fir trees and wet rotting leaves covering the earth. It was a short, very short rest. Pride pulled and jigged back and forth again and again. "Damn it Pride, I need to stop," I said. Rain dripped off my hood and onto my face, like tears I dared not shed. I adjusted the cinch before swinging back into the saddle. I stroked Pride's neck. "Okay, let's keep going." I knew he was confused. He still had home on his mind, but then so did I. "Stay awake, stay awake," I repeated as my eyelids sagged. I sang, rolled my feet, and stretched my arms. I talked nonsense to Pride, who followed the disappearing dog act

Claire performed before us. If Claire went to the right, Pride went right. If Claire went behind us, Pride would stop. Okay, I get it, just keep going.

I was weary from lack of sleep, from the excitement and apprehension of the first day of my journey, and from compressing my fears about all that could go wrong. I felt like I was squeezing through an oppressive dark room or a cave or squeezing through a birth chamber. Somehow through all this, I drew courage from the steady rhythm of Pride's movement. I attached myself to the beat like a dancer to a drum and was carried smoothly by Pride's powerful equine strength, and we kept moving.

Three o'clock in the morning. I had to stay focused. "Pay attention to Pride's movement," I told myself. "He'll carry you through this. Trust this horse. Trust the secret these two animals share, allow them to lead you forward."

ONCE UPON A TIME

My thoughts drifted back in time. As a child, I slept with my younger sister on the second floor of our old white Minnesota farmhouse. My parents slept on the main floor, and my four siblings slept in three bedrooms upstairs. My bedroom window faced the back of the house, and the horse pasture was less than twenty feet away.

I could hear the horses sipping and splashing water with their muzzles as they drank from the cast-iron water trough. Kneeling by the window, I held the faded curtains to the side and pressed my nose against the screen. A bold full moon rose innocently over the planet it illuminated. It cast a silent, potent spell over my eight-year-old mind. Wearing only a t-shirt and shorts, I slipped out the kitchen screen door, whispering to Butchy the family dog, "Stay. Stay." Thinking back, I wonder if my folks never heard me because they were simply too tired and prayed for much needed sleep. I ran silently around the house on calloused bare feet, surprising the horses and momentarily stopping the chorus of crickets. Scooping up a handful of dirt and rubbing it between my cupped hands, I could fool them into thinking it would be grain. They'd grow curious and step closer to the rickety wooden gate, broken and repaired numerous times. I sat on the top board, rubbing and shaking the dirt, setting the trap, teasing them closer. The humid July night had our five big-boned farm horses, Pepper, Chee Chee, Prince, Samson, and Corky, and a Shetland pony named Buttons moving about, swishing tails back and forth, flinging heads at the gnats and mosquitoes that bit their sleek summer necks.

I saw my chance and leapt. My bare legs gripped Chee Chee's warm glossy coat. I wrapped and twisted my fingers into her chocolate brown mane. I drew my knees up like a jockey and streamlined my body against her neck. Branches smacked and scratched my legs as the old mare slipped through the woods. The other horses followed. I ducked my head with closed eyes until we escaped the fortress of trees, moving with manes strung out into a luminous night, running just because they were horses leaving behind the farm buildings and yard light. I shared the wild, unrestrained freedom with only my legs wrapped in trust around my noble steed. I spread my arms like wings and flew in the balance of mysteries, of shooting stars and Milky Ways. The horses ran, tossing heads and bucking until suddenly they stopped on top of a hill, nostrils flaring, ears and heads pitched forward. For a moment no one moved. Suddenly one of the horses let out a fart and we were off again for no other reason than for the pure joy of racing in moonlight.

The danger never occurred to me. It was easy, natural. I wanted only to run silently with them, unnoticed on their backs. My body rode effortlessly, scarcely moving, carried on and on by an infectious exhilaration I knew captured me long before I had come into this world. I was not a little girl. I was . . . horse.

Four o'clock in the morning. The persistent "Lions and tigers and bears" would not give up. I thought of Dorothy and Toto, about the yellow brick road and just where was Dorothy going? And where was I going?

An owl hooted then flew off a branch after who knows what! Both Pride and I were startled by the alarming swish of feathers in flight. Pride darted to the right, slipping on the pavement; I lost my balance and hung precariously from the saddle. "Easy, easy, easy," I said as calmly as I could while grabbing for Pride's left rein. I pulled his muzzle around to touch my knee, bringing him quickly into a tight ball, and regained my seat in the saddle. Now wide awake, I thought about the "vision" that brought me here. It seemed ridiculous to even think about it. The vision that set me on this journey felt remote from the danger and risks now surrounding me.

Mile marker 16. Why am I leaving behind friends, home, and community and embarking on this unnecessary and foolishly dangerous pilgrimage? It had never been a dream of mine to ride across the country on a horse. If someone had asked me "What's a long ride?" I would have replied, "I have no idea." But this notion, this "vision" of riding a great distance lured me from safe routines, protective walls, and the daily wellworn habits that made up my life. I don't think I knew "why" I had to do this anymore than Dorothy knew why she was in the Land of Oz, or why she encountered what she did. A woman doesn't always know why she's compelled to do something. The reason comes later. She just knows she must do it. Dorothy proceeded down the yellow brick road, but it was much more than Oz that she discovered. What Dorothy did find along her path was courage, truth, and knowledge, among a host of other things. I contemplated what I might find along my own yellow brick road.

Not one car passed me that night. Dawn finally greeted us. She slipped in unnoticed, a whispering of light defining first the treetops then the road before me. Light struggled through Wolf Creek's dense watershed. It would be another hour until full morning light would make reading my wristwatch possible.

Five o'clock in the morning. The gentle sway of a horse's back, the up-and-down, back-and-forth, side-to-side movement lulled me into the arms of my greatest enemy: fatigue. I could go no farther. Minutes earlier, pulled off balance by sleep, I'd nearly fallen from the saddle. Rain began to fall and I sought refuge under a sprawling fir tree. "Please just let me doze a minute Pride, please," I pleaded with him as I swung stiffly from the saddle. Thankfully, Pride stood quietly.

I left the covered saddle and pack on Pride but loosened the cinch before crumbling into a wet heap under a protective canopy of branches. I sat on a chunk of wood with my head against the tree trunk. I took a soggy peanut butter sandwich from my pack and tore it in half. Claire devoured hers. I ate slowly. Still wearing leather gloves, my right hand held half a sandwich as my left hand gripped Pride's reins like an umbilical cord.

I took two apples from my packs—one for Pride, one Claire and I would share later. I pulled the hood of my blue nylon rain poncho over my wool scarf and draped the rest of it over my legs. It covered Claire's body, which had curled into a heater, warming my now icy feet. My weary head dropped onto my knees, the worthless straw hat at my side. We'd traveled but one day and covered less than twenty miles. Sleep lulled my eyes closed, last night's ride a lingering dream. I woke at eight o'clock in the morning still holding Pride's rein in my left hand. Nearly everything I carried with me was damp. My heart sank as I studied the tattered map, a beautiful scroll I'd worked hard to assemble and months to chart. The map let me feel organized and confident of my trek with carefully defined and precise steps. The map, however, now wet and frayed at the edges, neglected to tell me how nervous my horse would be all night. Nor did it bother to point out how dark and long the night could be, or what dangers lurked in the blackness, or what a pitiful sight I must be by now—weary, wet, uncertain. "Yesterday was only your first day out!" spoke my sensibility. "It's not too late—turn back!"

But it was too late. The long ride had begun. My boot reached for the stirrup, my hand for the saddle horn. I swung into the saddle knowing there would be many more nights like the one I had just endured. No, I could not turn back. I spoke the words aloud to Pride . . . to Claire . . . to myself: "Let's go."

Pride shuffled around, restless to move, as I swung into the saddle and turned his head south.

Claire's annoying "take off talk"—her barking and jumping at Pride's muzzle—sounded our departure. The air filled with excitement. Steel horseshoes struck the paved surface like a song that evokes memories and inspires movement. The song's message for me was "keep going."

CHAPTER FOUR

BALD GOLDILOCKS

Walk on a little further and you'll find the reason to keep going.
—Rupert Christiansen,
The Complete Book of Aunts

My body ached from ten-hour days in the saddle. I was beginning to realize that riding or walking the hundreds of steps that make up a thirty-mile day is damn hard. For days, excruciating lower back pain led me to think I had kidney problems. Each time I stepped from the saddle I wrinkled into a pile of discouraging muscle and bone pains that dropped me to the ground. I had to stabilize myself against Pride's leg, waiting for the pain to subside before I could stand. I had foolishly considered myself in shape, but this ride was infinitely harder than any ballet class I'd danced my way through.

We had traveled less than a month. My aching body would eventually adjust to its new routine, and the miles and weeks already traveled had consumed and dissipated the anxiety Pride and I felt at the beginning of our ride. Our nervousness had broken into mere pebbles of edginess as we sojourned on the matrix of gravel roads that was our route south.

We were in the nearly treeless valleys of southwestern Montana, nearing the Idaho and Wyoming borders. A red building, still miles ahead, was as noticeable as a dollop of red paint on a white blouse and my eyes kept coming back to it. I was looking for shelter in this naked landscape, wondering if it might provide an escape from the relentless

On the first ride, Pride and I follow Claire south. PHOTOGRAPH BY MICHELE IRWIN.

westerly wind and pelting snow showers holding us miserable through much of the day. Powerful gusts of wind twisted my head east as I traveled south. I'd catch glimpses of the Centennial Mountains rising more than 9,000 feet, lying in our path. "Good grief, how will we manage to get over those mountains?" I asked Pride.

The one-dimensional map I'd repeatedly studied was now coming to life. My fingers had routinely traced the route, imagining the course, pulling information from the flat, dull map that provided names of places, rivers, and highways, a sense of direction, and sometimes mountain elevations but no real clues of what lay ahead in my great adventure. I was a novice long rider on my maiden ride and the reality was so much more than I imagined. I was embraced by the actuality of doing what was once only an idea. My eyes were like long fingers, touching the dazzling snowcapped mountains ahead. I felt myself captivated by their beauty and the unexpected majesty that draws us to them.

I pulled my orange and black plaid wool blanket from the bedroll behind the saddle and covered my legs. A pair of jeans and long underwear was pathetically insufficient protection from the cold. I could not remain exposed to this wind much longer. I turned off Blacktail Road and headed for the red building in the distance. The slight change in direction set us headfirst into a brutal westerly wind. Pride held his head low, resisting the light snow that pinged into our eyes as we navigated down a narrow dirt access road. There were no new car tracks, no mailbox, and no power lines. Apparently no one lived here. The wooden corrals to my left contained only fresh blowing snow racing over dry cow patties. To my right stood a log cabin valiantly resisting its decline. Its roof had collapsed into four standing walls. A strip of tin flapped a lonely "bang, bang" near the fragmented door. Three small glassless windows stared at me with hollow eyes. These remnants of an earlier homestead were a reminder of a romanticized era that had come and gone. Odd ends and broken pieces of horse equipment lay about, marking the passage of time. I felt a kinship to this past. I felt like a ghost from the past traveling now at the same speed, seeing the world at four miles an hour, viewing life from the back of a horse.

As we neared the silent red building, a plump pack rat with long whiskers and smooth tail caught Claire's attention. She hesitated, poised to attack. The rat froze. Claire snapped and chased it with a leap and a "yap, yap, yap." Too late, the rat disappeared into a pile of old lumber behind the red building with Claire in futile pursuit.

Should I stay? Should I ride on? I would survive the night if I set up camp on the east side of the building, out of the wind. I wasn't thinking of going inside, not yet anyway.

The sixteen-by-twenty-foot structure had a white tin roof and red tin siding, a cement floor, windows on three sides, and a full-size window in the front door—it was actually a newer building than I first thought.

The doors and windows were locked. At least I thought they were when I nosed around.

Claire persisted to dig madly for the rat while I, still holding Pride's reins, peeked through the dirty window in the door. I could see cots with mattresses. It was a bunkhouse or maybe a hunting cabin. The room contained a dilapidated woodstove in the northwest corner, a table and a couple of swivel chairs covered in blue-and-white-striped vinyl covers, and—six beds! "And I am going to sleep outside in this weather?" I asked myself. There had to be a way in.

For weeks, night after night, I had remained attached to Pride, holding his lead rope, afraid he'd break and run. I'd sent my tent back home, convinced I'd have to do without. If something spooked Pride in the middle of the night, it was impossible to unzip and exit a tent fast enough to prevent a catastrophe. Even a zippered sleeping bag proved impractical. Most nights I slept with my boots on. "Camp" became a sparse shelter created by spreading my bedroll on half of a ten-by-twelve-foot gray plastic tarp. The saddle stood on its horn, protecting my head. With my packs and gear lined neatly along both sides of the bedroll, I pulled the other half of the tarp over me and Claire. Still worried I might lose Pride, I continued holding his lead rope like an umbilical cord precariously binding us as one. It was faster and easier to offer reassurances to him throughout the night, but I rarely got a good night's sleep.

Now, scouting out the little red bunkhouse, I cussed as hostile gusts grabbed the warm saddle blanket, tossing and tumbling it with the blowing snow.

Wind has a way of complicating every situation. Every action is blown into discord. This would have been a bearable day without the accosting force in our faces. I collected the saddle, blankets, and packs and stacked them on the east side of the red building. I checked the perimeter of the fence before turning Pride loose in the corrals. I'd previously made the mistake of turning Pride out in a set of corrals before checking the many gates. Of course, a gate remained open at the far end. He didn't run far, but tears were streaming down my face when I did catch him. I wouldn't make the same mistake again.

Snow and wind didn't stop Pride from performing his blissful horse ritual. He rolled, scratching and rubbing his head, neck, and back against the hard ground, first one side, then the other, coming back to stand, then violently shaking the dirt and snow from his sorrel coat before dropping to the ground and repeating the act of pleasure. I gave Pride the remaining grain we carried that day, then turned into the wind and walked back to the bunkhouse, still thinking I would set up camp on the east side of the structure.

I again tampered with the windows, checking and testing each one. "Maybe I can take the door off with my Leatherman tool," I said to myself. I jiggled the doorknob in hopes it might magically open. Trying again, I went from window to window, peering in at the beds. "There's got to be a way in there," I hoped. I pried a little harder on the window latch. The window slid—it was stuck, not locked! "Yes, yes, yes!" I sang out. I found a sawhorse I could stand on, propped it against the outside wall below the window, and squeezed in sideways. I tugged my hips one final time before dropping inside. I used the table's edge to keep from falling onto the cement floor. "I believe this is called breaking and entering, Bernice," I said to myself while opening the door. As if it were her home, Claire trotted in with a long tongue dangling out the side of her smiling face. I carried the saddle and gear inside, piling it into a heap on the bed nearest the door. The room smelled of working men, dirt, rat shit, and wood ash. Did I care? No, I was out of the wind and mercifully out of the sleet pressing against Pride's rear end. I wished I could bring him inside with Claire and me.

The humble cabin came furnished with the beds, table, swivel chairs, and woodstove, but it also came with other essentials: one quart can of B&B baked beans, a pint of Jack Daniels, candles, matches, and a pack of cards. The woodstove looked useless, but the wind and cold had me considering its use. When I opened the firebox door, I found the bottom filled with an inch of ash and water. The gray slurry mush had to come out before I could build a fire. Using a rusty dustpan and tin bucket, I scraped and hauled the mess out. The only wood small enough for use in the stove lay outside, wet. I lit the fire with paper and a few sticks I found inside and within seconds the cabin filled with smoke. The pipe had not been attached correctly; it would not draw, would not pull the smoke up and out the chimney. Black smoke billowed out of the stove as I scrambled to open the door and windows. The entire room was now thick with choking smoke. I thanked the accommodating wind as it quickly swept the room fresh, and with gloved hands, I wiggled and worked the stovepipe straight. After I added more crumpled newspapers, the fire flared, eventually going from damp wood to hot coals, warming the cabin and occupants. I lit the candles, drank a bit of whiskey, ate beans from the can, and then set myself to cleaning the cabin. For this night, I would call it *home.*

Outside, belligerent winds whistled and screamed, gusting and receding throughout the night while I enjoyed the repose of serene safety. I heated more water for tea. "Warm, safe, and dry, thank you," a phrase I repeatedly offered, grateful to have made it through another difficult situation.

While the sea of swirling snow and wind battled outside the thin walls, a cape of darkness lay over my hideout. The night-blackened windows imposed and reflected a faint solitary image of woman and dog. I felt insignificant, exiled, yet I was the center of my universe, sitting cross-legged on the shabby swivel chair. A single dim candle extended my evening as I wrote a letter to Mac and Evelyn. Claire slept in the other swivel chair near the stove. Her thick, black tail with its white tip lay gently over her nose. I agonized over Pride while picking out the least dirty mattress to spread my bedroll on. It seemed unfair that he had to be out there, while Claire and I were in here. The corral and bunkhouse offered considerable shelter, and earlier that evening I'd tied a wool blanket over Pride's back and shoulders; it would help.

Sleep came quickly. So did late morning when I awoke. The fire had gone out, the cabin was cold, and I refused to relinquish the comfort of warm blankets. I lay dreaming when all of a sudden Claire burst at the door like an attack dog, flaring a healthy row of menacing teeth. My heart pounded as I leaped to my feet in time to see a man standing outside the door window reaching for the handle. His black cowboy hat toppled forward as he rocked backward in surprise and disbelief. He had just discovered a raging guard dog protecting a bald Goldilocks in his bunkhouse bed.

Standing in long underwear, socks, and sweater, I scrambled for my red bandanna to cover my bald head. I'd lived with alopecia for more than a decade, yet still it embarrassed me. Claire's assault sent the tall cowboy staggering backwards. I wrapped my coat around my waist and grabbed Claire's collar while opening the door.

"I am so sorry, I am just so sorry for trespassing," I stammered. "Please, I am traveling across country on my horse. I had to come in. Oh please, I am so sorry, forgive me for trespassing." I kept rattling profuse apologies at the stranger as I struggled to hold back Claire who was now tail-wagging, anxious to greet rather than attack the cowboy.

I'd been caught! The owner of the ranch had arrived. He was a tall, lean, good-looking cowboy. Behind him, a four-wheeler loaded with blocks of salt for his range cattle continued running. I knew as soon as I laid eyes on him that he meant me no harm. But my first thought was, "Is he going to yell at me?" My second thought followed on the heels of the first: "He's going to tell me what a stupid and foolish woman I am—what the hell are you trying to prove?" he'll ask me.

With one long stride, he stepped inside, leaving the wind behind. I explained my intrusion and handed him a card, a postcard-size photo of me on Pride with Mac and Evelyn McCurry standing at his side. The back contained information regarding the ride, the route, Pride, and the McCurry Ranch. I'd hoped by the act of handing someone this card, it would validate me. Look here, it said, I am somebody. I'm really not a vagabond, homeless, nor worthless, it secretly said. At least I hoped it would.

"You coming in the cabin is the way it should be. If a man or woman in this case were traveling and ran into trouble like you had, well they should be able to come in like this, take shelter from the storm. The window had purposely not been locked so a person could get in, not have to break in. It'd have been plain stupid staying out there," he said, expressing sensible cowboy code and ethics.

After hearing my story, the cowboy, his tan face etched with outside work, insisted I stay another night, possibly two more nights. He said a winter storm warning had been issued. May weather in western Montana is temperamental. I was well aware of this, but I had remained convinced that I should start this ride as early as possible. He gave the woodstove a looking over, built a fire, and sat down to share his own story. The ranch had been in the family for generations. He said cattle prices were low and ranching wasn't easy, but it gets in your blood. "What else's a guy like me gonna do?" he said. Connected by my own childhood memories gathered on my parents' small Minnesota dairy farm, I felt firsthand empathy for him.

The red building was indeed a bunkhouse. The corrals were used in the spring and fall when cow and calf pairs are hauled from winter pasture to summer range. It was here this ranch family would come together with friends and often with "dudes" curious to rope in the experience of spring roundup. The cow-calf pairs would then go out on summer range where they grazed and fattened until October or November. In the fall, cattle would be gathered, sorted, and shipped from these corrals. I had already come across several wooden corrals built by early settlers or the cattlemen that followed.

The rancher didn't stay long. He said he'd be back tomorrow, then added, "I admire what you're doing. It's one of those things I wished I mighta done in my younger days, just get on a horse and ride across the country." Then he pushed open the door and quickly slipped out before the wind slammed the door closed again. By now I'd heard the phrase a dozen times, but coming from this cowboy it surprised me. Long riding is hard and often dangerous; it's not a pleasure trip, and it comes with a lot of responsibility. Did they know that each evening around five or six o'clock, as light receded and I hadn't found food, water, or shelter for myself, Claire, and Pride, a sharp prick of anxiety wedged into my gut? I had to take care of us. Claire and Pride depended on me just as I depended on them. A cowboy, someone who is used to long days in the saddle and hard work, and who works and cares for animals, would know this better than anyone. Why was it a dream of his to "just ride across the country"? It was never a dream of mine! Never had I said to myself, "I want to ride a horse across the country someday."

Actually, I had tried talking myself out of it, and it was strange to me that so many people along the way told me that it was a dream of theirs. A big part of me still struggled with the belief that women my age do not do such things. It was that part of me that had been told for years, "You should be married and raising a family." This was a block of resistance my mind continued to perpetuate—always afraid of what others might think. But in the days and miles ahead, I would discover why so many dream of riding a horse across the country.

I felt smug standing at the window the next morning, watching the sun rise and unfold over the black-and-white scene of grasslands and foothills. It was cold on the outside, warm on the inside. I could stay here for days. The big corral had enough spring grass to keep Pride satisfied. A clean creek close by provided drinking water for all of us, and the wind had stopped blowing. We were warm, safe, and dry. Later that day, the owner of the ranch arrived in his pickup truck bearing gifts: food for me and Claire and grain for Pride. He said I'd better stay another night. He didn't stay long, explaining, "I've got work to do." There's always work to do on a ranch, always.

As the day turned to early evening, I noticed Pride lying down with his blanket on, settling in for the night. In the cabin, the faint light of two candles encapsulated me. I would not let myself think of tomorrow or the journey ahead or what was out there in the enormous black space pressing against these four walls. Darkness can be so complete and fear always hungry for reason. Darkness became my fear and the light my reason. I knew the gnawing "what ifs" about this ride must stop or I'd never finish it. And the "what ifs" were spoiling my adventure. The anxieties eating away at me kept me from enjoying the magical, beautiful moments that mysteriously fall from the universe as we go along. I felt small in the bigness, in the inability to comprehend the whys and whats and hows of existence. Inside my head, thoughts circled out of control before I wrapped my arms around Claire and let sleep have its way with me.

Oatmeal and a horse, what better way to start the day?

Morning sunshine was tacking itself to the sky when I woke rested and clearheaded. After a breakfast of oatmeal, raisins, and a strip of beef jerky—half for me, half added to Claire's dog food—I cleaned the bunkhouse and began packing up. I don't know how it is that I've come to love "packing up," but I do. Assembling my belongings is a form of gathering. It reassured me; it said, "I'm going somewhere."

On my left, I looked at the Snowcrest Mountains, on my right, the Blacktail Mountains. I decided we'd follow Blacktail Deer Creek south. We would plant foot, hoof, and paw prints into the soft spring soil of the Centennial Valley, then go on to Lima Reservoir, Red Rock Lakes National Wildlife Refuge, and Henry's Lake. The map tells me what places are ahead, but it does not tell me what lies ahead. I must witness in person before I would truly know my path.

I heard a meadowlark and inhaled perfumed sagebrush air as I swung into the saddle. Pride's eagerness was as contagious as the promise of a new day. His tail was lifted high like a flag, a symbol of his equine nobility, as he instinctively moved forward. Where does this innate desire of his to move forward come from? Maybe from the sun, which always rises and moves across the sky each day. I can't help but believe that this daily picking up and traveling now very much suited this once-edgy horse that wanted only to go home. The traveling was a way of channeling his equine energy, giving this animal something he loved—moving across the earth.

"Don't leave me behind Pride," I said under my breath. "Don't leave me behind."

CHAPTER FIVE

IN MY OWN SKIN

Do not set forth in the spirit of acquisition but go forth in the utmost humility, experiencing the same fervor you would when choosing a lover, knowing a world of possibilities awaits you.
—GIACOMO CASANOVA

A n old red building, reminiscent of a big farmhouse, with a false front and green vines crawling up its side, welcomed us into La Barge, Wyoming. The sign read, "Location Bar, You push the bit and we'll push the beer." In this case, the "bit" wasn't a piece of horse tack but the business end of the drill in an oil rig.

Even from a distance, La Barge looked as if it were covered with a gray cloth. It spoke of steel and dirt, of noise and dust and backbreaking work. It spoke of the workers who produce the oil and gas that fuel modern civilization. This is work that "pays pretty good" but is damn hard on women, families, and animals. It seemed to be a restless town and for me a slap in the face when I was told, "You'll have a hard time finding a place to camp. No horses allowed in city limits."

I came into La Barge from the northwest, following the Greys River to its headwaters at the Tri-Basin Divide then crossing the historical Lander Cutoff Trail on Thompson Pass. The Lander Cutoff was a shortcut from the Oregon Trail to the Pacific Northwest. The rough route followed an already established Indian travois trail. In 1859, 13,000 emigrants bound by hope and dreams for the future traveled with 79,000 head of livestock over the Lander Cutoff in a single year! What

must the local tribes have thought? Their hearts must have ached with anger and sadness at this intrusion into their country and their way of life, just as the early settlers who came much later and some residents even today say, "Getting too crowded around here for me," followed by a nostalgic litany of the town or land "as it once had been."

I camped two days on Thompson Pass and wrote one word in my journal: "rapturous." I imagine mountain climbers experience the same exhilaration of height and arduous conquest when they arrive at the top of a mountain as I did. Each switchback, each blister, each step-by-step "we're almost there" in anticipation to reach the summit. After a long walk up the steep gravel road, we arrived at 8,756-foot Thompson Pass and collapsed in triumph. I was unprepared for and stunned by the vista before me stretching to the distant horizon. I was looking out at an intimidating panorama of the country I was yet to cross. The forests and creeks and grassy plains I had traveled along the Greys River gave way to a blanket of sagebrush and sand in a vast barrenness—the Red Desert. For this midwestern farm girl turned Montanan, deserts were something I knew nothing about.

From Thompson Pass, I followed the Greys River Road and the La Barge Creek Road through 100 miles of picturesque forests along the clear mountain streams of the Bridger-Teton National Forest. With each descending step we traded agreeable mountain shade trees and cold creeks for country wanting only to squabble with me—the high, dry desert. The map showed the land turning from green to brown for good reason.

I ate the last of my food early in the morning, long before I rode into the desert landscape of La Barge. My thoughts were preoccupied with food as I walked toward town. "Maybe I'll have a strawberry shake," I thought to myself. "No, first I will eat an omelet, a kitchen sink omelet with cheese. And instead of strawberry, I think a vanilla shake would go better with an omelet." Provoked by hunger, my mind ranted about food. Oddly, I rarely ate what I imagined I would. I carried enough food for three or four days: beef jerky, rice, lentils, sea salt, oil, raisins, and peanut butter in a plastic bag.

Sometimes I carried tortillas with cream cheese, apples or carrots, and dry dog food for Claire. I used a lightweight propane burner to cook with. A knife, spoon, tin cup, and stainless steel cooking pot completed my kitchen.

A few miles from town, I spotted a Hershey chocolate bar on the pavement. Before I could pick it up, Pride stepped on it and Claire had it in her mouth. I pried her clenched white teeth open, but she refused to believe me when I told her, "Chocolate is bad for dogs, bad, you can't eat chocolate, no, give me that!" The wrapper remained intact as chocolate oozed out. I didn't hesitate. I ate it—slowly—savoring the rich flavor.

The weight of 80-degree temperatures made the day seem sluggish and impossibly slow. There seemed to be so little progress and so far to go. I felt physically bankrupt. Annoyed by little things Claire and Pride would do, I needlessly yelled at them. I was frying like a slice of banana cream pie on a hot skillet. My old enemy fatigue had resurfaced.

La Barge is an island town fixed in an ocean of sagebrush, blue sky, and flat, open reckless space and bountiful oil fields. Row after row of trailer houses are squeezed onto town blocks while the spaciousness surrounding the town laughs. I heard it referred to as "a hell hole" more than once. It wasn't! What I heard speaking was tired, frustrated voices. An oil boom had descended upon La Barge, Wyoming. It may have lacked smalltown charm, but I met many people who momentarily cast aside their own worries and willingly helped a stranger.

We rode through to the south end of town before returning to the old red building, which seemed the most promising. The late afternoon breeze entered the Location Bar's open door and mingled with the chatter inside. I gave Claire water, motioned her to lie under a tree that lent shade, and told her, "Stay, stay," motioning with my hand. A young woman standing outside the saloon smoking a cigarette volunteered to hold Pride as he grabbed for green grass growing along the sidewalk edge. I loosened his cinch and watered him from a yard hydrant next to the building. After one last glance at dog and horse, I said to the woman smoking the cigarette, "I'll only be a minute," then turned and stepped into a commotion of testosterone. I had no money.

The Location Bar smelled like the end of the day. The row of working men leaning against a long wooden bar, its surface marred with knicks and initials, reminded me of my farmer father. Rolled-up sleeves exposed lean, taut muscles attached to strong shoulders and tired faces. Twelve- to fourteen-hour workdays had left layers of dry sweat on their furrowed brows, rubbed over and over again by tan and sunburned forearms now holding cold cans of Budweiser. They were comrades in labor, talking and drinking, all muscle and bravado. I took the only empty stool at the end of the bar; the place was jumping. Country music swept across walls splattered with large, colorful posters. One was a seductive photo of a cunning, lithe woman, her eyes fixed on the man that her leg wrapped around as he lifted a can of beer in salutation, "Cheers!"

The steady noise of truck and car traffic on U.S. Highway 189 rolled in from the open door behind me. I had walked into the Location Bar hoping to cash a check, and I would beg if needed. My broad-brimmed hat turned heads as I reached for the stool. "Where ya coming from?" asked a red-faced young man. His name was Josh, and he and his buddy John were both clearly drunk, as were most of the occupants of the Location Bar that afternoon. My answer was followed by "Where? You rode all that way? Well hell, let me buy ya a beer." I accepted. A cold beer on a hot afternoon is positively exquisite as it drains down a parched throat. It is, however, a mistake if you're dehydrated and have eaten only a Hershey bar since morning. I needed food and rest. There were two hungry bellies waiting outside the saloon and I had no cash. I told the two men, "I need supplies and I'm looking for a place where I can camp for the night." In a snap, chivalry grabbed Josh and John by the arm and slammed down their empty beer cans. Now occupied by a mission, Josh and John went off like Sir Lancelot and Sir Galahad to save the little lady. Fortunately, they fumbled around long enough for a woman, on her way out the front door for a smoke, to appear on the scene. She stopped and said, "Hey, I hear ya need a place ta stay for the night. My son-in-law's gotta place outside the city limits where ya can park your horse."

Which is how I met Katie Rose, the owner of this no doubt

prospering establishment. Her voice raspy, her words short, we both nodded with respect.

Why is asking always so hard? It makes giving seem easy. I needed help—it was that simple, but intolerably hard to ask for. In my journal I wrote, "Katie Rose, one tough lady, about my age, a face crimped with first-hand experience." Katie Rose cashed my hundred dollar check without hesitation.

Pride and Claire stood quietly when I returned. I was still lightheaded from the beer but came bearing treasure for the next four days: beef jerky, candy bars, nuts, and four fresh eggs from Katie Rose's backyard chickens. Katie refused to let me pay for anything. I also walked out with valuable route information. Katie said, "Ride the east side of Fontenelle Reservoir. You'll get ya self killed by them oil trucks if you go ridin' Highway 189 to Green River. It ain't that hard. A bunch of guys rode it a couple a years ago. There ain't any roads. They did it the old way. The bunch rode with authentic gear from the 1800s. Even boiled their water." At least I have a water filter, I thought, even if it was broken.

Charting the sixty-mile stretch of highway between La Barge and Green River had caused me concern, but not until I'd seen the traffic did I realize how dangerous it would be. "Great, that's great information," I said, thanking Katie Rose. Grateful and relieved to have the new route that kept me off Highway 189, I imagined shade trees and campsites along the waterfront. Yes, good news, I naively thought. I stepped outside to a casually descending orange and red ball of sun disappearing behind Oyster Ridge, the Tunp Range, and Mount Isabel. Pride nickered, and a hungry Claire, who had her Hershey bar stolen from her earlier in the day, jumped up and cheerfully wagged "Got anything for us?" in dog-tail sign language.

We zigzagged our way into the setting sun past pickup trucks and trailer houses. Shadows finally disappeared into a lingering haze of light as I led Pride and Claire through the back streets of town where I could "park my horse."

Pride had grown accustomed to the sight and noise of towns. Barking dogs, four-wheelers, motor bikes, and kids on trikes no longer upset him, but then maybe tonight he was just too tired to care. It had been a long day for all of us. He held steadfast if a truck and trailer honking its horn flew past, even with a whipping tarp carelessly covering the load. "I'm proud of Pride," I whispered into his muzzle as we walked along side by side. His ears were forward and he was walking with ease and confidence. Claire, Pride, and I had bonded: we stayed close to one another. We shared apples, carrots, tortillas, and assorted treats. Every day I brushed and rubbed down Claire and Pride, during which time we talked—I asked questions and of course answered for them. "Well how did you do today? I noticed you were frightened of that tarp hanging off the fence, you can't be doing that," I'd say. "But it startled me," I'd imagine Pride's reply, then say to him, "You must be brave." Our mutual trust grew deeper each day. Each day was a lesson in devotion!

Jake, my twenty-four-year-old host, owned the house and the ten acres he lived on. He'd gone to work in the oil fields right after high school. He admitted to being an alcoholic and laughed about it, saying, "How the hell else am I gunna get through this?" I wasn't sure if he meant work or life. Two more men working in the oil fields rented rooms from Jake. The house was definitely a bachelor pad. Chipped, peeling paint and a broken garage door signaled a house to eat and sleep in and nothing more. "I hope I'm not getting myself into something I'll regret," I thought, cautiously placing my gun within reach. I hoped exhaustion wasn't putting me at risk. I kept thinking, "Keep moving, just keep moving, another day will come, one more day, you'll get through it."

The three men were rough around the edges and hard-mouthed but helpful. I was old enough to be their mother and they showed a measure of respect. Jake had tattoos on every piece of skin not concealed by his clothes and maybe under there too. There were designs in red and black swirls, animal faces, and fierce warrior tattoos. "Oh my," I thought, raising an eyebrow, not sure what to make of it all. Jake found an ice chest that I could use as a makeshift water bucket. One of the men fixed my water filter. Another gave me batteries for my headlamp and duct tape for Claire's feet. "You would'a paid high prices for them at the convenience store if they'd even had 'em," said Jake. The three men were drunk with fatigue and beer by 11 P.M. I took a can of tuna fish, an apple, and carrots from the sack of groceries I brought into the kitchen and stepped outside.

It wasn't exactly a lawn extending from the front steps, but a good feed of grasses awaited Pride. I spread my bedroll out in a patch of tall grass and weeds and lay down. With Claire at my side, I lay listening to the sounds of a nocturnal town and staring at the stars—amazed at the light.

Full moons are always lustrous, and on this night, with nothing concealing the celestial heavens, moonshine cast a crisp moon-shadow behind every figure it found. Two rings of light circled the brilliant full moon. Typical of the long days of summer, day and night seemed to merge—the sun was reluctant to set and would be anxious to rise in the morning. The wind ignored my request for a stronger breeze to alleviate the oppressive sultry air and the mosquitoes descending upon us. The town of La Barge remained awake with barking dogs and rolling traffic through most of the night.

I lay awake thinking about the young men inside the house. Were they caught in a fishnet of work that would eventually break their bones and steal their dignity? Did they come to work in the oil fields seeking fortune or seeking merely to survive? How long can they push the bit and push the beer before they can no longer push the bit and can only push the beer? If they wish upon a star, do they wish for something more out of life, or do they wish to be the best at what they do and for a better, somewhat easier tomorrow? Their overworked bodies are a ticking clock that well before their time will be broken—their song of strength silent. These hardworking, hard-living men and women are part of the vast number of workers who do the backbreaking work, the digging and scraping, pushing and pulling, who toil hidden in the vast chain of professions that produce the cars we drive, the plastic bags we use, the toys we play with, the machines that do work for us, and the stuff that amuses us.

The three hardworking lives inside the house reminded me of my father. They reminded me of the long days he worked, of his frustrations and the gamble that farming must have been for my mother and him. Day in and day out, working to bring milk from his precious herd of Holstein cows to people who knew nothing of the milk's story and how it got to the store in its pretty carton, in the pretty stores, for such a low price.

I slept fitfully until dawn broke. The men in the house were at the end of their workweek and remained asleep. At 5:30 A.M., Pride was saddled and packed and Claire sat waiting nearby. My foot reached for the stirrup.

Good thoughts and a stunning sunrise escorted me out of town until I came upon the graveyard of bones and dry shriveled animal hides in the ditch along Highway 189. Ditches along major highways are often like this. Littered among the broken glass and beer cans are the carcasses of deer, antelope, coyotes, cows, rabbits, skunks, porcupines, and other animals attempting to cross a stream of deadly car and truck traffic to get to water. Here, the precious water in the Green River lures the animals to cross the busy, traffic-laden, black two-lane highway that runs the length of Fontenelle Reservoir on the west side. "I could easily be one of the traffic casualties," I thought. I had four miles of riding in the ditch along Highway 189 before turning up a dirt road and over a bridge crossing the Green River to the east side of the reservoir.

The highway was worse than I thought it would be. The ditches, besides being littered with animal carcasses, broken glass, and rough broken terrain, were infested with swarming mosquitoes rising up, biting our faces, as I moved us along slowly through dry, longstem grasses and stacked tumbleweeds while watching for rattlesnakes. The reel of irritating truck traffic caused a steady roar and blasts of wind, making the going even slower. It took two hours to ride the four miles. We crossed the Green River at 8 A.M. Pride drank, Claire drank and soaked, and I grumbled about the heat. It was already blazing hot.

GREEN RIVER

The Green River flows 730 miles southwest from its headwaters in the Wind River Mountains of west-central Wyoming, then through a small corner of Colorado and into Utah to merge with the Colorado River within Canyonlands National Park. The "Green" is the largest tributary of the Colorado River and forms the western boundary of the Red Desert. The Shoshone gave the Green River its first name: *Sisk-a-dee-Agie*, also pronounced Sees-kee-dee-Agie and Seeds-ka-dee Agie, which loosely translated means "Prairie Hen River." The river is famous among anglers for cutthroat and brown trout and whitefish, and the river corridor supports more than 200 species of resident and migrant wildlife. To the Shoshone and Ute tribes who once inhabited this country it must have been paradise.

RED DESERT

The Red Desert includes the Great Divide Basin and stretches across much of southwestern Wyoming. Red and purple rocks and soil appear to be flat and featureless like my map, when in fact, out there in that sweeping landscape are spectacular butte formations, badlands, and sand dunes. The entire area is a massive and mostly unprotected wildlife refuge. It is home to sagebrush wildlife: sage grouse, coyotes, bobcats, rabbits, rodents, mule deer, and pronghorn. Eagles and hawks fly overhead, and this vast high desert is home to numerous wild horse herds. It also contains rich gas and oil reserves.

I could not expect Pride to carry me in this heat so I walked, holding Claire's leash in my right hand and Pride's in my left, connecting us three rovers of the road. My feet and shins hurt something awful as we proceeded along the east side of Fontenelle Reservoir and into the daunting Red Desert beneath an unending sky.

My map, once again, deceived me. It showed a smooth, benign shoreline bordering the east side of Fontenelle Reservoir. In reality, deep cracks at the reservoir shoreline began as gaping eighth-of-a-mile-wide canyons that narrowed eastward. Negotiating around the crevasses added two miles east and west for every one mile I rode south. The reservoir itself was held unreachable by a fortress of precarious shale cliffs, shallow caves, and canyons that cut deeply into the shoreline. Four-wheelers had etched a maze of small tire tracks every which way.

Wildflowers and blooming cacti were scattered among the giant anthills, making surprising decorations on the desert floor. The thriving neighborhood of gophers, rabbits, and grouse took no particular notice of us.

To the east I could hear the sound of diesel engines generating power for pumpjacks in the Green River Basin oil shale field. The pumpjacks are also known as nodding donkeys, horse-heads, or sucker rod pumps. Their mechanical arms attach to reciprocating piston pumps to pull lazy, thick oil from the earth. These black, prehistoric-looking steel figures touch the blue sky, breaking the horizon as they rise and lower, up and down, day and night, creaking and moaning like old men that move without moving.

A strong southwest wind picked up; the hot air kept the mosquitoes away but robbed us of moisture. I'd reach a plateau and think, "Okay, from here it looks all clear," but the flat line of the horizon fooled me again and again. The deep crevasses in the earth were invisible until we neared their edge as we moved across the sagebrush-blanketed desert. Gullies and recesses appeared from nowhere. I tried cutting across, but the steep sides were rocky and treacherous. This was not fun. We were forced to walk around these ancient cracks in the land, while to my right the tantalizing and inaccessible blue water of Fontenelle Reservoir shimmered with light. "If only we could get down there," I thought, relishing the idea of a swim to cool off. But we couldn't—access points were few and far between on this side of the water.

Goathead thorns stuck in Claire's wrapped paws. Usually she'd wait for me and I would pull them out. But often she would stop and use her teeth to carefully pull a goathead and spit it to the side. Locals call the plant "puncturevine" because the thorn is sharp enough to puncture car tires. Texans call goatheads "Texas longhorns" because the thorns look like the head of a longhorn bovine. I frowned at myself for not foreseeing the need to better protect Claire's paws. Until I came up with something better or found doggie booties, I'd have to continue wrapping her paws with strips of cloth and duct tape. I knew the duct tape, even wrapped loosely, could not possibly be comfortable, but it worked, for the most part.

In the heat, I stopped at least every three hours, pulled the packs and saddle from Pride's sweaty back, and added strips of duct tape to Claire's paws before she crawled into the shade under some sagebrush. My heavy saddle tipped on its horn improvised as a chair for me and my tired, aching, sweaty body. I wrote very little in my journal.

As I poured precious water into Claire's collapsible canvas dish, I thought, "I'll be out of water soon." Katie Rose made it sound so easy. I was kicking myself for leading my animals into this mess. It was inexcusable to have done so. I drank less so Claire would have more. Pride would be okay, but Claire needed water often. What was supposed to be a one-day, twenty-four-mile ride along Fontenelle Reservoir would take two days at this rate, and the hot, dry desert yawned ahead for miles, uninterested in my mistakes.

I had no idea where the next fishing access would be, or even if one lay ahead, and I needed water, badly. I could make out trucks and dust trails in the same direction as the oil fields, so I headed east, hoping to flag down a truck driver to ask for drinking water. More trucks soon became visible, as did the patchwork of dirt roads they traveled on. Camouflaged by a thick coat of dust, a noisy flatbed equipment truck slowed to a stop. I'm sure the men in the truck were entertained by the sight of us three dusty, thirsty vagabonds. I hadn't even flagged them down. Two men with sun-dried crevasses like the land itself etched across their brown faces sat silent inside the cab. It must have been my hat they were staring at speechlessly. I was soon to learn that the driver was a "floorhand" with a "worm" in the passenger seat going to check on a "thirsty bird." Translated, the truck was driven by a laborer with rank, with an inexperienced worker as passenger, heading out to maintain a pumpjack at an oil well. Regulations required every one of these trucks to carry water. Most carried a five-gallon orange water cooler strapped to the frame behind the cab. The driver tipped his silver hard hat back and stuck his head out the window. "What the hell are ya doing out here?" he asked.

I stood beside the truck holding Claire and Pride by lead ropes and gave the men a condensed version of my story. As I handed the floor-hand my traveling card, a wave of dust pulled up behind us and a dirt-clad roughneck stepped from his truck to see what was up. A roughneck is an experienced member of an oil rig drilling crew. Given the grit and fortitude these men must adopt to survive, I suppose I should not find it surprising how they incorporate slang to communicate rank and position. It's a language binding them as comrades in common with the grueling work they do. "Hey there Slim," said Floorhand. "How's it going?" replied Slim as he stepped from his truck cab. "You and College boy [the worm] helping damsels in distress?" They didn't stay long, but long enough to fill my water bottles with good drinking water. We gave Pride water in his feed bag lined with a large plastic bag that I carried. College boy gave me a granola bar and Slim reached for an apple from his tin lunch box. They left me in their dust when they drove off to service another nodding donkey.

I thought my chances were better if I stayed near the water. I knew somewhere along this eastern side there had to be another fishing access. "At least water is there, you just have to get to it," I told myself. I could risk riding Highway 189 or risk not having water for a day and a half—neither one a good choice. We ate only apples that afternoon. I figured it would be the least dehydrating of foods I carried. There was very little grass for Pride. Four hoofs, four paws, and two human feet rambled along, with trepidation, toasting in the intense afternoon heat. Then, unexpectedly, a fishing access appeared in the distance. I got on Pride and rode, Claire padding along beside, hurrying down the dirt access road.

We were all smiles as we plunged into the water, splashing and drinking and then drinking some more. I stripped the saddle and pack off Pride and he rolled in the water and sand. I climbed on his wet, bare back and coaxed him into deeper water. He pawed with his front hoofs making big strikes at the water. It was horse play. Claire followed us as we swam and circled together in the private cove. There were no trees or picnic tables and we were alone. I wore only my wet long-sleeve cotton shirt and underpants. We stayed nearly two hours, indulging in a shoreline frolic, a welcome diversion from thinking of the miles that lay ahead.

I refilled the bottles with water from the reservoir. The water was for Claire and tasted awful, but I would drink it if need be. "At least I have a water filter now," I thought, "thanks to the guys back in La Barge." We climbed to the top of the flat ridge refreshed and feeling a little less defeated. The traveling was easier—the land ceased to crack and spread as it did fifteen miles ago. By 9 P.M. I could make out Fontenelle Dam, the end of the reservoir. Despite my earlier foreboding thoughts, much to my relief we had made it in one day! The map showed a campground and I could see trees near the dam. "Let's hope there's grass," I thought.

My journal read: "Camp 29, June 23rd, 2005 . . . south end of Fontenelle Reservoir. Earthen dam, Green River running fast, came in from desert just as light left the sky and a full moon proudly took its place. Hot and dry, no other campers, good drinking water, wind blew hard this evening. Pride fussy at first but settled down. It's an oasis. Trees surrounding us; lots of grass and the coolness, a great welcome. It has been a long day. We've been walking since 5:30 in the morning and it's now 10 o'clock at night."

I made camp, and Claire and I ate rice cooked with beef jerky. When finished, she promptly curled into a ball and slept. I watched Pride, bathed in moonlight, eating as I sipped hot tea from my tin cup thinking, "I don't know if I can do this, I really do not know if I can do this." I sat with Pride until 1 A.M., then tied him close to my bedroll and lay down with Claire. I convinced myself the worst was over and slept a few hours.

With great effort, I mustered myself from bed the next morning. I ate a hard-boiled egg, fed Claire, staked Pride in grass, packed up, and stepped in the saddle by 5:30 A.M. It was essential that I avoid traveling under the crippling desert sun as I had yesterday. Neither Claire nor I could sustain the heat; Pride would do fine, but none of us were seasoned desert travelers.

The Seedskadee National Wildlife Refuge begins just south of Fontenelle Reservoir. The refuge forms a corridor one to one and a half miles wide that extends along thirty-six miles of the Green River, protecting a diverse mosaic of riparian, wetland, and upland shrub habitats. It's a migration route and nesting area for a wide variety of birds, including trumpeter swans, bald and golden eagles, mountain bluebirds, and sage grouse. The habitat also provides cover for an array of mammals, including moose, mule deer, pronghorn, porcupines, bobcats, beavers, coyotes, badgers, and white-tailed prairie dogs.

Four-wheeler dirt roads just outside the refuge fence line were easy to follow and easy on Claire's paws, which were newly wrapped and taped for the day. I had an acute sense of rattlesnakes as we trod, still connected by lead lines. The morning proved hotter than the day before; it must have been in the high 80s by 10 A.M. I knew it would boil over into the mid-90s if not hotter by late afternoon. As often as possible, I sent Claire into the water for an essential cooling dip.

What a surprise and relief to see the first livestock access point. These are smaller fenced-in areas where range cattle (and in this case a long rider) on public lease land can reach the water while minimizing shoreline damage. But would there be more? I knew nothing about range cattle, open range, U.S. Bureau of Land Management lands, and water right-of-ways. Even with the water filter, I wasn't eager to drink from the Green River, but at least Claire and Pride would have ample water. All morning we struggled with more hard miles up steep grades and around sand dunes and crevasses. My legs and feet, with blisters taped like a ballet dancer's, hurt with each step. I had never ridden or walked across such land as this—it was brutal.

It must have been after 2 P.M. when I first noticed lightning flash along the western horizon. Again and again long jagged bolts struck at the earth from foreboding clouds. "It's still a ways off, but damn there's no shelter anywhere," I said to myself, taking a deep breath. I knew little about measuring a storm's speed and direction, but I could smell rain coming. Eventually, clouds edged across the incessant sun; it became surprisingly cool very quickly. Did that mean hail? I stepped into the saddle and picked up speed. I could see nothing remotely suggestive of shelter, and on my right four strands of tightly stretched fencing with locked gates kept me heading due south. The exposure sent a wave of panic through me. At a fast trot we quickly made a few miles, and then I saw vehicles traveling fast in a straight line without dust. My map showed Highway 28 running east and west through the center of the refuge. It was not far—a couple more miles—and we'd be safe.

"Locked!" I screamed. "The gate's got a chain around it and it's locked!" I bellowed, with Pride standing behind me waiting for the gate to be opened. An adjacent gate for vehicles was open, but it had a cattle guard—a section of steel bars spaced three inches apart spanning a shallow pit the width of the gate. Cars and trucks can easily drive over, but cattle and horses will usually never attempt crossing. "How the hell can this be?" I thought. I threw my head back and screamed, "NO!"

Gusty winds whipped at our faces as a few cars drove by, sounding a bump, bump, bump as their wheels ran over the steel bars. Livestock gates are not supposed to be locked on public road accesses, but this one was. I pushed my broad-brimmed hat back and pulled a wool cap from my saddle bag. An hour previously I had thought I would suffocate in the heat—now I was freezing. Panicky thoughts raced through my mind: "We have to go through this gate, there's no other way! I must go west here and I can see buildings not far once we cross this fence line." I swung back into the saddle. The cooler air had renewed Claire. She was no longer on a lead line, and I yelled at her in the wind and noise, "You stay, you stay with me!" I rode south along the fence looking for a break, another gate perhaps, maybe a weak section I could take apart, pass through, and reconstruct. But I didn't get far before being stopped by a soft, boggy wetland, too dangerous to cross. I turned back, retracing our steps, looking up at the storm bearing in on us and searching the fence for a weak spot. Finally, I saw it—a weak spot where the fence was slack. I pushed the wires to the ground and stood on them while Pride carefully stepped over. Pride sensed the urgency in my voice as I saddled up and urged him into the wind. We moved fast across the Highway 28 bridge to the west side of the Green River.

I knew I had very little time before the storm would hit. Trees along the river tossed about, offering minimal shelter. A small paved side road led us to a wooden information kiosk with a small over-hanging roof solidly blocking the now ugly, whipping wind. I pushed Pride up against the information signs, saying, "Easy, easy, you're okay." And then the lightning hit, shaking the sign and spooking Pride. I shuffled around, getting him back in place. The rain came with such force that within seconds the road began flooding. Fortunately, we stood higher on a concrete pad. Unfortunately, the kiosk walls didn't extend all the way to the pad, leaving a gap about knee high. Claire sat on my toes, using my legs as a windbreak. She watched nervously as branches and leaves flew through the air and rain and wind rushed in at our ankles. I quietly said a prayerful "Thank you" for at least having a roof overhead, even if it barely covered us. Terrifying hail hammered at the kiosk. "You'll be okay, just stand, stand easy," I said, talking close to Pride's head, perhaps reassuring myself more than the horse. I loved him so much at that point in our ride. I'd already asked far too much of this horse and he would give and give and give. He had been such a high-strung, fidgety animal when this journey began. Now he stood next to me, trusting me through this raging mess I'd gotten us into. Twenty minutes later and still mostly dry, we stepped away from the tiny lifesaving shelter.

Pride and Claire noticed the approaching truck before I did. The Seedskadee wildlife ranger stopped, obviously not happy to see me. He barked out a series of questions: "What are you doing here and where the hell did you come in from? This is a wildlife refuge, you can't be in here."

I wasn't having any of it. "Why was the gate locked?" I retorted. "It's a public highway. By law, the side gates allowing cattle or horse passage should remain unlocked." After I told him my story, he softened a bit. He said, "There's nothing ahead for another fifteen miles," and offered an empty trailer house three miles up the road at the refuge headquarters where I could spend the night. Pride would have a corral.

The corral, although solidly built, did not have a blade of grass in it. "Oh Pride," I thought. "How tired you must be and now nothing for you." I set two five-gallon buckets of water in the corral and gave him what I had—an apple, a few crackers, and a granola bar—before walking to the trailer where I'd laid my gear. The ranger's wife sent over food, mostly snacks for traveling.

WALKING THROUGH WALLS

Marathoners refer to it as "hitting the wall." Buddhists call it the "gateless gate," or "passing through the gate." My father would have said, "You're just stuck in the mud." I became engrossed in a nonstop dialogue between two voices in my head. From one moment to the next, I kept assessing, reassessing, and jostling my thoughts, desperate for insight into my dilemma. For the past 1,000 miles, I'd fought the desire to turn around and head home, back to the certainty of a world I knew, and forgo this misadventure of riding through a world I didn't know except as marks on a map. There was more desert ahead. Not having water for myself, Pride, and Claire sent a jolt of fear through me. Not knowing where I might camp the next night or the uncertainty of my food supply kept my mind zigzagging from one anxiety to another. My long-ride adventure had unraveled into something much harder than anything I'd ever done in my life, and all my planning could not have possibly prepared me for what I had already encountered and what would lie ahead.

Sitting in the empty trailer thirty miles north of the town of Green River, Wyoming, exhaustion and dehydration rolled together with the thought of facing 800 more agonizing miles. "It wasn't supposed to be like this," I sobbed. I sank to my knees like a tire going flat, releasing an uncontrollable fit of sobbing. "I can't do it!" I cried. I had hit the wall. The Red Desert had brought me to my knees. It bit deeply into my desire to continue with this daring adventure. Wave after wave of desperate, doubtful questions accosted me. Alone, I sobbed and talked with tears, snot, and saliva running down my nose, dripping from my lips. "If I go back now, that'll be 2,000 miles. No one will think I'm a quitter. I'm never going to make it—I can't do this," I sputtered.

Claire and Pride endured my stupidity and my mistakes, and of course it was me that had gotten us into this. My soul wept. The sense I'd never make it clutched my thoughts. Hidden fears and wounds long ago marked "closed" cracked open: my childhood embarrassment at being a dumb farm girl in a big-city school, the wins and losses in competitions, recklessly hurting my pony as a child and telling no one, saying "yes" when I should have said "no," and the pain of unrequited love. I'd been covering my baldness with a brave, independent façade and that bravado now lay shriveled and meaningless. Now I dreaded wearing a "loser" label and people telling me, "I told you so," knowing that I wasn't getting any younger and maybe was already too old to do what I had set out to do.

I woke late the next morning facing another unbearably long, grueling day of desert walking. I had already decided to go only as far as the town of Green River and no farther. Then I would return home.

ALONG CAME A TRAIL ANGEL

The day proved to be yet another hellish day of riding and walking across parched desert. It was slow going—by late afternoon, we were only about eight miles south of the previous night's stop. My mood was as bleak as the landscape. But then a thin line of dust in the air revealed the approach of a car. The driver-side window lowered slowly as the Ford Mustang rolled to a stop beside us, revealing a broad smile from a tan, thirtyish-year-old woman, curious enough to stop and inquire about the travelers on her road.

The woman, her long dark hair pulled back in a ponytail beneath a baseball cap, had just become a "Trail Angel." Later she told me I looked like a sheepherder. It was only when she drew closer that she realized that it was a woman atop the horse.

A Trail Angel is an unexpected helping hand, extending from

seemingly nowhere, to someone on a journey at a serendipitous moment. They can work "Trail Magic," like the unexpected Hershey bar or the drinking water we got from the oil field workers on the east side of Fontenelle Reservoir.

Claire trotted up with wrapped front paws and greeted our Trail Angel with a wagging tail. The woman and I exchanged greetings—she was Michele Sherwood-Irwin, a local. I asked what road we traveled on and did she know of a place I could camp for the night?

Maybe she could sense it, or maybe she could hear it in my voice or see from my cracked lips and disheveled look that I needed help. We did not talk long. It was 5:40 P.M. Michele explained that she worked the night shift at the Oci Big Island Mine and Refinery, a trona mine just east of the river, and she was on her way to work. She added, "The Hamel Ranch is about eight miles up the road. You'd be welcome to stay and rest up. I'll call ahead." Then she drove off. Her reassuring smile and invitation marked a passage through the narrow, rocky channel of my misgivings.

Three families live on the Hamel Cattle and Hay Ranch thirty miles northwest of Rock Springs, Wyoming. Don and Janet Irwin are the parents of Rob and Carolyne. Carolyne is married to Doug Hamel. Michele is married to Rob Irwin. Each family lives in their own home on the ranch.

Don and Janet, retired and in their seventies, were waiting for me when I arrived. I did my best at concealing the shadows of doubt riding with me. I didn't want them to know I was struggling and scared and skeptical of my ability to continue. I was no wonder woman!

After settling Pride and Claire in, Janet spread a feast on the kitchen table—leftover homemade stew thick with vegetables, beef, and lots of gravy. I ate two full bowls with homemade bread and followed up with more cake than I should have. I drank tea and lots of water, and then realized how hard it suddenly was to think straight. I wanted sleep. The Irwins insisted I use the guest bedroom and I didn't argue.

I tried leaving the next morning. A weary and wise Claire made it clear her vote was no! We stayed four more days.

Don Irwin had lived his entire life on the rough desert landscape and knew what I could never know about "desert riding." Don suggested we take a flight in his Cessna 172. "Let's go up and look around," he said. "It'll give you a better idea of what you'll be crossing."

The first step to moving through a wall is gaining perspective. This is the place where you will either confront or transform your demons or from there on it will be nothing but a variation on the same old themes. Passing through the gate requires a willingness to take a deeper look at what's keeping you from moving forward. It's about breaking the grip of your perspective, beliefs, and opinions about yourself and others. It's about changing the dialogue in your head—and it's a whole lot easier said than done.

"Ah, perspective!" I thought. I don't know if it really gave me a broader picture, or if the sight of this country from the air reinforced my skepticism for crossing it. The panorama of the enormous nothingness of my intended route was daunting. It frightened me more than anything I had confronted so far. It browbeat me with its seeming emptiness. "Such useless land," thought my Minnesota farm-girl mind. The harsh, intolerant reality of a desert, where everything pricked and poked in opposition of my being there, was waiting for me, daring me to come.

"And this was a wet year," Don told me. "You'd never have made it last year." The advice he gave me was smart and simple: "When you come to water, stay there for a few hours, overnight if possible. Let that horse and dog rehydrate before moving on." Then, the day before I left their ranch, Janet and Don took me on a drive south to the country I would be riding through in Colorado to give me even more perspective. It worked! Just knowing what was ahead, I felt a wave of confidence swelling in me.

Michele and I quickly became friends, shook our heads, and laughed about our fortuitous meeting. We talked often. The talks were lively discussions about women's spirituality, our journeys through the stages of womanhood (maiden, mother crone), raising buffalo, hunting, and Native American issues. We squeezed a newfound friendship into a brief four-day chance encounter. We spent a day in Rock Springs visiting

Don Irwin watches as I ready Pride. PHOTO COURTESY OF MICHELE IRWIN.

with her friends who owned Earthen Impressions, a new age bookstore. I found doggie booties for Claire and new clothes for me at the thrift store. Our quiet conversations consoled and encouraged me more than Michele knew. We have stayed in touch throughout the years.

Don knocked on the door at 5 A.M., and the aroma of venison steak, eggs, toast, and brewing coffee floated into my sleepy mind. Doubts of finishing my ride no longer held me hostage. Last week's discouraging miles were a lesson learned.

Don Irwin metaphorically filled my saddle bag with the "how tos" of crossing a sparse, arid desert country. Janet filled my belly with home-cooked meals. Actually, most often Don prepared pancakes and breakfasts if I remember correctly. Pride spent four days pastured with two of the Irwins' old horses. He grazed, rested, and was content. Claire received a continuing stream of attention and loved it. These folks, the Irwins and the Hamels, stood me back on my feet, dusted me off, and said, "Now see here young lady, you can do this!" Each in their own way had offered me more than they realized.

I'd been dehydrated and exhausted when I arrived—Claire, Pride, and I had all needed rest, food, and water. But my humanness needed more than that. More important than anything had been the Irwins and Hamels believing in me at this particularly difficult point in my journey. They rallied around me, looking at my wall of doubt and impossibility and rebuilding it with confidence. If these seasoned desert ranchers knew I could do it, if they believed in me, then maybe I could too. They gave me the courage to believe in myself again, and with it the will to go on.

NEW MEXICO BOUND

Before taking the lead, Claire pranced and danced around Pride's legs in real doggie booties, red with black Velcro straps. I'd replaced my old clothes with a sharp western look. The saddle and bridle were cleaned and oiled. I stepped into the saddle with confidence. A cool sagebrush morning kissed my cheek as the sun surfaced on the eastern edge. Pride stepped out with enthusiasm. Before me, historic Pilot Butte called out from the otherwise featureless landscape, "Here, this way, Rock Springs is right over here." Behind me stood the Irwins with all the faith in the world that I would make it just fine. We opened the imaginary gate to the land of the Red Desert and rode through.

From Rock Springs we continued slowly south through Colorado. When I rode out that morning I was 1,000 miles into my first adventure in long riding and I was beginning to realize how, magically, every night something had always come along, not always a Hilton experience, but I always got through it. The sun rose, the sun set, and no one yelled at me.

I came to realize that "giving" is a whole heck of a lot easier than the confounded difficulty of "asking." Stepping down from my prideful high horse and asking for food or shelter or water or directions would never be easy. But no one, as I had imagined, yelled, "You need what? You need water? Well, if you'd a just stayed home you wouldn't be needing any water!" I suppose a fair amount of people laughed or shook their head as I rode away, but most of the people I met along the way were considerate, helpful, and encouraging.

Bernice on Pride ready to ride on after recuperating at the Irwins' ranch.
PHOTO COURTESY OF MICHELE IRWIN.

When I look back on the ride from Rock Springs, Wyoming, south through Colorado and into New Mexico, it was hard, damn it was hard. It's a wonder I made it. Yes, I still got thirsty and hungry, and so did Claire and Pride, but we were okay. Every night we managed to be warm, safe, and dry. Each night I said thank you, and day by day I began to see the ride through a wider lens. When my eyes grew weary of the distance I studied my maps, combing for details, clues that might help me. The appreciation of a pleasant, quiet day with my horse and dog warmed me like a campfire. Claire and Pride received more attention and were relaxed, and we all seemed to be smiling in our own way. As we went along, I developed a "spiel" that I confidently repeated hundreds of times when we met new people: "My name is Bernice Ende, please forgive me for troubling you, I am traveling cross-country on my horse from the northwest corner of Montana. I need. . . ." I learned to ask ahead: "What do you hear for weather," "Are there any ranches between here and there, is there water? in the creek? in the dirt tank?

Two long-ride essentials: a journal and campstove.

Does the town have a farrier?" I stopped pushing so hard to go farther each day and found moments to breathe deep, enjoy and savor the miles we had already come, with an "Okay, we've made it this far."

As we descended into the northwest corner of Colorado, into more desert—rattlesnake country—the red rock canyons and rough rock formations brought to life those black-and-white cowboy movies I watched as a child that had so stirred my imagination. Only now the black-and-white cowboy movie was in color and I was riding in that magnificent western landscape. I let my imagination drift. Roy Rogers on Trigger galloped through country just like this. Now I was! As silly as it might sound, I enjoyed the thought, and for some unexplainable reason I felt that everything I had done in my life, however coincidentally, had prepared me for long riding. It finally dawned on me: I am riding across a desert, with my dog and horse, and seeing, feeling, and touching country close-up that until now I knew nothing about except for what was on a flat map. The further from the comforting familiarity of home I got, the harder became the challenge, the greater the adventure, the more about people and living I would learn, and the closer to the beckoning distant shore I would come.

By the time I reached my sister's home in Albuquerque two months later, I'd begun planning my next ride. For the first time in my life, I felt I was living in my own skin. I wrote in my journal: "I feel like a duck having just discovered it could float on water and fly with wings."

ROAMING THE WEST
2ND LONG RIDE

APRIL 2006 TO SEPTEMBER 2007
5,000 MILES

CHAPTER SIX

IF YOU WANT TO BE EXTRAORDINARY

There is no sin punished more implacably by nature
than the sin of resistance to change.
—ANNE MORROW LINDBERGH

A damp, raw morning crawled down my neck as I adjusted my leather gloves and wrapped my black wool scarf a little tighter under my chin. Honor's head dropped to the ground as she grabbed huge hungry bites of October brome grass. She'd kept Claire and I up last night; if one of us is up and nervous, so then are all of us.

Honor was now my long-riding horse. Pride, who I rode on my first ride and had grown to love and with whom I shared a mutual trust, belonged to Mac McCurry of Trego, Montana. Understandably he wanted Pride back. I needed another horse and had very little money. I answered an ad in a Washington paper. Honor was an eight-year-old, high-strung Thoroughbred mare with the famous Native Dancer breeding line. As a racehorse, she was a throwaway and apparently headed for the cannery when I answered the ad. When I went to see her, she was standing in mud and had rain rot on her back. I wasn't sure that this magnificent but pitifully cared-for animal could be a long-ride horse, but neither could I leave her here to face slaughter. I paid the price and took her home. When I tried to mount her or even lay across her back she fell to the ground. It took two months of care, massage, special feed, and doctoring one ailment after another before Honor was healed and

Honor and Claire on familiar home ground in Trego, Montana.

had her strength back. She was physically strong but still an emotionally fragile horse when we started on this journey.

Honor, Claire, and I were on a 5,000-mile ride through the Midwest and West. The ride would take sixteen months. We left Montana in April 2006, riding east through South Dakota, the corner of Minnesota, then south to Iowa, Nebraska, and Kansas. We were now seven months and 2,000 miles into the ride and were camped southwest of Dodge City. From here we would travel south, crossing the Oklahoma panhandle into Texas, then west through New Mexico, Arizona, Nevada, and into California, then north through Oregon, and finally east across Washington and back to our home in Montana.

Honor tugged and pulled at her picket line, distracted, walking circles, peering into the blackness at things I could neither see, hear, nor smell but that a horse can. Coyotes howled on and off throughout the long hours. Dogs replied with frantic, fast, barking jabs that came in across empty grain fields. I could hear traffic on Highway 56, a principal two-lane highway running east to west through the bottom half of Kansas just south of where we were camped. The road bore a stream of rattling, clattering semitrucks. The bang and whoosh from air brakes was audible throughout the night. Thanks to the direction of the wind, I did not know that the third-largest stockyard and meat-packing plant in the world were but fifteen miles west of us.

The night sky offered a broadcast of stars, and the smooth horizon was camouflaged with colored lights like stars fallen mysteriously from the black sky, now resting on the ground, twinkling and burning.

All through the night I was up and down, repeatedly walking over to Honor, comforting her with an "Easy girl, easy, it's okay." My reassurances did little good. "Will she ever settle down?" I wondered as I waited out the darkness with a discouraged heart.

I continued using the same camp setup as I had on my first ride. Claire waited impatiently, staring at the rice and beef jerky cooking in the blackened, dented four-cup stainless steel pot. Once I had fed everyone, I snuggled in under a sleeping bag next to Claire who was curled like a warm furry bagel. "We might not sleep but let's at least get some rest," I whispered in her ear. With Honor restless, I dared not sleep.

When I rose, a blanket of morning fog hung close to the ground. Visibility couldn't have been more than thirty feet in any direction. I later learned that methane gas from cattle manure can trap moisture and cause air inversions. A fresh west wind now carried a dominating odor as I maneuvered Honor across Highway 56. I grew up on a dairy farm and I know what a herd of cattle smells like. This odor smelled nothing like my father's dairy farm. My hand went over my nose. "What must it smell like to Claire and Honor?" I wondered as Honor came to a stop.

COFFEE STOP IN SOUTHWEST KANSAS

Except for grain elevators—"midwestern skyscrapers"—the Kansas horizon presents a smooth, undisturbed profile. From a distance, those 100-foot-tall grain elevators proclaim, "There is a town here. Stop and look." They are a measure of prosperity, storing a town's future, announcing a town's size, containing its continued livelihood. Nearly

Claire in her booties, crossing Kansas.

every small midwestern town I've ridden through has grain elevators, but too often the town itself has faded like an old black-and-white photo, and the elevators have been empty for years. Small towns and small farms have given way to the immense fields and feedlots of "Big Agriculture" on an industrial scale.

I sat in the saddle facing a cold southwesterly wind, debating my crossroad choices, "intersection pondering," as I call it. Which was it going to be? I could head south on County Road 10, a soft, lightly traveled gravel road promising a quiet, easy ride through this shamelessly naked Kansas farmland, or go southwest on Highway 56, a two-lane paved road with wide ditches, bearing load after truck load of live bovines going to their penultimate stop, the nearby feedlot, to gain weight before the slaughterhouse.

Honor tugged at the reins. Her long sleek neck lengthened as she reached for more grass, her eager black eyes attentive, ears twitching. Her head popped up, staring off in the direction of the ghastly stench. Claire was nearly hidden in dense longstem grasses. She circled and circled, flattening the grass with her paws into a small, round, soft bed.

Doing her best to make it comfortable, she looked serious and deter-mined in her actions. I smiled and looked back down the highway.

What was tugging at me? Why did I look west hoping to see the "skyscrapers" in Copeland? Why even consider riding beside a noisy, stinking, busy two-lane highway? Ordinarily I would avoid such "ditch riding." I ran the pros and cons through my head. I felt dreamy; the lack of sleep was getting to me. "Focus!" I thought. The wide ditch had recently been mowed, so Claire would be walking on soft grass, not gravel. It was also true that I would save many miles if I cut through the town of Copeland.

Or was it the possibility, the promise and comfort, of hot coffee that prompted me toward Copeland? No, I knew it was more than saved miles or hot coffee that had me looking west instead of south. This town promised more than that. I saw my cold fingers wrapped around a mug of hot coffee, steam rising onto my wrinkled face. Despite the noxious feedlot aroma enveloping me, I imagined breakfast cooking. In my mind I could hear a radio in the background, filling farmers' sunburned ears with weather updates. They would be wearing blue-and-white-striped bib overalls, worn and patched at the knees like my father's, and like my father they would wonder aloud at the economy or crops or the new tractor they could not afford but purchased anyway. Talking and drinking dishwater coffee, sharing stories that unite them in their struggle as farmers.

I had no idea if Copeland even had a cafe—I was merely dreaming. The wind had swept away the morning's fog, and I thought I could glimpse the top of Copeland's grain elevators and a tall water tank. Together, those giant totems promised that the town living in their shadows might very well be alive. Claire looked up at me. "Well, which way should we go?" I asked her. The question ignited her "take-off talk." She came up with this on her own. No amount of discouraging could stop this performance. Until we moved, she would whirl around, mak-ing short jumps, barks, yaps, and dances. Hiding her excitement was impossible; apparently she approved of this way of life.

At the bottom of that imagined cup of coffee would be the

exchange of humanity as it woke to another morning. What had me considering "ditch riding" was the chance to sit with others, inside, leisurely, comfortably laughing, smiling, and sharing. I wanted the nourishment and warmth that comes from human conversation.

Equestrian travel is of another period, something from the past. Gray overcast days like these would leave me feeling as if I'd slipped between the cracks. I felt like a ghost from the past—I was "out here" and everyone else was "in there." "Okay, okay, you win," I whispered to Claire. I hoped there would be a cafe in Copeland wearing an "open" sign in its window. Honor, Claire, and I turned and faced a putrid westerly wind.

The spectacle of a horse packed and loaded for long-distance riding, ridden by a woman, with a dog trotting beside is, granted, an uncommon sight. It is a startling "Oh, my gosh! Did you see that?" sight, and it coaxed waves, smiles, and honking horns from the cars and trucks rolling past us.

I ignored the long stares. My travel was slow, deliberate, unlike the urgency of those soaring by at seventy miles an hour. I kept my mind in the ditch. I watched for snakes and gopher holes, but I also had to keep an eye on the traffic. I tipped my hat at a honking horn but didn't look up. Causing an accident was the last thing I needed.

"Copeland, 8 miles," the green sign read. The gentle swell of a Kansas horizon is an illusion. It appears smooth, frame after frame of "boring" for many travelers who ride low in cars. But on a horse, at ten or eleven feet above the ground, I was elevated just enough to see a great distance. From the ground, the horizon looked empty, barren of inhabitants. But from my perch, a distant black mass on the western junction of sky and land soon grew into tens of thousands of mingling cattle, lying down or eating in one-acre dirt feeding lots. I'd never seen or smelled anything like it.

Prior to entering a feedlot, cattle will spend most of their life grazing on open range land. When they reach roughly 650 pounds, the cattle are transferred to a feedlot and fed a specialized diet consisting of corn by-products (derived from ethanol production), barley, and other grains, as well as alfalfa, cottonseed meal, and minerals. The conditions necessitate antibiotics. The animals will gain an additional 400 pounds during their three to four months in the feedlot. Once cattle are fattened to a desired weight, they are transported to a slaughterhouse, then to McDonald's or your dining room table.

Herds of cattle preparing for their next and final step answered my question of why Honor had been restless throughout the night. Undoubtedly, Claire and Honor picked up the scent or may have even heard them the previous night though we were miles away. I later learned that within a seventy-five-mile radius of Dodge City, 5 million head of cattle are "processed" each year. Thousands of living cattle passed us that morning in semitrucks. They were mostly brown and black cattle loaded tightly together, eyes wide with fear, peering out double-decked stock-trailers heading for slaughter. The smell assailed us.

Honor was hesitant; her ears flickering back and forth voiced her opinion. I covered my nose with my gloved hand. I noticed traffic had been slowing, and I soon knew why. Ahead, a flagman—a young man I guessed to be in his twenties—stood sentry holding a tall white pole with a red sign attached at the top. Slow! Stop! A crew was repaving the highway. The young man, wrapped warmly in a blue hooded sweatshirt, dark jeans, and winter boots, stood stoic like a soldier. This stretch of highway belonged to him and he controlled the masses with authority. I waved and smiled. Honor, Claire, and I could safely ignore his authority because we were in the ditch. To us, his orange vest and red sign meant only added color in a gray landscape. He called out, "Where y'all comin' from?" "Montana," I replied. He shook his head and gave me a big smile. While pushing his hood back he said, "You done rode all that way by ya' self?" Cars and trucks were lined up behind his stop sign; more were slowing to a stop. It was difficult hearing him over the noise of the paving machinery. I kept my hand over my nose. The nauseating smell of hot tar mixed with cattle manure was almost more than I could bear. The scents and sounds of this world were unknown to the passengers traveling in the clean protective shells of their vehicle with music blaring on their radios, holding a hot beverage and heaters warming their feet. "Oh my, I done always want ta do that," he yelled out. We stopped and Honor reached for grass. Claire stood nearby, shifting her weight and looking up at me, waiting for a cue. To understand his deep southern accent, I listened more closely. "I gotta friend who's gotta horse," he said. "I'm just gonna get that horse, I might just do it, go for a real nice long ride." "Well," I yelled back, relaxing in the saddle, "you've got time, you're not dead yet." He flashed another beautiful smile and said, "Hey, you mighten just see me out there ridin' along someday." "I'll look for you," I said and gave Honor a gentle squeeze with my legs as she grabbed one last bite of grass. "So many dreams," I thought as I signaled Claire ahead. We moved past the line of idling cars and trucks loaded with moaning and mooing cattle. So many dreams that never bear fruit, so many dreams blowing in the cold Kansas wind.

As if on cue, sunlight cast a brief flash upon the green and white highway sign that read, "Copeland 1 mile." I reached down and patted Honor on the neck, saying, "Come on, let's see if this town has a cafe." Turning away from the haste, urgency, and clamorous sounds of Highway 56 onto Main Street, like turning a page in a book, our scene dramatically changed. The sharp, solid, rhythmical sound of steel horseshoes on pavement announced our arrival to an all-but-empty Saturday morning street. At the far end were one car and one dirty pickup parked head first in front of a Dr. Pepper sign that read "Copeland Cafe." "Yes," I sang, "Yes!"

Midwest towns are unique in their look and character. Broad, spacious streets are lined with brick buildings occupied by agriculturally based businesses. Towns boast of not having a stoplight within their city limits. They are uncluttered, somber, but friendly and functional towns. As one woman put it, "We aren't a fancy lipstick and hairspray kind of town." In Copeland, several buildings were closed and obviously had been for years. City Hall sat across the street from the cafe. A block away was a tiny library, closed on Saturdays. I studied its simple architecture with appreciation. I don't take for granted our public libraries and post offices because, traveling the way I do, they have become increasingly important to me. At libraries, I am able to send emails and post to my website, and post offices enable me to receive and ship supply boxes and letters. Both are vital places for information.

I could see our reflection in the cafe's large window as we rode past. Inside, heads turned, fingers pointed. First, Honor had to be tied securely away from pedestrians and traffic. This presented no problem in Copeland. The cafe signpost would do. Next, Claire and Honor had to be visible from where I would sit inside. I saw an empty table near the window. Good! And finally, Honor had to be parked where no one would mind horse poop piles. The empty lot next to the cafe was weedy. Perfect!

I dismounted, knowing every move I made was observed. I removed the bridle and the packs from the saddle, then loosened the saddle girth and made Honor comfortable. I felt the warmth of sunshine on my neck as I spread Claire's blanket on the ground. I reached down with reassuring strokes, saying, "Stay, you stay Claire." A routine she knew well. "I promise I'll bring you food," I said. I left her in the sun already making herself comfortable against the red building trimmed in tan.

I reached for the door and stopped. The reflection of myself was alarming. I was wearing a filthy beige down jacket patched with silver duct tape and faded blue jeans rubbed with stains and dirt. On my feet were ill-fitting tennis shoes that were given to me by a family in Nebraska when Claire carried my boots into deep grass—after hours of searching, I had given up and left them behind. Looking at myself in the window, I wiped the back of my hand over my crusty lips and smoothed my wrinkled face. "What a mess," I thought. "They may refuse me service." I pulled my leather gloves off, tipped my broad-brim hat back, stepped inside, and realized how hungry I was.

"You must get pretty good gas mileage!" came a comment from an older gentleman with a broad smile as he swiveled around on a round silver stool to face me. He joked with his two friends sitting with him at the counter. At the corner table, two teenage boys dressed in jeans, t-shirts, and tennis shoes sat with a woman I guessed to be their grandmother. She wore traditional Mennonite clothing: a plain, homemade light blue dress and black scarf on her head. I guessed that she was taking her grandsons out for lunch. As I looked around, it occurred to me that the interior of the cafe matched the exterior of the land—bare, colorless, and flat. There were no booths, only tables and a counter with five swivel stools. Three of those were occupied by jolly farmers, one of whom had on blue-and-white-striped bib overalls with a patch on the knee. After my entrance, he resumed a conversation about tractors with his neighbors.

The waitress, a confident young lady of sixteen or seventeen, had everything under control. She came over with a glass pot of hot coffee. "Yes, please," I said energetically as I took my jacket off and settled into my vinyl-covered metal chair. Just as I'd imagined, steam eased my wrinkled face and my precious cup of hot coffee warmed my hands.

Two more teenagers—the cook and dishwasher—emerged from the kitchen wearing long red aprons. They'd brought with them their breakfast and sat at the table next to me, immediately firing questions: "Where did you ride from? Where do you sleep? Don't you get scared? Does your dog run all the way?" Their young curious minds reminded me of my ballet students. They blushed with potential.

I rarely order food at restaurants, not on my $20-a-week budget. But two breakfast burritos for $4? Okay, I decided, I'll take it. Hunger makes everything taste sensational. The cooks expressed delight watching me eat what I'm sure were over-sized burritos. "Oldies" played softly in the background. I looked out the big window and saw Claire sleeping in the sun against the wall. Honor's head nodded, her back hip cocked, resting. The ride along Highway 56 in a ditch now seemed worth it. Contentment poured from the coffee pot as I sat in this quiet, simple cafe.

One of the boys from the corner table came to the counter. He wore a striking turquoise t-shirt with the words *If you want to be extraordinary you have to stop being ordinary* printed on the back. "That's quite the statement," I said. He smiled shyly, paid the bill, and returned with change that he handed to his grandmother. The grandmother got up and came toward me, talking as she walked. "Don't you have anyone in a car or truck watching out for you?" she asked. I shook my head no. Without hesitation, she continued talking, her tone clearly that of matriarchal authority. "Don't you think it's awfully dangerous for you, a woman to be out riding alone? Do you have a cell phone if something happens to you?" She stood over me, a short, shapeless figure, like a one-room schoolmarm looking sternly down at her disobedient student. Her hair was tied in a precisely bunched bun under her black scarf, and a black purse hung from a strap looped through her arms crossed over her waist. She must have overheard the girls questioning me.

The two young boys stood waiting by the door, obviously embarrassed, looking in any direction but at their grandmother. "Well, what happens if you get hurt?" she asked. "Do you mean that you contact no one, that no one knows where you are?" I assured her that I called once a week to let my family know I was alive. None of my answers satisfied her. She simply could not understand why any woman in her right mind would pursue something so dangerous or foolish. Her concern was genuine, and I truly did not mind her taking the time to walk over and give me the once over. My mother may have done the same. I assured her that I used caution as anyone should when traveling by horse; that long riding is not for everyone; and yes, it's dangerous but then should I not do it? True, it's not an ordinary method of travel, but I find it interesting and challenging. "Sometimes we must step outside the ordinary to find what we're looking for. I think your grandson might agree," I pressed on in defense. Up till that point, everyone in the cafe had been silent, with heads turned, watching and listening to the entire exchange of words. We all moved our focus to look at the young boy in the striking turquoise shirt who then slowly turned around for us. The waitresses, customers, cooks, and myself listened as the grandmother read aloud, "If you want to be extraordinary you have to stop being ordinary."

"I think he knows what I'm talking about," I said, smiling at the blushing boy. He did know what I was talking about. This produced a faint smile across the concerned grandmother's face. I silently wondered how this young boy came to be wearing such a statement. The two boys were not dressed in traditional Mennonite clothing. Had the grandmother's daughter or son chosen an alternative lifestyle, leaving behind their religious path? Or maybe the son-in-law or daughter-in-law had influenced the boy's choice of a turquoise and extraordinary life instead. But then I thought following a Mennonite faith was not exactly ordinary. It was a faith most people would find impossible to follow. Mennonites oppose taking of oaths and infant baptism; they are pacifists and refuse military service or the holding of public office. Their manners and clothing speak for them; they favor simple, plain living.

What else could I tell the worried grandmother? I told her that I felt I'm forever being watched over. That people stopped every day for roadside visits and for the most part were always generous and helpful. "I ride wrapped in prayers," I said. This helped ease the tension on her face and produced a nod. She seemed satisfied. With arms still crossed at the waist, she took a deep breath, heaving her thick arms up then down. We all looked at one another—the boys at me, the girls at the boys and then at the woman. The grandmother looked out the window one last time and then she turned toward me and with a genuine smile she said, "Well it must be quite the adventure." With that, she turned toward one of the boys, who helped her on with her jacket, and she proudly led the procession out the door that was held open by her other young escort.

Two more men, one dressed in overalls and a green John Deere cap, entered the cafe. Time picked up again. One more cup of coffee? Okay, but last one! The girls brought food from the kitchen for Claire and carrots for Honor. I left a big tip under my cup when they refused to accept my money. "But girls, I drank five dollars' worth of coffee," I said. "Let me get a photo of you with my horse and dog." We took the photo and the three girls ran back inside, back to their teenage lives and futures. I thanked them for breakfast and left one of my cards. On it I wrote, *If you want to be extraordinary you have to stop being ordinary. Copeland Cafe.*

Claire ate her table scraps, Honor chomped down her carrots, and they both drank water. With saddle and gear safely secured, I waved goodbye and, leading Honor, walked down the middle of Main Street. Traffic noise grew louder and I stepped back in the saddle as we neared Highway 56. We proceeded past the towering gray concrete silos.

The friendly crew at the Copeland Cafe.

"Thank you for calling my attention your way," I thought as we continued west, leaving behind a town still very much alive, past a few more stockyards, until once again we were wrapped in the humorless Kansas landscape with me thinking, "You never know what kind of extraordinary people you'll meet in an ordinary Midwest cafe having an ordinary cup of coffee."

CHAPTER SEVEN

PIE À LA HOME

The trick is not to satisfy our longings but to cherish them.
—GIACOMO CASANOVA

As I saddled Honor, a cascade of brilliant sunlight lit three inches of fresh snow that had fallen the night before. The sun's warmth on our backs did not last long. By noon, shortly after we crossed the Continental Divide, it began snowing, not heavily but enough that I kept my face down. It was cold enough to keep me walking for warmth. Honor held her head at my back, using me as a windbreak. Claire found this weather glorious. I longed for home.

I was not well. I was running a fever and needed rest. I was also confronted with a long, twenty-mile day from Datil to Pie Town, traveling Highway 60 across central New Mexico. It was after 3 P.M. and already the light was dim. There was a fair amount of traffic on the lonesome stretch of highway that runs like a black ribbon through the belly of New Mexico's expansive high-desert country. I held Honor's lead rope in my left hand and Claire's lead rope in my right. We walk on the right side of the two-lane pavement. The snow built up under Honor's hoofs, packing hard between the steel horseshoe and the warm sole of her hoof. In no time, she was walking on three-inch snow stilts and I had to stop frequently to clean out the hoof. As much as possible, we walked on the pavement that was clear of snow. We were "pounding the pavement," as the saying goes.

74

Claire stayed off the hard surface and trotted in the grass where the snow was sticking and growing deeper. How good that must have felt on her paws, but the accumulating snow added worry to my steps. I had tried several commercial doggie booties on Claire, but nothing fit well. They either chafed or fell off or were otherwise uncomfortable. Claire hated them. In one of my creative moments, I made two pairs of booties from deer hide. They were custom-fit moccasin-like booties laced up with baby socks inside to keep sand out and were a great success. But soft snow on bare paws must have felt good to her.

Snow skimmed sideways across the desolate twenty-foot-wide path we were following. The winter of 2006-2007 was dropping record snowfall and was threatening bronco-bucking winds again. "It's probably going to blow all night," I thought to myself. I was halfway through a 5,000-mile ride, exhausted and sick, and I was finding little meaning in the lonesome daily routine. You can ride the same road twice, but ride in different seasons and you'll have two completely different experiences. Hot summer sun is not considered an unreasonable riding condition. Fall and winter riding can be brutally hard and often lonely. People don't stop as often.

We were a lowly looking sight—horse, dog, and woman wrapped in foul weather. Riding a horse cross-country though winter months when it's snowing, blowing, and damn cold is beyond the sensibility of most people. People in cars pass a bleak-looking image. They can't take their eyes off the unexplained sight as they race by in their shells of steel. They are warm, listening to music, chatting about life, thinking about family issues, jobs, or what they're going to buy. They have food and they have water and maybe hot coffee and maybe chips and maybe a sweet roll or. . . .

As we plod down the road, the imaginary list ran through my hungry mind. "And they don't even have coats on!" I thought to myself, with envy of their warmth. As they passed along, their head-twisting stares sent pity washing over me. I felt like a homeless woman and, yes, momentarily a little sorry for myself. "Why am I doing this?" I wondered. "This is stupid. Go home."

A few juniper trees in the ditch along the highway were not much of a wind break but there was grass here for Honor and Claire needed a rest. I sat on my heels with the wind at my back, bundled in a beige down jacket, black scarf, and wool cap. I pulled a sandwich from my saddle pack that Janet Coleman had sent with me that morning. I chewed slowly, returning a passerby's wave with a nod of my head. "Maybe someone will stop and give me hot coffee," I said aloud to myself, but no one stopped.

I had spent the two previous nights in the tiny town of Datil at the home of Janet and Jim Coleman, waiting out another snowstorm. Seventy-five-year-old Jim Coleman would tell you that "riding in winter in the Southwest is not hard." And he could tell you a hundred stories about riding winter to prove it.

In his younger life he'd been a rancher and a cowboy. "We all rode, all winter, and never thought anything of it." he said. The horses do better in cold weather than in hot, there's snow and water puddles across a land that makes you reach and stretch for a drink of water any other time of year. Tall brown grasses in the ditch will easily sustain a healthy horse. "Ride between snowstorms; find hay and grain when you get into town," Jim would say. He reminded me of my dad. They were about the same size, and both had large, calloused, working-man's hands. Like my dad, Jim wore bib overalls and had the same farmer sensibility and can-do-ness.

I broke off a piece of sandwich for Claire; she got half the baloney sandwich with mayo and iceberg lettuce. She grabbed at snow with her mouth, gulping it down. With her back legs stretched behind her like a frog, she dragged her hot belly through virgin snow and slid slick as an otter down the ditch. This was perfect weather for her. The snow kept her feet damp, soft, and cool. Her thick calico-colored coat was exquisitely designed for this 30-degree temperature. I swear she was smiling as she rolled in the snow over and over again.

There's a reason I hadn't stopped the ride and waited out the winter. In the coming month, I would be crossing Death Valley and the Mojave Desert. The heat of New Mexico and Arizona deserts would make it very difficult to cross any other time of the year. February would be the best time to do it. "Keep moving," I said to myself.

PIE TOWN, USA

"Pie Town 5 miles" read the green sign. At three or four miles an hour, I had another hour and a half of riding. My wristwatch read 3:30 P.M. It would be dark early, and I could tell another storm was moving into my path. I stepped into the saddle and rode the remaining miles to Pie Town.

Until that time, I had not really considered what Pie Town might hold for me. But now the word "PIE" stood out like a carrot in front of a horse. "Pie's?" I wondered aloud. "Will they really have pies, like lots of pies?" I asked Claire. Is this a town I could not only see but taste?

There is very little foreplay when riding into small Southwestern towns, no huge seducing billboards coercing, luring the hungry, the weary, and the lost. Pie Town at first sight did not look hopeful. I rode past a community park and a set of old corrals, which I mentally filed as a potential campsite.

According to a sign on the door, the Pie-o-neer was "Closed for the Holidays." My heart sank. "Bernice, it's getting dark, you have to find hay, grain, and a place to camp," I thought as I tied Honor's lead rope to the steel handrail outside a tiny adobe-style building. A wooden handmade sign hung above the door proclaiming it the "Pie Town Post Office." The hub of any small community is the post office. I have found this to be true in small towns wherever I've traveled. It's a good place to start asking for help, as word will spread quickly. "A lady just rode into town from where? Montana? No way!" "She needs. . . ." I do not know why it's so hard stepping down from my high horse to humbly ask for food, water, and shelter, but it is. Admitting I don't have at the very least the bare essentials was admitting failure or at least misfortune, and inviting pity, which I did not want. But I went in the post office in Pie Town and asked anyway.

I knocked on the first door I was directed to, but the person who answered said, "No, sorry, we sold our horses this summer, go ask so and so." Still leading Honor with one hand and Claire with the other, I walked down the empty street with snow blowing in our faces. I felt anxious and wondered how this was going to work out. I knocked on another door and heard, "Try the Daily Pie Café, someone down there might be able to help you."

"What, another Pie Café?" I thought as we headed for the west end of the tiny, dreary, deserted-looking town.

I felt the urgency gnawing in my stomach as I wrapped Honor's lead rope around a juniper tree behind the Daily Pie Café. Temperatures were dropping fast; I urgently needed a place where we could camp—the snowstorm had arrived.

Peggy Rawl's smile could warm a snowman. It could disable a fierce warrior; it could make sunshine obsolete. Her smile could stop a war, and when I saw that smile I knew I'd been saved.

Peggy's striking red hair, a neat thick braid trailing down her back, matched the red apron she wore. She flashed her, "Of course I will help you smile," as she stood in the doorway. The café had closed at five, but Peggy remained, cleaning up by herself. No, she was baking pies!

In the glow of the yard light behind the café, I could see how hard it was snowing. "Come in, come in and warm up," she said, wiping her hands on her apron. "You'd better stay inside, they're predicting a snowstorm tonight."

"I think it's already here," I said, stepping in behind her. I was abruptly stopped in my tracks by the aroma—that rich, welcoming scent of fresh baked bread and pies. The café felt warm and funky, and yes it was HOME I was smelling. HOME!

Minutes after I explained my situation, Peggy called local rancher Dave Zable, who braved the near-blizzard conditions to bring two bales of hay from his ranch three miles west of town. The juniper tree behind the café offered some shelter. I pulled the saddle and packs off of Honor and covered her back with a wool blanket. "It's not the best," I said, stroking her neck and reassuring myself. "It's going to be cold tonight," I thought. "But Honor is out of the wind, she has a blanket, warm water, and good hay." I carried my gear inside and found Peggy had already

The Daily Pie Café, Pie Town, New Mexico.

cleared away a table in the corner by the woodstove. I spread my bed-roll out on the rough-cut floorboards and set my gear neatly against the wall. I let the heat of that old woodstove soak into my cold bones. Claire was already asleep on the bedroll. "I'm glad you're here," Peggy said. "My husband and son are gone for a few days, you can keep the fire going, and I won't have to come down tonight." I felt better being of some use. I wished Honor were inside with me. It's agonizing when I'm sheltered and my horse must be outside. It's not right! I feel I should be out there with her. Temperatures dropped into the single digits. A silent wind slowly covered the high desert with six inches of spectacular snow. I watched it growing as I stepped out from time to time, checking on Honor, taking her carrots and apples from the fridge. The woodstove snapped and cracked when I put another log in. It poured heat and contentment into my weary bones. I felt safe, I felt at home.

In the morning, clumps of sagebrush peaked from beneath a transformed horizon. What a sight for this northern girl. By 11 A.M. that brilliant Southwestern sun began melting the frozen landscape. Peggy came in early, cars began pulling up to the parking lot, and within minutes the café erupted into activity. Customers with excitement in their voices began arriving. Snow in the desert is an event.

I started the coffee brewing as I gathered my gear and moved it aside, then checked on Honor. She was gone. I panicked, dropped everything, and Claire and I set out, following a clear trail through fresh snow. Honor is a Thoroughbred racehorse. She had taken off on me before and ran for miles.

Fortunately, this morning she had decided not to go far. I found her pawing for wet brown grass, standing nonchalant in the morning sunshine. "Come on you two," I said. "Let's find us a place to call home for a few days."

When we returned, the café was circled by older, beat-up pickup trucks. It was the last day before Peggy closed for the holidays. Inside, windows steamed more from talk than from hot food. I was hungry and couldn't stand it any longer. I dug into my pocketbook of dwindling money and ordered a "kitchen sink" omelet. Claire remained outside, happy with snow and sun, successfully begging for treats from the young girl washing dishes. I also saved her half my breakfast. The talk in the café was of weather. "Looks like its gonna snow all week," I heard Dave Zable say. My heart sank.

Obviously I wasn't going anywhere. I'd have to find more permanent accommodations. Several people offered their houses or a barn, but what I really wanted—needed—was to go home. I'd been longing for home for days now. Homemade pies and the holidays only intensified my longings. There's much visiting as a long rider, always a guest, night after night in someone else's home. The animals and I are stopped day after day by the curious and the interested, but what I needed now was home—quiet, rest, being alone with my family. But how?

When I walked back to the café after retrieving Honor, I noticed several shacks, apparently abandoned. One shack just up the hill from Peggy's café looked habitable. "What do you think, Peggy?" I asked when I got back to the café. "Would anyone mind if I held up there for a few days? The tiny tar-paper shack isn't too bad inside. The yard is sort

Honor and Claire relax at their temporary home in Pie Town, New Mexico.

of fenced in—I could fix it up for Honor." Dave Zable said he'd bring more hay over. I'd have to haul water up the hill from the café, but I could manage okay. No one seemed to know just who owned it "Some guy from California; he won't mind," was the general consensus of the coffee-drinking, pie-eating customers.

"We have a new home," I wrote in my journal on December 29, 2006. "Nothing fancy, a tar-paper shack with a million dollar view, a still-standing remnant from the past."

Some of the windows were broken and patched with cardboard, plastic, and plywood. The whole shack was lopsided, resting on its right side like a tired old man. I dragged a usable mattress and a faded green, chipped drop-leaf table from the front room into what would be my bedroom in back. I brought my gear into the middle room, which had, amazingly enough, a small parlor woodstove with a good stovepipe sticking haphazardly out of the roof. The side of the firebox had a crack that I could see through, which worried me; I would have to be careful. I closed off two rooms with blankets and found a five-gallon

It might not look like much, but the old shack felt like home.

bucket outside for a chair. I patched the fence surrounding the yard well enough to secure Honor. The front yard was littered with sticks and wood I could use for firewood. A small shed in the back would work as a hay shed, and there was a handmade shovel for keeping Honor's pen clean. We were set.

On top of all that, this tar-paper shack had an extraordinary view of New Mexico's western horizon, the immense snow-covered sagebrush expanse splayed out before me. Simply breathtaking! I had a tar-paper shack with a million-dollar view.

Honor was happy with the alfalfa hay. I gathered wood, built a fire, then cleaned and arranged my belongings. It took no time at all to feel at home. And what is home but a place where families and friends come together. "Go home and rest, go home and eat, go home and be with your family." We were family, Honor, Claire, and I. We needed home-time as all families do. Shacks can make very good homes—it matters less what they're made of than what you fill them with. The most luxurious, spacious houses can be beautiful on the outside but void of home on the inside.

"It's supposed to get down below zero tonight," Peggy said as we climbed the snow-covered hill to my new home. Peggy came armed with a staple gun and blankets. I carried other essentials: cardboard boxes, duct tape, and large plastic bags for patching up the windows. We were self-sufficiency in motion, collaborating in the act of creation— a shack becomes a home! We giggled with excitement, not to mention a little wine. We saw the potential in this shack and it made us laugh. A candle burned on the table, the woodstove easily heated the room. We toasted "To Home," sharing a bottle of wine. "Now here I am," I said, "already entertaining a guest in my new *home*."

Snow continued to fall hard. Geez, I thought, I may be here forever. Peggy did not stay long. Honor stood outside covered with blankets, her nose touching the dilapidated front door that did not shut tight. She was hoping for more treats, perhaps an apple, carrot, or grain. Claire liked her new home; she curled in a ball on the mattress, taking long, deep sighs. More snow fell and long icicles hung outside the window. It was a picture-perfect winter holiday scene.

I borrowed a kerosene lantern from my next-door neighbors, its dim light casting shadows against faded rose-flowered wallpaper. I imagined a woman carefully preparing this room for her family. Adding color, she had hung bright yellow curtains, now faded and tattered, with red pull back ties. She trimmed the windows in white and covered handmade wood shelves behind the stove with red-and-white-checkered plastic contact paper. Even the linoleum, its brightness lost, cracked and stained, tells me this humble space must have meant something to her. I imagine a young woman taking pride in the home she'd created.

Pie Town had many vacant shacks, and I wondered what had happened to the families that once lived and loved in them? Where had everyone gone?

The next morning, I sat at the Pie Town Café counter with hot coffee and read a story Paul Hendrickson wrote for the *Smithsonian* in the February 2005 issue, "Savoring Pie Town." According to the article, a miner named Norman opened a general store at this red-dirt crossroads. He baked pies and sold them out of his store. As Hendrickson

A brief history of Pie Town on the Pie-O-Neer's front porch.

reports, "Mr. Norman's pies were such a hit that everybody began calling the crossroads Pie Town. Around 1927, the locals petitioned for a post office. The authorities were said to have wanted a more conventional name. The Pie Towners said it would be Pie Town or no town." The Dust Bowl of the Depression years drove people here, west from Oklahoma and Texas. Hendrickson says the town peaked then with a population of around 250 families, and it boasted a school, hotel, and its own baseball team. But then drought came to Pie Town and people left for bigger cities or greener pastures.

"It must have been quite the place! Still is!" I thought, smiling to myself. Then I raised my focus toward the pie case. "Should I?" I did, and there is nothing better than a Pie Town pie.

Later that day, I set out to explore Pie Town and exercise Honor's Thoroughbred legs. Claire couldn't hide her enthusiasm—she barked and danced in the snow. I rode past Lester Jackson Park when I first came into town, and it was there that I discovered a famous home once belonging to Bob Sundown. Sundown, as he was known, spent forty years traveling

Bob Sundown's home on wheels, Pie Town, New Mexico.

the Southwest in his little shack on wheels pulled by a team of donkeys. When he passed away in 2004, his wagon became a shrine, exactly as he left it at Jackson Park. His wagon home looked like a big tent on wheels covered with layers upon layers of faded blue, green, and brown plastic tarps. When one tarp wore out or tore, it stayed, and Sundown simply layered another tarp over the old one and tied it down in the most creative way imaginable with ropes and twine or wire.

Sundown had made a heat stove from a five-gallon drum and used coffee cans to fashion a stovepipe out the side of his precarious setup. He slept on a plywood bench in the back of the wagon and cooked food with a green two-burner Coleman stove. Inside were wire scraps, nails, and cups with broken handles—probably stuff he'd found on the road.

I gleaned a bit about Sundown from a January 9, 2003, article in *Southern New Mexico* online magazine that was written by Carla DeMarco and titled "Freedom in a Sheep Wagon."

Oldtimer Bob Sundown is a dropout in the true sense of the word. For 40 years he has voyaged about 20 miles a day along the

West's gritty highway shoulders in a donkey-drawn sheep wagon he and some kids built from discarded materials. "Thousands of friends," a few live-in chickens and his knowledge of edible plants form his sometimes tenuous security net. Although he intentionally draws no pension nor social security, he claims he's the richest man on Earth because he knows how to "use his mind." The seventy-something, slow-and-steady traveler espouses hard-won creeds borne of stark life experience. It's apparent this slight, one-eyed, leathery-faced man in dusty clothes has conquered concepts cerebral seekers grapple with perpetually. As his story unfolds, he untangles fear, worry, surrender, attention to the moment, freedom and peace of mind sagaciously in the rough, unfeigned tongue of cowboy slang. Sundown bears his Nez Perce Sioux mother's name. After his wife was killed in an automobile accident, he decided the fast lane was not his friend. He relinquished his worldly goods and properties to his children. He eats plants, jackrabbits, chickens and eggs. His burros, he says, "always have hay." Sometimes, if he has money left over after his burros are fed; he treks to town and treats himself to some store-bought food. "I'm not afraid to go hungry," he says. "It never killed me yet." Humans will be free when they learn to surrender their fear-based need to control, says the cowboy, intimating that the mind can expand to a clear perspective when aired in nature's open spaces. "Lots of people are afraid to do the way I do; they say they can't. I say, How do you know? Have you ever tried?". . . He believes humans from all walks of life face tough roads, and the key to peace is in learning to handle the fear that accompanies struggle. "People are worrying about, 'what am I going to do tomorrow?' Let a person who has real heavy duty fears of life just go someplace away from every place else and just give up on everything and relax and start to thin—use their mind. Then they figure, 'Hey! By golly! I made it through today!' They realize, 'Hey, I could have done this but I was afraid.' Then they figure again, 'What was I afraid of?'"

By most people's standards it wasn't much of a home, but Bob Sundown found it more than suitable, more than enough. His shrine, the "wagon home," is a legacy, a lesson in the possibilities of home.

HOME SWEET HOME

Snow continued falling on and off throughout my respite week in Pie Town. "A record snowfall," I was told. But each day the sun warmed our faces for a few hours and we walked around town, exploring. A "free box," like a mini secondhand store, sat in front of the community center. "FREE" was written in large black letters painted on the side of the big wooden box. It was filled with household items, clothes, bedding, books, and junk. I picked out winter pants, blankets, sweaters, and books, all of which I returned when I later left town.

I encountered an interesting lawn decorated with toasters. Yes, all manner of silver toasters hung from pinion trees, making an arched entrance. Some were on the steps leading into the tiny shack house, some were creatively arranged on a peeling white picket fence, and some were stuck in the unmowed lawn. In my travels, I've seen fences made of snow skis, cowboy boots stuck on fence posts, and mailboxes made of car parts, but never had I seen a yard landscaped with toasters.

On Wednesday the commodities truck arrived. Like a pack rat, I was looking for more useful items in the "free box" and noticed people inside the community hall standing at long tables filled with food. There was outdated canned food, baked goods, crackers, rice, and pasta in torn packages but no fresh food. I hesitated to ask—I wasn't a resident—but there were no grocery stores of any kind in town and I couldn't possibly afford to eat at the café every day. I had my own stock of oatmeal, sea salt, molasses, and peanut butter, but not much of that was left. The two ladies in charge welcomed me in, saying, "Yes, yes of course, come in, there's plenty for all of us." As I moved down the long table, they said, "Here, take some of these, better take some of this," while generously loading plastic bags with food. In my mind, I was thinking, "Okay, what will my horse and dog eat?" Honor liked crackers and donuts and Claire would eat anything. I did not tell the ladies I'd be sharing the food with my family, who just happened to be a horse and a dog.

Back at my shack, the back porch steps I sat on were broken. I ate breakfast under a clear, crisp Southwestern sky. Steam rolled off my oatmeal cooked on the woodstove with lots of sea salt, molasses, and olive oil that I borrowed from Peggy. It was a delicious feast for this lady long rider. Honor left her hay and came over, bumping and nuzzling against my shoulder. She obviously thought this meal should include her. Claire finished her breakfast of oatmeal, sea salt, raw egg (from Peggy), and olive oil and was dragging her belly in the snow, rolling in sheer delight. Home was like this for us; we ate and shared our meals together. In one short week, I'd comfortably settled in at Pie Town and made friends. I knew the neighbors and became a temporary resident. I did not welcome the thought of leaving this home. "Why don't you just stay?" I thought to myself.

Peggy reopened her café after a four-day holiday break. Cars drove in and out all morning. Peggy was busy filling bellies with homemade pies and hot coffee and warming hearts with her smile. Many customers considered this restaurant "home," and if there was an unhappy face that walked out the door, well, they apparently had not eaten a slice of homemade pie or shared a story over a two-hour cup of coffee. All manner of people leisurely connected with one another. Oh, how our human heart longs for that!

As much as I felt at home in Pie Town, I couldn't stay. Curiosity wouldn't let me. The lure of the horizon would pull me back into the saddle. "Tomorrow," I thought, "I'll pack my saddle bags and head west on Highway 60. As I ride out of town, I'll turn in my saddle, turn and say thank you, thank you for this time of home in a tar-paper shack with its million-dollar view." Bathed in the aroma of homemade pies, I realized that I'd learned an important lesson about home and how I could take an empty space and fill it with "home," fill it with love, wherever I went. Maybe home is a choice; wherever you hang your hat, wherever you feel respected and secure, engaged in life and appreciated for who you are is a place you can call "home."

"It's all downhill from here."

At the café, Peggy's coffee mugs were engraved to read, "Pie Town, New Mexico, on top of the Continental Divide, it's all downhill from here." Ironic, I thought, to be halfway through this 5,000-mile ride. We were standing on the Continental Divide at 8,000 feet above sea level, and after a week of rest at home in Pie Town, USA, it was quite possible the last half of this adventure would be "all downhill." We three rovers were energized and heading west through Arizona, Nevada, and California, and then north to Oregon and Washington before turning east to our home in Montana.

CHAPTER EIGHT

NIGHT OF THE BLACK STALLION

(THIS CHAPTER IS EXCERPTED FROM THE AUTHOR'S STORY
OF THE SAME TITLE THAT APPEARED IN THE
WINTER 2014 EDITION OF FIDO FRIENDLY MAGAZINE.)

As we crossed the high desert of northwest New Mexico, Claire and I had been sleeping under the open sky. It was too windy to use the tent and I slept in my clothes. One night, Claire dashed out from under the warm down sleeping bag, waking me with a jolt. A full moon flashed like a beacon on and off as broken, troublesome dark clouds sprinted across a rebellious looking sky. Belligerent winds whipped a layer of dust and dirt into my face. A few feet to my right, Claire's rigid stance signaled danger and her barking quickly turned into snarling rage. Flaring rows of sharp teeth appeared out of the dark, and I knew we had trouble. But not until I heard the wild, high-pitched squeal from the distance did I know what was happening.

When I heard the high-pitched squeal, I quickly slipped on my head lamp, grabbed for my boots, and yelled, "Claire, no! No, Claire, stay!"

In a flicker of moonlight, the outline of an enormous, rangy black stallion standing on his hind legs flashed before me, his front hoofs beating out defiance. I knew in an instant the stallion was determined to take my beautiful eight-year-old mare Honor into his harem, and he was just as determined to kill Claire and me if need be. The stallion let out a throaty, menacing scream, flattened his ears against his head, barred his teeth, and lunged for us.

Claire on alert.

Earlier that day, as the sun set on a long, twenty-five-mile day, I chose to make camp near an ancient but functioning windmill. The windmill churned with dizzying speed in the high winds, pumping precious water into an overflowing tank held together by rusty corrugated steel. I chose to make camp there because we needed the water. The mistake I made—the lesson I still had not learned—was never camp near water in the desert! I had naively broken a golden rule. Animals large and small, wild and domestic, would surely come in at night for a much-needed drink from the wheel of good fortune. We had already disturbed a herd of wild burros and half dozen cantankerous, wretched-smelling feral pigs. Now I faced the screaming stallion.

My hand gripped Claire's halter as she raged back at the stallion's challenge. "I have to get us out of here," I yelled in my head. "Get out of here! Leave us alone!" I screamed aloud, swinging my thick picket rope at the stallion who wheeled, kicking his hind hoofs at me before plunging back into the darkness. Claire broke free and dashed out after the stallion. My heart dashed out with her. "No, no, no, Claire! No!" I screamed. "No!"

Bernice, Claire, and Honor in the high desert.

Honor, who was tied near my bedroll, began pulling and thrashing in distress. Claire's barking and chasing suddenly stopped. She cried out and suddenly appeared at my legs with cactus needles stuck in her paws and nose. "Oh Claire," I said in desperation, snapping a leash on her before swinging again at the fierce shriek and charge of the stallion now coming in low. His black neck stretched long, my headlight picked out his aging yellow teeth. I swung again and again. He momentarily ricocheted off.

In a fit of frantic speed, I pulled the cactus needles from Claire's paws then threw together the camp gear and saddled Honor. Claire stayed with me, barking out warnings and fierce indignation at the black stallion that was now madder than ever. He charged and tried pulling the saddle from Honor's back. I had never seen anything like this raging equine wildness. I needed to move, to act, to respond. But move where? Which way was out? I had to follow the fence line and find the cattle guard where I could cross and the wild horses could not.

"Which way is it?" I pleaded in my head. I unsnapped Claire from her leash with faith she'd know the quarter-mile path leading us back to the gate. "Okay, Claire, okay, let's go!" I said. The stallion darted in front of us, savagely shrieking at Honor. The stallion's herd, what little I could see of it, was running on our right. The range stallion had only one thing on its mind—Honor. He had no use for Claire and me; we only stood in the way of his instinctive plans. I threw rocks and swung again and again with my picket stake as he weaved from one side to the other, roaring and charging. We wove our way in and out of sagebrush and thorny mesquite bushes, stumbling through the wind and night-marish darkness.

Claire was now guiding us with uncanny precision, leading Honor and I to the gate and out of danger. As we passed through the gate, the angry stallion stood on his hind legs and let out an infuriating scream. Then he spun, flinging dirt and pebbles at his loss, before returning to his already running herd.

We were like runners at the end of a race, exhausted and bruised by the impending risk of losing but finally winning. I grabbed Claire, hugging and praising her. I wrapped my arms around Honor's neck and with Claire leaning against my legs I cried, "Oh, Claire you are the best dog that ever lived!"

CHAPTER NINE

JEWEL OF THE COLUMBIA

Claire Dog, Honor, and I were 4,000 miles into our 5,000-mile ride. Claire had easily walked the entire distance. I walked half my miles each day to relieve Honor of her burden—me. On this long ride, we had circumnavigated the flat spacious farm and ranching communities of the Great Plains. We had ridden and walked south onto the red dirt roads of New Mexico and Arizona, tromped across Death Valley, and then climbed our way north up the intimidating Sierra Nevada. We found our way through the dense rainforest of the Cascade Range and then over the Coast Range south of Astoria, Oregon, where we met the Pacific Ocean. I understood the exhilaration that Lewis and Clark must have felt when finally, after months of exhausting trials, their weary expedition reached the Pacific and he exclaimed "great joy in camp, we are in view of the ocian." I felt that joy in a smaller way when, after sixteen months of equestrian travel, the Pacific Ocean came into view.

Astoria is a jewel wedged into the cheek of the Columbia River. After a winter of relentless rain, the townspeople of Astoria spill out into the sunshine, filling the streets with playful events. Farmers markets and wine and music festivals miraculously sprout on the sidewalks. Brilliantly designed kites catch and play on the ocean winds. Tourists stroll the paved walking and bicycle paths, while not so ambitious onlookers lounge on park benches and bask in the exotic scents and sounds of waterfront activities. Seagulls pilot the sky with death-defying

acrobatic maneuvers over lazy, blubbery sea lions hoisting insults at one another.

The day we rode into town, a cruise ship had docked beneath the Astoria-Megler Bridge and unleashed a flood of curious, happy travelers, creating a carnival effect upon the already festive streets of Astoria. Generous smiles and waves were pitched our way from joggers running side by side with their canine friends on their trails to good health and fitness. Claire, Honor, and I were but one more group of welcomed visitors to this friendly town celebrating summer. We simply clip-clopped our way into town on a glorious summer afternoon and joined in. Claire pranced in her leather moccasin booties as a television news crew came looking for a story about the odd-looking adventuress and her traveling companions.

Claire had cut her hind foot and needed several weeks to recuperate. We met the Clatsop County Sheriff's Posse at Astoria's famous Pig 'N Pancake Restaurant. They had offered to haul us across the busy 4.2-mile-long Astoria-Megler Bridge that reaches like a long arm from Oregon across the mighty Columbia River to the steep, rocky shores of Washington.

Astoria was our farthest point west on this trip. Once across the bridge, we rested for nearly a month in the tiny Finnish community of Naselle, Washington. From here we would turn our heads east into the rising sun, facing another 1,000 miles before completing this bold 5,000-mile adventure we had begun in May 2006. Like a brilliant jewel cast securely into its setting, Astoria sparkled and winked at us from the southern shore of the Columbia River. I heard it, I am sure I did. I heard Astoria call out, "Happy trails, until we meet again, happy trails." Waves slapped against the gray, moss-covered boulders as the tide changed. We made our way east, following the formidable river, heading for Montana and home.

In Astoria with the Clatsop County Sheriff's Posse, ready for the haul across the Columbia River. PHOTO COURTESY OF LARRY ZIAK.

DESERTS, PLAINS, AND SMALL TOWNS
3RD LONG RIDE

FEBRUARY TO OCTOBER 2008
3,000 MILES

CHAPTER TEN

ESSIE PEARL YOU BEAUTIFUL GIRL

Gypsy gold does not chink and glitter.
It gleams in the sun and neighs in the dark.
—GYPSY SAYING

When I returned from my second long ride in September 2007, I had decided Claire Dog, who had already walked 7,000 miles on long rides, needed a horse of her own. I mentally listed my requirements for such a horse: safe; not very tall; strong; safe; with a wide, flat back to carry a pack with Claire riding on top; and, most of all, safe.

By coincidence, some folks in Fortine, Montana, had dreamed of farming the old-fashioned way, using draft horses, and had purchased three Canadian Norwegian Fjord draft ponies. Unfortunately, their dream did not materialize. They had insufficient equine knowledge, and after a short difficult venture trying to farm in the old ways, they decided to sell the horses. Two of the horses had already been sold when I went to look at the Fjords.

Norwegian Fjord's are ideally suited for long riding with attributes that my previous horses did not have. Fjords have a thick skin, coarse hair, and short, flat backs, and they are "easy keepers," meaning a little food goes a long way. They are scavengers and will survive on twigs and coarse roughage. Their ancestry goes back to Mongolian ponies. Genghis Khan conquered most of Eurasia with horses much like these. The Vikings stole breeding stock from the Mongolians, and those hardy horses survived on seaweed on the long ship ride to become the horse of Norway.

Most importantly, I felt their mild dispositions might let them tolerate a dog riding on their backs, something most horses would not allow.

Standing alone in the corral was a fat, dumpy Norwegian Fjord with a cantankerous, no-nonsense, "leave me alone" look in her eyes. She was six years old, had a large head, and at slightly over 14 hands was taller than most Fjords. I did not reach out to her as I often do when I am considering a horse. I didn't dare. One look and I knew that this horse needed help, and I didn't have time for another rescue project horse.

Her neck and belly bulged from overly generous rations of food and no exercise. Her feet had splayed, with huge cracks down the front hooves. She moved with a stiffness common among foundering horses, a condition that leaves a horse's feet sore and lame. The owners told me that a veterinarian had diagnosed her with chronic navicular problems (pain in the rear of the foot and attendant lameness) and a farrier confirmed her condition. She also had a stubborn equine pushiness few people would care to deal with.

"What will become of her?" I wrote in my journal that night. "Try, just try. See what you can do with her." The next day, I could have been called a fool for good reason. The owners asked way too much for a lame horse. "I can still sell her as a brood mare even if she's lame," came the reply when I tried to dicker. And sure enough, three weeks into her training, she came up lame. I eventually discovered abscesses in both front feet. I dug into the holes in the bottom of her hooves, cleaned them out, packed them with wool and oil and covered them with leather booties I had fashioned for her hooves. Exercise, diet, attention, daily brushing, rubdowns, more attention, piles of attention, not all of which she agreed with, slowly brought her relief.

She still had an attitude but she showed interest in what we were doing and I could tell she was beginning to like Honor, Claire Dog, and me. She had been named Essie Pearl after one of the previous owner's aunts. I called her Essie Pearl You Beautiful Girl.

I instinctively knew Essie Pearl needed the dry, hot climate of desert country where her weak, soft hooves could set up and harden, and she also needed movement. She needed to walk all day, slow and easy. In

Essie making the most of a good dirt bath. PHOTO COURTESY OF JOANN WHITCOM.

February, I arranged to haul all of us to Mohave Valley, Arizona, in the Sonoran Desert to escape Montana's snowy, wet spring that would still last for months, and to begin a 3,000-mile ride with Honor and Claire Dog and my new pack horse, Essie Pearl.

I had met Suzanne Evans in 2007 on my 5,000-mile ride. I stayed at Suzanne's family-owned Triple Farms Stable in Mohave Valley, which is just east of Needles, California. It was there I had staged the crossing of Death Valley the year before. I called Suzanne and asked if she would mind another visit. She said, "Sure, come on down!" We stayed at Triple Farms for four days, putting gear together and doing short practice rides with my two mares. When we were ready to leave, Suzanne, who was always busy giving riding lessons, training horses, and managing the stables, found time to mount one of her horses and escort us out of town. So we began our 3,000-mile long ride.

The weather felt glorious to me, but the horses were hot in their winter coats. We moved ever so slowly, with blustery warm winds urging us eastward across Arizona into New Mexico. I visited my sister Mary Ann near Albuquerque before pressing on for Kansas.

Bernice on Honor, Claire on Essie Pearl, riding the roadside through the desert.
PHOTO COURTESY OF JOANN WHITCOM.

On the move across the Southwest. PHOTO COURTESY OF JOANN WHITCOM.

Claire on her new mount and friend, Essie Pearl. PHOTO COURTESY OF JOANN WHITCOM.

After walking 7,000 miles, Claire is happy for the lift.

Essie's hooves did as I had hoped. They grew stronger and so did her desire to join with us as a team. By the time I arrived in Kansas four months later, Essie wore steel horseshoes and the cracks were slowly closing on her front hooves.

Claire liked her new accommodations on the back of Essie Pearl, and Essie Pearl seemed content to have the responsibility of being Claire's horse. Claire easily clambered up Essie's haunches to her seat on Essie's back, but she also often chose to walk. During this ride, Honor and Essie Pearl became inseparable even though they constantly bickered like sisters as we walked along. We were already a good team, but it would take many more months before we were a well-oiled team moving with unity. So far, it was a good ride. I was proud of my riding family and particularly proud of how quickly and how well Essie Pearl adapted to this life. Her Fjord nature proved well suited for patiently enduring the traffic noise, packs of dogs, bicycles, four-wheelers, trains, and plastic bags clinging to fences. You name it, she braved it and did it well. I was humbled by her show of affection toward me, her soft nuzzle that gently let me know she needed something, or the quick response I got when I asked something of her. And with Essie Pearl carrying the packs, Honor's load was greatly reduced, which allowed me to ride more and walk a little less.

A GOOD RIDE

When we left Suzanne's, we dropped south to Blythe, California, then turned east, crossing the Colorado River into Arizona again, and headed toward Maricopa in the Gila River Valley to visit my Aunt Carolyn and Uncle Joe. Then we rode north along power line roads and county dirt roads to Rainbow Valley.

As I later reported to the Long Riders' Guild, along the way we camped in an empty lot in Maricopa, in backyards, along canal ditches, and in several campsites in the vast Sonoran Desert. I saw beautiful desert flowers and had more than one rattlesnake shake a warning at me. We stopped in the old mining town of Crown King, Arizona, in the

The General Store in Crown King, Arizona.

Bradshaw Mountains for a weeklong visit with friends I had met on the ride the year before. I visited with the Colemans, who owned the Bear Creek Cabins. I saw Susan Hite and Mike and Darla from the Mountain Suites where I stayed to wait out a snowstorm in 2007. I even had a chance to again visit Mike and Debbie Shivers in Palace Station, once a stagecoach stop. In Prescott, we also stayed with other friends: Gary and Sharon DeLanoy, who had also kindly hosted a stay the previous year.

I was enjoying reconnecting with friends and exploring new places. I walked many miles and rode even more, washed up in cold, clear running creeks, and slept under brilliant stars. We lost only two horseshoes and one Easyboot. It was a good ride through Arizona and New Mexico.

Having Essie Pearl added much to the ride in unexpected ways. One was the response from people to the sight of a dog riding a horse. It became a dog and pony show starring Claire Dog and Essie Pearl You Beautiful Girl. People were curious about Essie Pearl. So few knew what breed she was and they were drawn to her unusual looks. "Is this a mule or a henny or what?" they would ask. When I gave a talk at a school, one little boy asked, "Is that a zebra?"

Essie Pearl, a Norwegian Fjord.

According to the Norwegian Fjord Horse Registry, the Norwegian Fjord horse is one of the world's oldest and purest breeds. The Fjords of today retain the wild dun color of the original horse and the primitive markings, which include zebra stripes on the legs and a dorsal stripe from the forelock down the neck and back and into the tail. All Fjords are dun in color. About ninety percent are brown dun and ten percent are red, gray, white, or yellow dun. The mane of a Fjord is unique: the center hair is dark, often black, while the outer hair is white. These horses are generally affectionate and mild tempered—they don't get excited about much of anything and tend to take things in stride. They love to work, but they can be stubborn and require firm, consistent handling. Fjords are strong, easy keepers. They are agile and sure-footed in rough terrain, which makes them ideal for mountain riding and rides in a variety of terrains. They love to eat and will take advantage of any opportunity.

CHAPTER ELEVEN

LEGENDS OF KANSAS

We rode on to Flagstaff, where I gave a talk at the local library and, as usual, the horses and Claire were the stars of the show.

Then we skimmed Colorado's southeast corner and into Kansas to visit the town of Nicodemus. Although I had been here before, I wanted to spend more time exploring this historic town. Nicodemus is the oldest and only remaining community west of the Mississippi established by African Americans after the Civil War. I was hoping to have an opportunity to visit with historian Angela Bates and learn more about what freedom meant to the descendants of the former slaves who settled here.

I had met Angela two years earlier in 2006 on my 5,000-mile ride with Honor and Claire. I liked her immediately, and I liked her enthusiasm and determination to keep the community of Nicodemus alive in our memories. To say Angela is ambitious is to say the obvious. She is the catalyst behind Nicodemus becoming a park and a National Historic Site.

Angela is a direct descendant of the early settlers, and she believed from childhood that Nicodemus is a unique place. That it speaks to the unwritten chapter in American history when African Americans governed themselves in their own all-black towns. Angela created the Nicodemus Historical Society and has for twenty-nine years worked to collect, preserve, and interpret the history of Nicodemus. She set up the Nicodemus Historical Society archives at the University of Kansas Spencer Research Library. The collections include thousands of photographs and written materials. Angela is also the executive director of the Nicodemus Historical Society and Museum and works closely with the

Essie, Claire, Honor, and I ready to give a talk at the library in Flagstaff, Arizona.

National Park Service as a community interpreter. She has also written a series of children's books titled *The Adventures of Nicodemus Annie.*

While I was in Nicodemus in 2008, Angela and I sat visiting in the museum, a restored small white building with ghosts of the past sitting in the empty chairs around us as we shared their photos, newspaper clippings, and stories—stories that were heart-wrenching, stories that were heart-warming, and stories that must be remembered.

"What did freedom mean to the new settlers of Nicodemus?" Angela repeated my question. Then she said, "Well, freedom was land ownership. Kansas was the promised land where they could start new without the dark cloud of oppression and Jim Crow. It was the expression of free will to do, to go, and to be what they wanted to. It meant autonomy, self-government. It meant self-control versus others controlling every aspect of your life from the choice of your name to who you were to have children by. Freedom meant they had choice . . . the freedom to exercise their own free will. Freedom to live versus die for what they said or did that was

Historian Angela Bates welcomes the long-riding family for another enlightening visit to Nicodemus, Kansas.

not acceptable to their white owners or counterparts. Free to travel. Free to move about. To raise their own children without the fear of having them sold or taken away, or even murdered in front of your own eyes. The freedom to worship what they chose to believe such as their own interpretation of the Bible, rather than being forced to believe they were born to submit to their owners. Freedom meant to be a human rather than chattel. Freedom meant to have basic 'choice' in any matter in their lives that had been formerly chosen by another." She paused, collected her thoughts, then spoke of courageous people facing enormous adversity and about the determined people who landed in a place of hope.

THE STORY OF NICODEMUS

The following story of Nicodemus is quoted from the Nicodemus Historical Society archives at the University of Kansas Spencer Research Library.

> Kansas had an appeal to African Americans living in the post-Civil War South. In the minds of many of these recently freed slaves, Kansas represented a land of freedom and opportunity due to the actions of John Brown and other abolitionists. Promoters such as Benjamin "Pap" Singleton encouraged African Americans to move to Kansas. Nicodemus would become a destination for these new migrants, and railroads and steamboats offered them cheap passage. Eager to escape the persecution and poor living conditions of Reconstruction, thousands left the South and headed west, seeking economic opportunity and a sense of freedom.
>
> On April 18, 1877, a group of seven Kansans, six of whom were black, established the Nicodemus Town Company. W. H. Smith, an African American, and W. R. Hill, an experienced white land speculator, served as the town's president and treasurer, respectively. Most of the group consisted of former slaves from Kentucky in search of a new livelihood. The goal was to establish the first all-black settlement on the Great Plains.
>
> The early settlers found life in Nicodemus to be challenging. Some people turned around after seeing the scarcity of resources. Most were impoverished farmers who came without money and other provisions. Without proper tools and equipment, such as plows, wagons, and horses, farmers could not efficiently develop the rough land.
>
> New groups of settlers arrived in Nicodemus in 1878 and 1879

Early homesteaders near Nicodemus, Kansas. LIBRARY OF CONGRESS,
HABS KANS, 33-NICO, 1—6.

from Kentucky and Mississippi. Unlike the early migrants, they had the resources necessary to develop and cultivate the farmland; they came with the horse teams, plows, other farm equipment, and money that the early settlers did not have. Soon the town began to grow and businesses became profitable. Two newspapers, a hotel, and two stores were established, and a school and three churches were built.

After a legal battle over land errors in the filing record, the town finally received its official title on June 6, 1886.

Beginning in 1886, the town began another campaign of promotion. The town's two newspapers, the *Western Cyclone* and the *Nicodemus Enterprise*, were central to the new campaign. The papers sought to broaden the appeal of Nicodemus by reaching out to other populations, both black and white. Descriptions of the town's numerous social clubs, activities, celebrations, and business opportunities were spread in the hope of attracting new migrants. The failed attempt to attract the railroad, however, marked the end of growth for Nicodemus, and most of the businesses in town relocated elsewhere. The Great Depression and the Dustbowl each had a serious impact on Nicodemus; the population of the town fell to as low as forty people. Starting in the 1970s, Nicodemus underwent a process of revitalization and restoration.

Donations from former residents led to efforts to repair damage to deteriorating buildings. In 1976, Nicodemus was named a National Historic Landmark. New improvements were made to the town, including construction of low-income housing units and a 100-foot-tall water tower, and the pavement of the major town streets. These efforts succeeded in preserving Nicodemus and rebuilding its popularity. The town developed a new identity as a retirement destination for former residents. The annual Emancipation celebration, renamed "Homecoming," changed to become a gathering of old residents who celebrate their roots and common history which continues to be celebrated to this day.

TORNADO WARNING

Later that day, the miserably hot and sultry afternoon clouded over and cool, strong southerly winds swept in. By 5 P.M. it had grown dark and tornado warnings were out. Kansas tornadoes are legendary. Fearing the worst, Angela and I moved my tent and gear into Juan Alexander's daylight basement. Juan was Angela's cousin and lived near the museum. He looked at the threatening sky and said I'd better get inside.

Yes, but what about my horses standing outside in the pasture, with angry winds, rain, and debris beating at them? Juan, who suffered from Lou Gehrig's disease, punched the garage door opener and said weakly, "Bring them in here!" I pushed a few things aside. Claire did a concerned dance, perhaps trying to herd us in as I led the horses into the garage, telling them, "Easy, easy, stand easy." Juan's frail body stood at the kitchen door. He pressed the switch and down came the door, slowly closing the storm from us. He thought the whole thing was pretty funny, horses in his garage! I stayed with the horses, holding their halters and talking to them in a low, quiet voice. Claire sat at my feet—the storm made her nervous. Lightning strikes cracked nearby, a drain gutter broke off the house, and the lights flickered, going out momentarily. Honor and Essie stepped from side to side. We heard a crash, a loud blast, and the house strained. And then it was over except for the rain pouring from the dark sky. Juan opened the garage door and cool, wet air rushed in. We learned later that a tornado had touched down in Nicodemus! We were fortunate.

My packs were full of more than just food the following day as I prepared to leave in a refreshingly cool morning. Angela's words bulged out the seams of my panniers. She gave me a lot to think about. Angela's words and the story of Nicodemus continued roiling around in my head. They were words to think about, words to pass on. "Freedom for all."

DOWN TEXAS WAY AND AROUND THE WEST 4TH LONG RIDE

MARCH 2009 TO JUNE 2011
6,000 MILES

CHAPTER TWELVE

A LONG WINTER'S NIGHTS

My fourth long ride began in March 2009. It was a 6,000-mile ride starting and ending in Montana and looping around the vast intermountain West. It took two years and three months to complete. During this ride I learned even more about the joys and hardships of long riding and especially about winter camping. I also endured a terrible loss and sadness that led me to acquire an even greater appreciation for the kindness and generosity of the people of this country.

Halfway through this ride I lost Honor. Up until that time I had been lucky. I had ridden more than 13,000 miles in five years without a serious accident. On February 22, 2010, I had to have my dear Honor put down after an accident in a corral left her right front leg too badly shattered to save her. Exactly how her injury happened I do not know.

But I do know what happened! I broke a golden rule of equine care: keep your horses in separate pens when you leave them unattended. All the mistakes, all the blame are mine. I continue to agonize over it to this day.

Honor was one of the greatest teachers to have marked my life. From the get-go until the very end, that magnificent flea-bit gray mare dotted with pebble-size brown spots became a lesson in patience, hope, and perseverance. Her crazed Thoroughbred spirit challenged me nearly every day, but she had won my heart with her black radiating eyes and her infinite willingness to move forward. We filled each other with courage.

We were in the heart of Texas, staying at the Wimberley VFW Rodeo Grounds. I thought I was doing the horses a favor by opening the large arena to give them room to run and play while I went to visit my sister in town. While I was gone, Essie Pearl kicked Honor. Later x-rays showed several blows. Honor's leg was shattered. She was in horrific pain and I could not let her suffer so. I had her put down.

Holly and Tommie Nixon and Odie and Hedy Wright came to my rescue, as did many others living in the "Heart of Texas." I had met the Nixons and the Wrights a few weeks earlier riding through Menard. This happened to be a particularly difficult period in this two-year ride; heavy rains had set in, I had an abscessed tooth, and crossing the vast Texas plains was no piece of cake. The Nixons graciously provided a room in their unique ranch home where I came to my senses after the tooth had been extracted.

Several people offered horses to replace Honor, but few were suitable. I finally settled on Lucky Kid, a big, 16.2-hands-tall paint Quarter-Thoroughbred gelding owned by Odie Wright. I renamed him Hart because he came from the heart of Texas. I worked with Hart and Essie Pearl a few days at the Nixons' ranch and then headed north for open space where Hart and Essie could safely mesh into a long-riding team. It's difficult thinking about those events even now. I never would have made it without the generosity and kindness those many Texans showed me.

It's ironic that the grand image of a long rider is of self-reliance and independence. Actually I am for the most part dependent on others for food, water, and directions. Time and time again, people have opened their homes, shared meals with me, offered a shower, washed my clothes, repaired tack, shod a horse, and encouraged or supported me in one way or another. I am truly indebted to hundreds of people.

Hart, Claire, Essie Pearl, and I left Texas heading north through Oklahoma, Kansas, Nebraska, and Iowa. In Minnesota, I visited with family, and then we rode west through North Dakota. By October 2010 we were in eastern Montana, heading for Miles City.

AMBASSADOR OF GOODWILL

Claire lay under my sleeping bag, curled like a warm doughnut. "That was a two-dog night," I said to Claire, pulling the sleeping bag over my head, hiding from the cold, reluctantly giving up my dreams. Mornings come late in October and there's no sense getting up before the sun. A candle burned inside the tent for light. The water bottles were tucked inside the bag with Claire and had not frozen during the night. All was well.

Hart and Essie Pearl had a bounty of grama grass. They were intent on eating and were not distracted by a grand flock of Canada geese mingling along the Yellowstone River south of our camp. But Claire lifted her head, her eyes following the sound of hundreds of long black necks stretching, honking, and flapping as strong gray wings pull dense bodies into a crisp blue sky. A huge mass of synchronized geese rose up and over our campsite.

Breakfast was hot tea, Earl Grey, with lemon and honey for me. Claire got cooked oatmeal with sea salt, olive oil, and a raw egg. I slowly ate a hardboiled egg but quickly reached out to hold Claire's bowl with both my hands before it could spill as she licked it clean.

Riding horses into Miles City, a legendary cowboy town, wasn't an odd sight, but a dog and pony act riding into town still turned heads. People on the sidewalks stopped in surprise, pointed, and cast a disbelieving grin. Cars rolled to a stop, the windows slid down, and, at least once, out poked a camera with an "I don't believe it" look from the driver.

I had to pick up supplies, and I wanted to stop at the local elder care facility where Claire and Essie Pearl would pull wide smiles from even those not feeling well. Claire was an ambassador of goodwill, as are most beloved dogs. They remind us of the goodness in life. On our long rides, we were often guests of elder care facilities and senior centers where a few hearts and souls might need a little dusting off. There is nothing like a "rare breed of unknown origin" sitting confidently atop a fat Norwegian Fjord horse to slice a smile onto a sullen face and smooth a furrowed brow.

Truly an ambassador of goodwill.

Miles City greeted us with gentle fall breezes against our faces and warm sunshine on our backs. Claire loved the excitement of entering a town; she loved the people, the attention, and the treats. I strung a decorative red ribbon around Claire's neck. "A girl's got to look good," I said to her with a grin and gave her a kiss. She waved with her paw in the air, reaching for the curious people who stood next to Essie Pearl and looked up with admiration at Claire Dog extraordinaire.

When we visited senior centers, I would lace up moose-hide moccasins on Claire's front feet. Why? Because my dear Claire could not help herself from reaching out with a doggie handshake, her canine version of, "Hello, my name is Claire. I just rode in on a horse. Pleased to meet you." Without her moccasins, even her well-worn toenails would have scratched fragile skin on frail hands and legs, leaving behind a dreadful, bloody trail. Not good for public relations! Her tail beat enthusiastically on a wheelchair behind her as she reached for the hand in front of her. "Do you have a treat?" beamed Claire. She didn't mean to scratch anyone; she simply wanted everyone to pet her as she

Smiles all around at a senior center.

shook hands with every single resident in the facility. You could feel her delightful soul in action. A resident pulled out a bit of food wrapped in a paper napkin they had saved from lunch and made an angelic offering to the shaggy ambassador of goodwill. This benevolent dog patiently waited as a wrinkled hand rested gently on her luxurious calico coat. "Nice," I said, "take it nice," reminding her not to grab for food. Once again Claire, with her amusing doggie antics, had successfully brightened the hearts of many aging residents and left behind a colorful afternoon of stories for them to tell and retell about "the day a dog rode into town."

We had already stayed at the senior center longer than we should have. As leader of the pack, I still had to find a campsite and unpack before settling the family in for the night. Claire's "take-off talk," a series of barks and twirling dance moves, created a commotion that Essie and Hart completely ignored. Essie Pearl patiently waited as I lifted Claire up to her doggie box. Claire appeared satisfied with her day's work as she silently snuggled down with her head resting on the edge of the padded box she rode in. I prepared the horses, gathering reins, pulling us close, before moving into the flow of traffic. "Okay, let's go!" I called out with a bravado voice. Claire jolted upright and sat as statuesque as a queen. This time I did the waving. Claire and the horses were looking ahead, expectant. "Okay," they seemed to say, and "What's next?" They know it's the end of the day.

I turned in the saddle and called out, "Happy trails" to the senior citizens. A few residents piped up with a chorus of, "Happy trails to you, until we meet again, happy trails to you." They waved goodbye as we were swept into a current of car and truck traffic.

ONLY 600 MILES TO HOME

As we rode west from Miles City, winter was fast approaching. The nights were cold, the leaves were dropping fast, and the riding season was nearly done. I had been out nearly two years and ridden 5,400 miles on this latest ride, and home was another 600 miles—another month of riding—to the west. I knew I couldn't make it over the Rocky Mountains in winter, and I was too tired to try. Instead, I hatched the crazy idea of camping through an eastern Montana winter. Madness! Yes, but I had to see if I could do it.

I could think of only one person who might let me pitch camp on his property—Bill Straw. He was the only person I knew who would not try to talk me out of it or call me crazy or say, "No way!" He would understand.

Bill Straw was eighty-seven when I met him on my second ride in 2006. I had been riding across eastern Montana in late spring when a set of gray weathered corrals and a little flat-roofed red barn appeared on the horizon. I had ridden Honor on that 5,000-mile journey, and she had thoroughly tested my equine skills. Every day presented itself with challenges, much like my first ride. Honor refused to quiet down at night, she seemed to be in heat all day and night, and she remained ridiculously excited whenever we passed horses in pastures. Her nervousness had worn her thin and had me on the edge of collapse. It was

Claire and Bill head into town.

hard going. I felt beat up, defeated, and emotionally fatigued. At a small ranch outside of Forsyth, Montana, I stopped to rest.

Claire, Honor, and I were leaning against the corral rail when a couple of ranchers rode up at a fast trot while rounding up some escaped bulls they owned. I expected they would yell at me and tell me I'd better move on. Earlier, I had pulled Honor's saddle from her back and found two sores near her withers. "Shit," I swore, "just plain shit," as I sank to my heels, my forehead pressing against her lean, muscular leg. We needed help and a place to stay for at least a couple of weeks. What a pathetic sight we must have been to the cowboy husband and wife team in chaps and spurs sitting on big, well-bred Quarter horses looking down on me. As we talked, their horses shifted about, tugging at their bits, jiggling the lasso ropes tied to their saddles, reluctant to stand still. I felt like crying and probably looked like I was about to. "And I've got another 4,500 miles to go," I said under my breath.

The ranchers—Keith and Vickie Gilje—said their neighbor owned the little red barn, corrals, and the flat 640 acres of unobstructed, open range land they rested on. The Giljes contacted him and that's how I came to meet William J. Straw. For the next two weeks, Bill just sort of took care of us. He brought a cot for me to sleep on, an ice chest and food, and always, always something to read scribbled with little notes he'd made while reading the articles himself. He drove Claire and me into town for groceries or mail, or to the library. Claire sat between us with a serious look on her face. One ear up, one ear down, she sat close to Bill like a long-lost buddy she'd recently found, the effect of daily bones and treats from his sturdy, tan, wrinkled hands. I'm sure he had an ongoing conversation with Claire waiting in his truck while I ran in for groceries. Each stop produced nodding heads, smiles, and handshakes, giving old Bill and I a friendly teasing. He was a well-liked fixture in the town of Forsyth. By the time I left two weeks later, Bill's friends, with warmhearted kidding, were asking about the "girlfriend living in his barn north of town."

Well, we did complete that 5,000-mile ride. Now, four years later, I was riding into Montana's westerly winds again. This time I was riding Hart. Claire was still at my side, but now she was riding Essie Pearl and we had an additional 8,400 equestrian miles strung out behind us.

WINTERING ON THE PLAINS

Now in 2010, Bill was expecting me. We had stayed in touch through the years, but he had no idea what I held in my mind. Even I had my doubts that I could winter in a tent through a Montana winter. I had wintered over on previous rides but always in southern climates. I didn't want to go in. I wanted to stay somewhere with my dog and horses and I wanted to live in my own home—my tent. Could I do it?

That was the question: could I live in my tent through a brutal eastern Montana winter? I thought if anyone would let me try, it would be Bill Straw.

Bill's lower lip usually protruded over a plug of chewing tobacco, and he held a rusty old tin can for a spittoon. He was always neatly dressed, even color-coordinated, and clean shaven. He was about five

Bill Straw, gentleman Montana rancher.

feet, six inches tall and stood straight and strong. When Bill worked, he wore a black and red wool cap and faded blue-and-white-striped overalls that snapped on over his shoulders. His dry sense of humor came out unexpected, surprising me, sometimes even shocking me. "Forty miles from water, forty miles from wood, forty miles from hell, for all I know I'm done for good," he would chuckle. He had a hundred sayings. He was one of those people that appears one way yet is very different inside. "Even a blind pig can find an acorn," he'd spit out with his snoose. Ask him how he was doing and he might reply, "Well got no holes, no worn places." How could that have come out of this mild looking little man? He read like mad—newspapers, magazines, pamphlets, books. His stories were long-remembered tales told in detail. He'd feign a smile when I told him how sharp he looked. His wife had died years before I had met him. Besides his memorable overseas war years in the navy, Bill had lived in Forsyth all his life, managing the grain elevator for over twenty years. His father had built the ten-stanchion red milk barn and corrals north of town during the 1920s and 1930s, eking out a living during the Depression for his family by selling milk and cream.

OCTOBER 17, 2010: WINTER CAMP

"So here's my idea, Bill," I said. He listened, shook his head, listened some more, and then spit out a disgusting wad of snoose and said, "Well hell, you can't move in with me, but you're welcome to stay in my barn. Go ahead and try it, I suppose someone'll come haul you out if you run into trouble." He chuckled and left.

I had been thinking how I would do this ever since I rode across the Minnesota–North Dakota state line a month ago. On the inside roof of every tent I've used on my rides, I have written: "I love my life as a lady long rider." I love living in a tent. I love living on the ground with only a thin line between inside and outside. I love hearing and talking to my horses at all hours of the day or night. It's much like playing house. I become a child with imaginative ways of improving my campsites. It's like building a tree house or snow fort or any other childishly creative endeavor. It was with this sense of play, and a little excitement and nervousness, that I set about constructing a winter camp. It was the first of many winter camps I would eventually create.

Protection from the wind was the most important. The wild open Montana prairie invites a brutish, unforgiving wind, even encourages it—"Come play, look at all this open space, do as you please," it says. And the wind smiles, perhaps sneers, before roaring on and on and on across the playground of eastern Montana. Of all the weather conditions I face, the most difficult, the most dangerous, is wind. Curse it and you'll be left to suffer in a sweltering of bugs and heat. Welcome the wind and it will gladly freeze you or simply blow you off the face of the earth like an insignificant thought.

Bill Straw's twenty-by-twenty-foot red barn was built a hundred years before I arrived. It had electricity, a cement floor, was pretty clean, and had a low, flat ceiling held up by handmade wooden stanchions. Entrance to the barn was through two large Dutch doors in the front and one small door that opened at the east end. The barn and stock tank were surrounded by wooden corrals and a windbreak made of tin. The windbreak was a daring wall that defied fierce northwesterlies but easily

My winter home inside Bill's barn.

could have been mistaken for a six-foot-tall piece of abstract art. It was a patchwork of old tin signs, corrugated roofing tin, flat smooth tin, and crinkled tin with hundreds of nail holes now rusted like a patina mural. We literally had a fenced-in yard. I swept and cleaned, filled the gaps in the barn walls with paper, layered the cement floor under my tent with cardboard, washed the four small southern windows inviting sunlight and heat into my living quarters, and then set about constructing a home. Over the course of a week, I made a yurt-like structure from a cheap nylon tent. It was four feet high and provided six-by-eight feet of floor space. I layered it with blankets, tarps, and anything else I could find at the thrift store in town. A wooden pole I found outside became a center support beam. I purchased long quarter-inch-diameter PVC pipe for additional ribs. A plastic pop bottle with the bottom cut off poked out of the ceiling for a vent.

Vicky Fink, manager of Forsyth's fairgrounds, donated a small floor heater and a stock tank heater. "I can't believe you're helping me like this," I told her. "You must think I'm nuts." I thanked her again and again. The barn came with a shovel and a stable fork, and I made a sled for hauling horse manure with a rope and piece of tin. I found a twelve-inch length of corrugated culvert in a pile of junk outside the corrals and used it for an outdoor fire pit ring.

Forsyth's only thrift store was a disorganized department store if ever I saw one. It was cluttered and stuffed to the brim, with narrow walking paths through the maze of stuff. A person had to step carefully to keep from falling or knocking something down while hunting for just the right item they wanted. Somehow, June, the owner, a friendly woman my age with long brown hair, knew exactly where to find things. I became her steady customer. In addition to a dozen or so blankets, I also purchased a small electric radio, kitchen pots, a spatula, rugs, a bowl, a plate, winter boots, and sweaters. For lighting, I made do with candles and a mechanic's trouble light.

Bill lent me an ancient double-burner electric stove with a dubious cord, so for the most part I cooked on my single-burner propane camp stove or I cooked on the fire pit outdoors. We were settling in, establishing a routine that would carry us through the winter. Claire and the horses now sported winter coats and I felt less anxious about us wintering in a tent in a cold barn.

LOVING A THREE-MILE RIDE

Lonely Castle Butte was the only interruption in the panoramic view on the three-mile ride from the red barn into Forsyth. Essie, Hart, and Claire would all go unless I walked or caught a ride with Bill. I rode west on narrow, zigzagging cattle trails a couple of miles, then south on Highway 12 across the bridge spanning the Yellowstone River that led us into the west end of town. The surrounding scene on my three-mile ride to town no longer intimidated me. On the contrary, I'd fallen in love with it.

Hidden below the earth's southern skyline, thick with hundreds of migrating Canada geese, flowed the Yellowstone River. For days, the morning sky filled with flocks of long, graceful necks reaching for landing space, their powerful wings whistling, gliding, and circling for the earth. The Lewis and Clark Expedition traveled through this country in 1805 and 1806. I couldn't help but wonder what the natives before Lewis and Clark must have experienced. What did they see? I'd heard stories, such as, "The skies blackened from migrating birds," and, "With a single shot into the sky, a dozen birds would drop."

TELL ME ABOUT YOUR DESPAIR AND I WILL TELL YOU MINE

Journal Entry, November 14, 2010: *My birthday is in two days. November has always been a time of struggle for me. I wonder if I didn't struggle to keep from being born, that I knew somehow life was safer, warmer, tucked in my mother's womb, floating in her fluids. The outside world would not be so easy or to my liking. I would enter a loud, noisy, cold world and share my mother's own hardships.*

My mother, Cornelia Francis Hoy, became Mrs. Lawrence Ende in 1947. Both my father and my mother had served four years in the U.S. Armed Forces and both were "by chance" working at Glacier Park in Montana in 1946.

Like my grandmother, my mother ventured west from Minnesota, most likely lured by my grandmother's tales of adventure. She met my father while waitressing at Many Glacier Lodge. From the stories my father and mother told, I learned that my father worked at the park for nearly sixteen years and wore several hats. He was a wrangler, maintenance man, mechanic, and guide. He charmed my mother, they fell in love, married, and started a family on my grandparents' failing Minnesota dairy farm. Mother became a farmer's wife and already had three children when I arrived. At times she must have wondered what had become of her life. She gallantly endured the physical fatigue of arduous farm life and a house ruled by the chaos of six children. She never totally attached herself to house and home as many farm wives did. Her life could hardly afford the time let alone the money for what she loved—travel, books, and time to play with her children.

I remained unwilling to extract myself from the comforts of my mother's body. No wonder we must be pushed out. Once out, I wasn't sure I could or would breathe. Our father chain-smoked in the house and no one thought anything of it in those days. At six months old, I came down with pneumonia and struggled to live. My fifteen-month-old brother Lawrence and two older sisters still needed my mother's attention. I was hospitalized and once again torn from the warmth and security of my mother. For some reason, whether or not it has any truth, I find comfort in perhaps understanding that maybe in my infant mind I formed a secret resolve; I learned to breathe on my own! I've come to know myself in the absence of others' company. Maybe it explains why I fell apart during my divorce or why I fall apart when one of my beloved animals dies and leaves me. Maybe it's what this womb-like tent is all about! Maybe it is that same desire for a safe, secure, warm space. The feeling of closeness, wrapped as if in a womb, my thoughts free to float, indulging in the space of only me. Maybe it explains why I love this life so.

MEANWHILE, THE WORLD GOES ON

I look back on those childhood years and marvel at my mother's ability to create joy in our poor farm life. She wove books, piano lessons, letter writing, and art projects into her strenuous work schedule. Between my father's daily routine of milking cows, planting and plowing, baling hay, and harvesting crops, and mother's canning and gardening and household chores, we produced plays (Cinderella and Dudley Do-Right), and we learned to cook and sew and work outside, helping with farm chores. She would manage somehow to find time for a field trip to the Minneapolis Institute of Art, or a train ride, or a boat ride on Lake Superior. I think how remarkable this kind, loving woman, my mother, had been. She found delight in decorating for everything: Valentine's Day, Thanksgiving, Easter, birthdays. From the attic of our old, white, two-story farmhouse, she extracted large colored Easter bunny cutouts for the walls, the old yellow tape from the year before still hanging off the edges. Then out came the assortment of Easter baskets with green shiny grass, large yellow and green plastic Easter eggs from the year before all nicely arranged on the dining table. I'm not sure how we decided who got which basket. No doubt there was squabbling over it. The kitchen became a factory of creativity with a half dozen children and teens at the table and kitchen counter coloring eggs, experimenting with new techniques my mother or my older sisters had discovered in *Good Housekeeping* magazine. The grand finale came on Easter. Our baskets mysteriously filled with candy, then we had an Easter egg hunt, went to church, and feasted on a ham dinner. We must have been wild from so much sugar. She went all out for Christmas too—candle lights, long looping strands of colorful tinsel highlighting doorways, angels stenciled in frost on the windows, a tree decorating party. We baked dozens of cookies and cakes and made candy. She pulled from the attic Santa cutouts with legs that moved. We strung cranberries and popcorn and drank hot chocolate. With my older sister at the piano, we sang carols or listened to holiday records—*Christmas with the Chipmunks* or Bing Crosby's *White Christmas*. As we grew older, the decorations grew more elaborate as my mother's contagious enthusiasm affected us all.

Because of my mother, what could have been a dull or even hard life became an adventure. But my mother also had interest in the bigger world. Her love of "What lies over the horizon?" had poured down from her mother and from her mother's sisters who had inherited it from their mother. It lured her as it lures me. Later as an adult, I often wondered if her children and her farm life were enough for her.

My rides are dedicated to my mother. I honor what she has passed on to me and believe that I am exploring the country the way she would have liked to.

CHAPTER THIRTEEN

MIGRATING WITH GEESE

I long to be, but where do I belong?

Wintering outside of Forsyth, let's let my journal entries tell the story.

NOVEMBER 20, 2010

Tonight I combined raisins, cream cheese, sea salt, sunflower seeds, honey, cinnamon, and uncooked oatmeal—violà, a new dessert creation! I have been in and out of town more than two weeks and already many people have offered help. It's possible they think I'm crazy, take pity on me, and are afraid I might die out here and they don't like the idea of reading about it in the local newspaper.

My new friends are ninety-year-old Bill, eighty-seven-year-old Swede, ninety-eight-year-old Howard Lee and his wife, ninety-three-year-old Vera, and Bill's aunt Berniece who is ninety-one. Oh, but they are young at heart—lively, quick witted, and charming. They dote over me with smiles and gifts: food, hay, bones for Claire, a folding chair, coffee, and doughnuts. We sit and visit. Their concern reassures me, but when they leave I must dig deep for courage. Why must I do this, live like this? Why can't I just go into town and live normally like other people? Why must I see if I can do it? I'm okay for now, but the wrath of winter has yet to come. Temperatures will dip below minus 20 degrees and wind chills of minus 30.

Dapper Bill in his home.

It's unlikely there'll be a repeat of last year's mild winter. My two horses will need three tons of hay, mineral salt, and oats. I have about $400 that must be spread thinly through the next four months. We have good clear water from the stock tank. But the electricity is an old precarious mess, not working correctly. I'll never survive without electric heat!

I'm anxious as days like minutes tick, tick, tick into December, moving into the heart of winter. "Are you sure you can do this?" I ask myself every night as temperatures drop lower and lower. I feel a sharp edge daring me. I've never in my life found myself so exposed, so alone. I reason that sometimes it's easier doing things alone because there's no one to cooperate with. I can face it all at my own pace and do it my own way.

DECEMBER 7, 2010

I look out at the distant horizon and I'm surprised by how the country makes me feel. At first, the vast emptiness filled me with fear. I had spread my vision across the land before me and thought, "You are going to ride across that?" The flat, straight line between me and those horizons is filled with hidden ravines, gullies, dips, and cracks in the earth as deep as the buttes are high, causing an equestrian traveler to sometimes ride miles around. It momentarily yanked big ideas from my head and turned them to mush. But I have grown accustomed to it and now I find it calms me. I feel embraced by the space. The earthly distance is soothing, the whole world lying motionless in all directions, the stillness steadies me, and the distant land formations appear as islands. The direction and distance of a storm is easily determined. I can see the layout of roads twisting, rising, and falling into the sunset. Light slowly emerges until the sun blinks a brilliant but silent morning wake-up call. It makes a long slow procession across the blue-domed sky, then lingers, oh how it lingers, squeezing out and contorting every last ounce of color it can manage. Montana has a show-off sky.

DECEMBER 14, 2010

Another cold frosty morning keeps me inside the tent listening to Canadian Broadcasting on the radio. I'm hibernating like a bear in its den. Voices fill my tent and head with hopelessness. I am crushed by the world at large, tunneling through despairing reports. Where does anyone find hope after a dose of news? The radio teeters from humorous stupidity to extreme religious factions fighting a never-ending conflict.

Claire is curled in a fur ball, her nose tucked under the white tip at the end of her long tail. She's part of the heating system. The red barn is sturdy and offers protection. It even holds in a bit of heat, but outside my tent it was a cold minus 5 degrees last night. I balance precariously between a thin line of frozen and fluid. The heater cannot be turned on if the 100-watt lightbulb is on. I must use a candle when I run the heater. I can use the old hot plate from Bill only if everything else is turned off. It would be easy to overload the circuit breaker and start a fire; I must be careful. Heating a space this small is not difficult, but I may find myself adding more blankets to my yurt-like tent. I've already purchased half a dozen blankets for five dollars each from the thrift store and layered the tent again and again. I then bagged leaves in large black plastic bags and lined the base of the tent. The idea came from a memory of my dad lining the foundation of our Minnesota farmhouse with straw bales.

The sun shows itself often on the open prairie. Oh blessed be when it does! Three small one-by-two-foot windows on the south side reflect and pull glorious sunshine into my little abode. When the sun is beaming, I open the south door and lean against the outside wall, squatting on my heels. I raise my face with closed eyes and take a deep sigh for the joy of being right there in a clean, cold, silent winter warmed by a generous sun. On days like that, Hart, Essie Pearl, Claire, and I hang out together. Claire is maddened but ignored when the horses hang their heads inside the barn door wanting part of the action, wanting carrots, apples, a handful of oats, a cracker, treats.

Today the sun hides and so do I. I give the horses more hay. I make another cup of tea. I read, I write. I don't think I've ever been happier, more satisfied, and quiet. I regard with contentment the distant, familiar sound of a long coal train making its way through Forsyth, blaring out the railroad crossing signal: two long, one short, and one long.

DECEMBER 16, 2010: CHRISTMAS PARADE

Like most western towns, Forsyth's main street is wide and lined with brick buildings. Detailed historical scenes have been painted on several buildings by local artists, giving the town warmth and personality. The murals on the fire hall are a must-see. A busy railroad track lines the south side of Main Street. The laundry, library, post office, senior center, grocery, and hardware store are all centrally located and now beautifully decorated for the holidays.

I provided a short, amusing Christmas parade for the hospital patients, nursing home residents, and townspeople consisting of a colorful holiday dog and pony show. Hart, Essie Pearl, and Claire were decked out in red and silver tinsel, long streamers, red Santa hats, and whatever

Claire and Essie ready for the Christmas parade.

else I could find at the thrift store for cheap. The star of the show in a red hat was of course Claire, her front white paw reaching out as if waving, calling people to, "Come over here. Come pet the Christmas pup." She is such a ham! I think the townspeople appreciated the Christmas cheer, but then again, they may have been smiling, waving, and shaking their heads because they thought I was just plain nuts. At least no one complained about the poop piles in the street.

DECEMBER 25, 2010: CHRISTMAS DAY

Claire and I rode into town with Bill this morning because ninety-two-year-old Berniece Higginbotham is having us over for dinner. Berniece's kitchen has become as familiar to me as if it were my own mother's. She is Bill's aunt, his mother's sister. She spells her name with a "niece." I spell mine with a "nice."

"Come on in and look out!" she says. Like Bill, she has a million sayings and chuckles at every one. I love that part about her, that she

Bill Straw, Bernice, and Berniece celebrate Christmas in Forsyth.

laughs at her own clever jokes. She's like a big sister, a mother, a grand-mother, and friend all wrapped up and rolled together. I love being with her; she nourishes my soul. We laugh a lot and her simple ninety-two-year-old ways ease my unnecessary worries.

Like Bill, Berniece is always dressed neatly if she goes out. She is a tiny delicate woman, and on this Christmas day she is dressed in black nylon slacks and a yellow sweater. Every Thursday morning Berniece gets in her 1968 Chevy Nova, which is in mint condition with only about 10,000 miles on it, and drives the few blocks to Paula, hair dress-er extraordinaire, to get her blonde hair washed and perfectly curled.

If I catch a ride into town with Bill, I am dropped off at Berniece's. Naomi Rusdal is another friend and we make a threesome, Berniece, Naomi, and I. We sit at Berniece's metal kitchen table, drinking instant coffee or tea, and talk of nothing really, just chattering, laughing, and loving one another's company—like normal people, I tell myself. They have no idea how much I appreciate these two newly acquired girl-friends that have so unexpectedly come into my life.

Bill, Berniece, and I sit down for Christmas dinner. There is absolutely nothing fancy about our table except for the red plastic poinsettia flowers I brought from the thrift store. I made Bill and Berniece each Christmas cards. I gave Bill a framed photo of him and Claire riding in the truck and Berniece a pretty red scarf a cowboy gave me in Texas. Bill pulls a little holiday cheer from his back pocket—a pint of whiskey. What he doesn't know is Berniece and I have been, slowly, sipping on eggnog and brandy all morning.

JANUARY 30, 2011

More snow, more cold, more time in the tent because there's nothing I can do outside. It's wearing on me. Five and a half months in a tent. I don't feel well. The hardest part is keeping this thin mind of mine stable, keeping it from collapsing in a mound of goo. These days, sitting alone in my tent, I am haunted with a sense of failure, of not having accomplished anything worthwhile. I reflect on failed attempts and hurtful mistakes I've made and they haunt me. How do any of us walk through this life without bags full of regrets, mistakes, should haves, and if onlys?

Day after day I listen to the radio. I hear stories of remarkable men and women, young and old, and I think, "What have I done? Have I sincerely tried, have I given all I could have? Or did I wrap myself in a selfish cocoon, to never break free, never mature?" In the aloneness of my tent, my mind wonders through a plethora of unruly thoughts; what most of the world accepts as truth I question. When I step out of the tent and barn each morning, the horizon my eyes lock on is billions of years old. Me? A mere fifty-four years marks my existence. I'm an infant, yet death seems far more real than it once did. I've peaked. Now it's downhill, and when I step from the stage will anyone notice?

I slept very little last night. I am restless and blame it on too much news of Egypt, Haiti, storms, economic troubles, and war. In this isolation and solitude there's no one but me to digest, console, and move through what I hear. Yikes, I would like to put my head in the sand until it all passes. Yes, give me sand and give me spring. I want sunshine! I want the unknown space between earth and sky calling me down a dirt road. It's in those moments I feel complete and that I am somehow following the path I was meant to follow.

FEBRUARY 14, 2011: VALENTINE'S DAY

I wrote myself a valentine:

> Will you be my valentine
>
> If I sing you a sweet rhyme?
> Will you be my valentine
> If I hand you a red tomato ripe off the vine?
> If I give you nine hundred and ninety nine
> Bottles of rosy red wine in a long straight line
> Then . . . then . . . then will you be mine?

FEBRUARY 16, 2011

Wash feet, hands, and face, between legs, read aloud, stretch.
Ride if weather permits.
Spend time with horses scratching, rubbing, spreading harmony
between human-equine-dog.
Pass out love in generous amounts, write letters—write!
Dance, cook, and eat simple foods slowly, with appreciation.
If these and other activities are maintained, it will help comfort
your mind—your silly human mind.

FEBRUARY 23, 2011

I have come in from a brief run to feed and water horses. Temperatures hang frozen at minus 4 degrees. Winds have it feeling much colder. I crawl like an animal on all fours into my tent and the heat quickly saturates my body. Sitting cross-legged, I pull off one long scarf wrapped around my face, then another, then peel off layer upon layer: two caps, three sweaters, a jacket, and two pairs of heavy wool socks. Finally I reach my dirty, once-were-white long underwear that hasn't

been washed in a month. Going outside each time I pee is not an op-
tion—it's just too cold—so I use two empty red plastic Folger's coffee
containers. One is a gallon with a black lid and one is a pint container
that I pee into then empty the warm steamy liquid into the larger
container sitting outside the tent. There is a dilapidated outhouse in
the northeast corner of the pasture about thirty feet from the barn for
more serious business.

Outside, Hart and Essie Pearl, when not eating, stand motionless under a metal roof shelter. I wonder where their waiting, resting minds go,
what they think or dream as they patiently stand, periodically shifting
weight from one hind leg to another. In a couple of hours I'll reassemble
myself and carry water to them in a white five-gallon bucket. In this
weather, the bucket of water will freeze in fifteen minutes. On nights
like this, I keep the fifty-gallon water tank covered with plywood, the
electric tank heater in it.

Claire runs in her sleep, yips, stops, starts again. I run my hand
through her thick, lustrous winter coat. She pulls in a deep sigh and
readjusts her curled position.

National Public Radio plays "Wait, Wait Don't Tell Me," a silly question and answer panel show. Books lay about—a biography of Julia
Ward Howe by Laura Richards, Mary Oliver's poems, Wallace Stegner,
a book about Mark Twain.

Naomi and Berniece drove out for a visit this afternoon, as they do
often. We sit in Naomi's van drinking coffee and eating graham crackers.
Claire jumps inside with us. It's cold and Naomi keeps the van running.
Essie and Hart circle the van, finally poking a head into an open window. Berniece laughs when Essie's big lips reach for her cracker. "Oh
careful," I wince. "Don't take her thin, delicate fingers."

Sunshine beams off the snow-covered landscape as we visit. They
brought me a package from Mel Evans, a friend in Trego. I'm feeling
poetic again and write the tale of two Bernieces.

The tale of the two Bernieces (Bernice) is a story of many pieces,
two colorful gals that became great pals.

"Do you know what I heard (herd)?" said Berniece "What?" asked Bernice.

"Sheep," replied Berniece with a serious smirk, causing both to laugh with quick jerks.

When Berniece and Naomi left, I went back to my tent. Mel had filled the box with chocolate, peanut butter, orange marmalade, crackers, dried fruit, fanciful snacks, and a scarf and a hat she had made. Like a happy child, I have scattered these prized gifts all over the tent looking at them.

I continue checking on the horses throughout a frigid night.

MARCH 1, 2011

Today, to quiet my troubled mind, I copied Mary Oliver's poem "Wild Geese" into my journal as a reminder that I'm okay and in my proper place in the world. The lines in "Wild Geese" are a balm, granting approval to be ourselves and follow our passions, however quirky they seem. The poem speaks of ways we sometimes punish ourselves, doing penance for the sin of pursuing what we love. Oliver's response is forgiving and emboldening at the same time, and I imagine she's talking to me.

Writing in my journal helps me acknowledge my doubts and loneliness and then face them down. Again, "Wild Geese" offers a way forward, inviting me to share my "despair" while assuring me that the world will go on. Yes, the world, my world, goes on—feeding the horses, feeding myself and Claire, cleaning and repairing tack, readying for the first steps of the next long ride. A flight of geese calls nearby and I too feel the urge to be on the move.

MARCH 7, 2011

Thank goodness it's warmer.

The sun halfheartedly pushes slowly from behind the undisturbed eastern skyline, rising with effort. Melting snow drips from metal roofs. Coffee boils. A calendar with torn edges lies before me, saying, "Come, prepare, ready yourself for travel. No lapse of time—no nearness of grave shall change my heart's behave." Who wrote that? I don't know.

I let the noon sun dance on my skin. I entertain myself with the thought that I've survived an eastern Montana winter in a tent with sound mind and body, but who knows, perhaps by this time I am delusional.

MEANWHILE, WILD GEESE ARE HEADING HOME

Spring is a marvel, the unfolding, opening, thawing, streaming, and pooling until all spills out, softening the frozen earth into thick, gooey clay impossible to walk on without leaving boots stuck heavy with mud. Mother Earth takes a long gulp. She bathes in spring rains, then, refreshed, she rises with her new brood of tiny green grasses zealously sprouting with ever more seedlings waiting for the right moment. Spring is calling, "Come on, come on, we only have so much time here, wake up. Let's get a move on—it's time, its time!"

Each day I wake to hundreds of migrating Canada geese flying overhead, circling like swirling black clouds toward the earth, landing in empty sagebrush fields surrounding me and the horses. They're everywhere and the sound is miraculous. I wonder if it's a joyous reunion for them and if their honking talks mean "Yes, good to see you here. Land by us! Oh look who's here already! Came up a little to the west, did you? Hard winds? Got shot at? Oh there's so and so, I'm surprised to see they're here again." On and on they honk.

MARCH 13, 2011

Bare from the waist up and in long underwear from the waist down, I'm now warm enough for such displays of nudity in the privacy behind my secret enclave. I'm spring cleaning—burning empty feed sacks and trash that have accumulated and organizing for departure. But the warmth and freedom doesn't last long. As it often does on the plains, the wind comes up and I have to add more clothing before finishing my chores.

Enjoying a sunny day at the barn.

At this point, just before setting off after a lengthy stop, my mind pauses. How many times have I found myself like this, pausing with the thought, "Can I do this again?" It's a moment not of doubt but of remembering what lies ahead: the routine of equestrian travel, the daily packing, unpacking, setting up camp, and morning tea in unfamiliar settings. It's riding into towns hungry, needing food, water, and shelter and knocking on doors asking for permission to camp. It's the thrill of horizons that pique and tantalize the smile on my face, the *aah* of life that comes from surprise and spectacular panoramic views. It's the challenges placed squarely in my path that bring me to, "Okay, let's see if you can do it."

APRIL 1, 2011

Bill greets me with a honk; he's driving me and Claire into town. "It's we're all fool's day," he says, then spits snoose into a dirty can on the floor and smiles. This country is all sky and today it's a wild, blustery morning with clouds rolling by in large gray and white shapeless clusters. A flock of geese hurdle themselves toward the soggy spring earth. "Springing into action!" says Bill. He thinks he's so darn witty—and he is. I smile.

In a few days I'll be leaving Forsyth on the wings of spring. I'll be heading *back out*, finishing up the 6,000-mile ride I began in the spring of 2009. I'll be completing a big circle that looped from the northwest corner of Montana to Portland, Oregon, south to Wimberley, Texas, then north to Minneapolis, Minnesota, and now I'm on the home stretch west, homeward bound.

Lately I feel I have really gone over the edge and I'm on the other side. This feeling is stronger now than ever before. I remember thinking on my first ride, asking myself, "How will I ever go back to a normal life?" And now I know how truly content I am as a nomadic equestrian traveler devoted to my horses, my dog, and my journey. I look up at the flock of geese flying overhead on a journey of their own and whisper to myself, "Be devoted to your journey Bernice, no matter what journey that may be, be devoted to it."

CHAPTER FOURTEEN

OUT OF THE PAST, PAULETTE

MAY 26, 2011

On May 26, 2011, I was riding into Boulder, Montana. I stopped the horses on the four-lane concrete bridge leading into town. Below us, the Boulder River roared loudly as it ran wild with muddy spring runoff. "Easy, easy," I said, quieting the horses. Thankfully the stream of semi-trucks on Montana Highway 69 graciously slowed as they passed two horses, one ridden by a dog and one by a woman with an enormous hat.

On the other side of the river, the town's wide Main Street stretched out lazily. Western and midwestern main streets have always fascinated me. I've been told the streets had to be wide enough for a team of horses with a large wagon to turn around. I thought it may have merely been the capacious amount of land available to build their towns on. Anyway, there's room to breathe. These small towns feel safe. They often have a sleepy no-nonsense look, with ample parking, unless it's rodeo weekend or a parade. The storefronts don't glitter and shine and the streets don't shake, rattle, or roll like a busy city's. Boulder is a small community of plain brick buildings, businesses, and small homes and a striking, majestic courthouse.

Food being foremost on my mind, I tied the horses to the dump-sters outside the grocery store. Nods and stares accompanied me as I entered the store until someone finally asked, "Where ya from, where ya headed?" The store clerk asked, "Finishing up a 6,000-mile ride?" Suddenly everyone standing in the checkout line was friendly and we

talked. I'm surprised anyone spoke to me the way I looked when I rode into town. My weathered wrinkled face and neck were engraved with dirt. I had patches on my riding pants and my boots were covered in dust. I looked rough, but in this ranch country, that rough look is not as uncommon as it is in many towns I enter. The word is out—there's a lady long rider in town.

When I returned with my groceries, a crowd had gathered around the horses. Claire was standing in her doggie box on top of Essie. She had an audience and was reaching with her front paw for handshakes. Her white paws gave her the look of wearing white gloves. The world is apparently short of dog and pony acts, and Claire and Essie never failed to please a crowd. Hart, Essie, and Claire's attention quickly turned to me and the grocery bags because they knew I had treats for them in those bags. They temporarily ignored their newfound fans while I loaded the panniers with fruits and vegetables for all four of us and headed over to a laundromat to wash clothes.

I tied the horses to a fence next to the laundromat and pulled the saddle and packs from their hot backs. I don't like leaving weight on their backs when we stop for any length of time.

Fortunately, the building was shaded by trees and the dirt parking lot out front was car-less. The laundromat was empty inside except for me and two rows of older white Maytag washers and dryers, a sparse bulletin board, and a lost-and-found box, which I went through but found nothing of use. Nearly everything in my packs needed washing. After slipping coins into three machines, I left the horses standing with cocked hips, bellies content with apples and carrots from the grocery store stop. Claire stayed on her blanket near the horses, gnawing on a chunk of raw meat as I set out to run the rest of my errands.

I caught a glimpse of the library and senior center across the street, made a note in my mind, and continued on with errands. The town was quiet except for highway traffic. At the thrift store, I found a wristwatch to replace the one I had broken. Now I needed a battery for it so I walked over to the hardware store. I passed a few people on the sunny concrete sidewalks; the women nodded, tall cowboys tipped their hats.

I nodded back with my broad-brimmed sombrero. My handmade heel cleats made from flat steel washers keep my boot heels from wearing down, and they added a crisp click with each step. I walked fast—my animals are always on my mind, and I don't like leaving them alone.

The horses nickered and Claire's tail greeted me with a rapid wag. They were always glad to see me, but they always trusted that I'd come back. That's unconditional faith and I loved them each day for it, and trusted them in return.

I neatly packed the well-worn panniers with clean clothes, the tent and tarps, and food, then loaded the packs on Essie Pearl. Claire jumped into her doggie box on top of Essie Pearl and off we went to the Jefferson County Fairgrounds. I hoped they would let me rest a few days. On the way to the fairgrounds, I reconsidered the library and stopped. I wanted to ask about using their computers to send some messages. I walked up the concrete steps leading into the Boulder Community Library and as I reached for the handle on the glass door I saw squarely before me a poster with a photo of myself. The poster read "Lady Long Rider Bernice Ende will be speaking Thursday." Thursday was tomorrow! "Okay, okay, okay," I thought. "Hold still, compose yourself. What in the world is going on?" As I entered the library, my big hat, riding pants, and boots were a giveaway. They knew immediately who just walked in. "Yes, well I am here, I made it, you have a nice town," I said calmly, concealing my dumbfounded look as best I could. I made the necessary arrangements for the unexplained talk I'd be giving the next day, walked out the door, and stood looking across the street at the Boulder Senior Center. Why not? The world was already upside down; I would see if the town seniors were interested in a lady long rider giving a talk.

The room smelled deliciously of roasted chicken, potatoes, and gravy. A middle-aged woman remained in the center of the room cleaning up after lunch. "They're all gone except a couple of women downstairs," she said. "Go ask them." Down the stairs I found two portly gray-haired women working a crossword puzzle at the end of a long table. They seemed totally uninterested when I asked if they thought the community of seniors would like to hear a lady long rider talk. "What's a lady long rider?" they wanted to know. Without looking up from their puzzle, they told me to come around Friday and talk with the director. I handed them each a card with my information and photo. "Okay, see you then," I said. As I was leaving, I heard them whispering, "I don't know what it's all about, I ain't never seen her before, don't know who she is."

I headed back to my horses. It must have been nearly 5 P.M. by the time I rode into the Jefferson County Fairgrounds about a mile south of town. A carousel restoration project was under way. I was greeted by attractive red buildings and spacious green lawns surrounded by white fences. Throughout the years of long riding I have stayed at dozens of fairgrounds, some nicer than others. This was well cared for and lovely.

I don't know why, after all these years, I still feel the gnawing anxiousness of finding a campsite. Rarely has anyone ever turned me away, but what if they say no? I inquired around and finally found the person I needed to ask. He said I could stay and I was all smiles because until that moment I did not have a place to camp for the night. Relieved, I settled in for a few days.

By the time evening came around I was tired, hungry, and maybe a little crabby. But before I can eat or rest, a well-rehearsed two-hour ritual of work awaited me. I had to unpack the horses, let them roll, and brush them. I had no hay, so I had to stake the horses out on long picket lines in the grass. The saddle pads, which I sleep on, had to be dried and brushed soft. I was in a horse barn for a couple of nights, which changed the usual camping arrangements. I hung bridles and saddles on a rail, I put my hat over there, Claire here, Essie there; I made it all very tidy. I loved this part of the long, drawn-out day, a chance to reflect on the events of travel. It was a time to settle into darkness, to pull my family together, hand out treats, and appreciate this life.

My thoughts rolled over the library talk announcement mystery. Back in Forsyth, I had met Emily McKee, a young college graduate and instant friend from Massachusetts. She had recently been helping me set up talks. I wasn't aware of a talk scheduled in Boulder, but she must have arranged it. Geez, how did we get this so mixed up? What a coincidence that I rode in like I did.

Resting after a long day.

A woman walked into the barn as I unpacked the horses. "Hey there, how's it going," I said without really looking at her. I hoped she wouldn't stay long at this inconvenient time of my day. I continued working as she asked questions. She had a sharp but deep voice and asked, "Are you that woman riding around the country?"

"That's most likely me," I replied, thinking about how much there was yet to do and glad to be inside for a couple of nights. I'd spent the night before I came into Boulder weathering a snowstorm. Northwesterly winds coming off the eastern front of the snow-covered Rocky Mountains pelted us with freezing rain and snow that nearly blew us off the face of the earth. I stayed awake most of the night, checking tent stakes and encouraging the flapping, struggling nylon tent to stay upright. The wind never did die down, but fortunately sunshine and warmth greeted us the next morning.

"Are you from Minnesota?"

"Yes, I sure am," I replied, continuing to unpack the horses.

"Are you from Rogers, Minnesota?"

That question made me stop and turn toward her. I looked at the woman, really looked at the tall, husky woman with thick, fading blonde hair and bangs covering her forehead and the rest pulled back in a ponytail. Her hands were shoved in her waist-length blue nylon jacket as she stood staring at me.

"Paulette?" I murmured, my eyes narrowed, my head tilted, not quite registering the moment. "Paulette Axt?" I asked softly.

I swear life is nothing but mystery and serendipity. What was going on? What was this? First the surprise at the library, now this?

Twelve feet and fifty-one years stood between me and this long-ago childhood friend. It surprised me I could recognize her. "How could this be Paulette?" I thought. Of all the crazy, wonderful, mysterious things that have happened to me while long riding, this one event was particularly poignant. How do these things happen? I don't know, I have no answer. But when they do and I am spun from my monotony, jarred awake by unexpectedness, I am delighted. I love it. I like surprises. Who really knows why such things happen, but I don't need an explanation. I do know mysterious chance-like acts arise often when I am not attached to my ride, when I'm not disposed to planning, expecting, assuming, but rather when I let the ride simply unfold. Is the universe playing with us? Is God playing with us? Is it the fates, destiny? I know everyone has experienced it and called it coincidence. I can only shake my head and smile.

Needless to say we hugged and screamed.

Remember those two portly gray-haired ladies working the crossword puzzle at the senior center? One of them happened to be Paulette's mother, Donna. She showed my card to Paulette and asked if she thought it could be the same Bernice Ende they had known years ago in Minnesota.

Paulette Axt, now Paulette Smith, and I had been childhood "best friends." She lived with her mother, father, and younger sister on a neighboring farm. Her dad milked a few cows and raised pigs. Small dairy farms like the ones we lived on in central Minnesota began fading from the land by the mid 1960s. The Axts had moved off their farm because of declining agricultural prices nearly ten years before we did.

But for six years, from the ages of six through twelve, we were "best friends" as only children of that age can be. We rode our ponies like raging storms, carefree, wild, ruthless—unsupervised. We rode bareback, defiant and daring, racing between rows of cornfields, crouched low on our ponies' necks, our dirty fingers wrapped tightly in long manes, our eyes closed. We raced recklessly to the other end of the field, the sturdy eight-foot-tall stalks of corn knocking against our legs. We'd stop in our tracks, grasping a moment of silence in a forest of exotic green stalks smelling of corn and horse. Our ponies, held by tight reins, danced side to side, refusing to stand still for long.

Wearing only t-shirts and shorts, our bare legs were wet with horse sweat. "Listen," Paulette whispered, pausing for a long while, and then yelling "Go!" Our ponies knew the game and leaped into a gallop as we rode for the Crow River bordering our farm to the west. Our ponies pawed and splashed in the water with their front hooves while our dirty bare feet dangled in the muddy, cool water. We would break off thin willow branches to swat flies and mosquitoes. Nudging our ponies in a little further, the water would cover our knees until we reached the drop-off and away we'd go, horses swimming and plunging through dirty brown Minnesota river water. It wasn't all that deep, but it could have been the ocean for the thrill we felt.

Even at that age, Paulette was brazen, fearless. She'd pick fights with boys or challenge ones that dared tease us. I'd step aside and watch her, thinking maybe I should hold her back but knowing nothing would. "Yeah, ya wanna fight about it?" she'd say, hands on hips, her lean legs standing wide, her hair wild with loose ends hanging from her long blonde braid. Most of the time, but not always, the boys would back down. Our long school bus ride provided plenty of time for the boys' continued and annoying teasing. They'd pull on her braid from behind our green vinyl bench seat. She'd go after them and have them down before you could think about it. The red-faced school bus driver squeezed in behind the steering wheel would yell, "Get back in your seats!" But Paulette didn't care. She wasn't afraid of what others thought. I loved her for that, or maybe I just wished I had more of what she was made

My childhood friend, Paulette.

of. I wanted the kind of courage she had. I wanted her toughness, her smart, quick, and daring ability, but I wasn't like her, not really. "How can she be like that?" I would say to myself as I stood frozen, amazed, watching and listening and sometimes embarrassed as she stood her ground with kids or even adults. She was probably labeled "mouthy." I worried too much what others might think or that I would be caught doing something I damn well better not be doing. But she wasn't like that. She was just out there, brazenly out there.

When we rode together on Minnesota's dirt farm roads, roads that no longer exist, drenched in sultry summer sunshine, the world belonged to us and everything was worth trying at least once. With Paulette, I found a courage I don't think I rediscovered again until much later in life as a long rider.

It had been years since I'd thought of Paulette. When her family moved to northern Minnesota, I was left with a lonely, empty hole in my life. My best friend was leaving me. Waving goodbye, she rode away in her Dad's old Dodge flatbed truck. The whole family was packed in the cab, and behind them, piled high, was all the junk a farmer thinks is valuable, and usually is if he waits long enough.

Outside the stucco house they were abandoning, an ancient oak tree still dangled our tire swing by a long, not very safe rope. The ground beneath it, once soft and powdery from so many bare feet swinging and dragging on it, turned hard. The swing never thrilled us again. I missed her so much. We wrote for a while, but our lives went in very different directions as so many childhood friendships do. I never imagined I'd see her again, ever!

Paulette married a man twenty years her senior and they eventually moved to Boulder, Montana. Her husband passed away a few years ago, but she continues to enjoy her life under the Big Sky.

I realized in the few days we spent reconnecting that I had many more memories of her than she did of me. I also realized that our childhood days had left a powerful imprint on me. Our time together as children "seeded" my future long-riding years, perhaps explaining why I love long riding as I do. In long riding, I had climbed back into those memories, into my childhood, into me. I'd found a secret passage to my youthful soul. I had rediscovered the fearlessness, the determination, the sense of freedom, and the love of life as when I was a child and Paulette and I were riding with child's minds, needing only the backs of our ponies and the wind in our face, daring us to live.

VACATION RIDE

AUGUST TO OCTOBER 2011
600 MILES

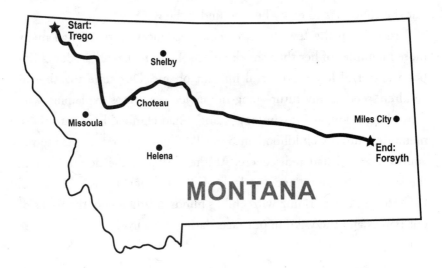

CHAPTER FIFTEEN

MONTANA HERE AND THERE

I was on vacation and riding at vacation speed—600 miles in three months—and I didn't have any talks scheduled. The horses were rested from a six-week stopover in Trego and Eureka and were eager to be out. It was August 2011. Summer was still in full bloom, with warm, dry, clear skies and starry nights, when I left Trego headed for Polebridge, Montana.

I had surprise guests the first two nights out. The first night out, four women friends gave me a rowdy sendoff with a campfire cook-out and music and laughter that filled the starry night until late into the evening. The second night out, my late night guest was a grizzly bear that stopped by my camp. He was not troublesome and quickly went on his way, although he did give Hart, Essie Pearl, Claire, and me something to think about. Toward daybreak, when I regained my composure, I rode into Polebridge for morning coffee and a freshly baked cinnamon roll. The road to Polebridge was busy and dusty. Several cars stopped beside us, their curious occupants saying, "We read about you in the paper." After I answered a few questions they drove off smiling, their curiosity satisfied.

From Polebridge we rode south to Columbia Falls. Along the way, the horses, Claire, and I went for a delightful swim in the North Fork of the Flathead River. I ate tiny, tart buffaloberries and huge, juicy service-berries by the handful and feasted on chokecherries and huckleberries the size of blueberries. I even found and devoured my favorite berry, the delicate thimbleberry. I also picked delicious greens to cook or eat

Major road work along Hungry Horse Reservoir made for a ride free of traffic.

raw—lots of dandelion greens, nettles, lambsquarters, and watercress. The weather could not have been more cooperative.

In Columbia Falls, we stopped at Outfitters Supply for two nights to pick up supplies and visit with Russ Barnett, the owner, and the crew that manages the store. Outfitters Supply is one of my most valued sponsors. We talked about next year's ride and what I might need.

It's a short seven-mile ride from Columbia Falls to the town of Hungry Horse, and we arrived in the early afternoon. Before we could move on, we had to wait for the construction crew that was working on the road on the west side of Hungry Horse Reservoir to end their workday. When the road crews were gone for the day, we slipped around the big machinery and rode a car-less, quiet, tree-lined, shady road for nearly a week, making our way toward the Bob Marshall Wilderness. Every campground was empty. We swam in deep cold water again and again.

Swimming with a horse is a free-for-all. You never know what they will do. In the water, their ears are pricked forward, eyes wide with surprise, backs wet and slippery, muscles taut. Hart and Essie Pearl splashed, pawed, snorted, and delighted in the cool water.

Bill Workman leading his pack string in the Bob Marshall Wilderness.

North of Spotted Bear Ranger Station, two friends from the Trego area caught up with us. They camped with us for two days and left me with panniers full of food. It was enough to keep Claire and I fed for the ten days it took to cross over White River Pass into Mortimer Gulch and then east along the canal road past Pishkun Reservoir and into the town of Choteau. This was the first time I had ridden across the Bob Marshall Wilderness. I was amazed at the good condition of the trails and impressed by all the work that must be done to keep that wilderness open. In a designated wilderness, clearing trails and fighting fires is done manually, without power tools. All equipment and food is hauled in by long strings of pack mules. As I rode the trail, I happened to meet up with a pack train and moved over to let the string of eleven mules pass. Bill Workman, from the Eureka area, who has thirty-two years of legendary service with the U.S. Forest Service, was leading the string. We talked awhile, then each of us moved on. This was my first Bob Marshall experience and I promised myself I would return and spend a summer traveling this spectacular country.

Hart and Essie thread a tree-lined trail in the Bob.

TIES TO THE PAST

We arrived in Choteau on September 13. I had deliberately routed us through Choteau in search of information. In 1896, my great-grandparents, the Hoys, homesteaded in a settlement called Blackleaf, north of

My grandmother, Francis Linda James, on the ranch at Blackleaf, Montana.

Choteau and west of Bynum. They owned the Blackleaf Ranch, and I wondered what I would find behind my great-grandparents' door.

As mentioned previously, my grandmother taught in the Blackleaf School and my grandfather broke horses, but I knew very little about my great-grandparents. I knew that Hoy Coulee and Hoy Grove were named for them and that my great-grandmother was the Blackleaf post-mistress for a few years.

I met ranchers Anne and Larry Dellwo, who own the land now. Anne was kind enough to show me the homestead site and spend an entire afternoon answering my questions. Anne's folks, the Pollock's, bought the ranch from my great-grandparents. The ranch is snugged up against what is now the Lewis and Clark National Forest and spreads east from the forest boundary. What I learned is that the Hoys ran horses and cattle and made a good living for many years. Then suddenly they sold out and were gone—why and where they went is still a mystery.

The horses, Claire, and I left the ranch and went to Choteau. Choteau is a lovely, quaint town with friendly people. As I stood on

Blacksmithing demonstration at the threshing bee in Choteau, Montana.

the west side of the historic courthouse looking down Main Street, I could not help but feel the spirit of my ancestors as I am sure they also stood there years ago with new hope and many dreams to fill the broad, open land.

We stayed a week at the rodeo grounds. The annual Choteau Threshing Bee was on, and members of the Northern Blacksmith Association were there, pounding out the shapes of yesterday.

MOVING ON

The prairie landscape of central Montana unwinds itself. It rolls out in dramatic buttes, razorback ridges, and long, smooth, sloping mountains nude and colorless in the fall. Creeks and streams carve deeply into

From her perch on Essie, Claire enjoys the rolling prairie near Cascade, Montana.

ravines and coulees. Ranches are separated by long straight stretches of barbed-wire fencing and open space. It is not welcoming country. It's rough country and completely indifferent to a lone long rider. It makes a rider wary and careful, but it offers by far some of the most stunning vistas I have ridden.

We headed south to Cascade, where Harlan and Iris Denboer furnished a corral and a place to set up camp. Iris showed me around town where I saw the cabin that painter Charlie Russell and his bride honeymooned in and also the home of J. Robert Atkinson, founder of the Braille Institute of America. Then we headed toward White Sulphur Springs.

The September afternoon sun was unusually strong and the heat unbearable. It did not last long—only two or three hours—but it was stifling. We had enough water every day from creeks and stock tanks, but the long, steady climb up and over Millegan Pass wore us out. I knew we needed a break before we reached White Sulphur Springs where we would stop to visit Kate and Darrell Dunkin. The map showed a corner of the Helena National Forest that looked like a good spot for a solitary layover where we could rest a few days along Vermont Creek. Late in the afternoon, we rode in and made camp.

HART IN TROUBLE

The next morning I woke and found that Hart was unable to walk. He had either suffered a stroke or a seizure or had caught himself up in the picket line and hurt his neck, perhaps a spinal cord injury. I immediately began massage, movement exercises, and prayers. Soon he could walk but it was as if he were drunk. I found myself in one of the most difficult situations I would ever face while long riding. I asked myself, "Do I need to put him out of his misery, using my gun?"

Hart displayed no outward signs of injury. He ate and drank well, and his temperature and respirations were normal. What had happened? I spent every waking moment with him, taking long walks. I kept him moving. But in my heart I wrestled with the thought I might have to put him down at any moment, right then and there.

Bill Loney, the owner of the neighboring ranch who had stopped by for a visit, hauled us to a nearby ranch veterinarian. The vet could only guess at what was wrong and concluded, "He's never going to be any good." Bill hauled us back to my campsite and came every other day to check on us.

Bill filled me with calm reassuring advice. I so appreciated his visits. Kate and Darrell, my friends from White Sulphur Springs, were kind enough to bring us food. We stayed camped on Vermont Creek for seventeen days while I worked on Hart, and I did see improvements. But Hart was still in no condition to be hauled any great distance, so I held fast at my campsite.

Darrell Dunkin happened to mention Hart's situation to Trudi Rioux, an equine massage therapist in the area. In her business, Range of Motion, Trudi does craniosacral massage and acupressure on horses. She drove twenty-three miles to treat Hart. I watched Hart go into a trance within minutes of her touching him. Hart eventually recovered, and I can only think that this was in large part due to Trudi's gifted healing hands and energy. It left a profound effect on me, on my ideas of horse healing, and regarding the ability to communicate through transmission of energy between horse and healer.

Even though he was doing better, Hart could not tolerate a 250-mile walk to our winter camp in Forsyth. We needed to be hauled. Delva and Spencer Gibson of Lewistown, Montana, are friends from the years they lived in the Eureka area near Trego. They had helped me in 2006 when Honor was having back problems. Now, once again, they came to my rescue. Delva drove to White Sulphur Springs with her truck and trailer to haul me, Hart, Essie, and Claire to their picturesque home north of Lewistown where we spent a restful two weeks. Hart did very well. Delva then hauled us to our winter camp in Forsyth on October 30, so ending our 600-mile vacation ride. I am deeply grateful to Delva and Spencer Gibson, Kate and Darrell Dunkin, and all those who helped me. Hart made it through the vacation ride, but I knew in my heart he would soon have to retire from long riding.

OH, CANADA
FROM FORSYTH, MONTANA, THROUGH SASKATCHEWAN, ALBERTA, AND BRITISH COLUMBIA TO TREGO, MONTANA
5TH LONG RIDE

APRIL THROUGH SEPTEMBER 2012
2,000 MILES

CHAPTER SIXTEEN

OH, CANADA

In early April 2012, I set out from my winter camp in Forsyth, Montana, heading north to Canada. It was my fifth long ride, a planned 2,000-mile horseshoe-shaped ramble through Saskatchewan and Alberta, then back home to Trego. This ride started out differently than my other rides when I would pack up, mount up, and go. In addition to my seasoned, faithful companions Hart, Essie Pearl, and Claire, during the previous year I had acquired a third horse and a new friend who was game enough to come along.

MONTANA SPIRIT

I received the new horse through another bit of serendipity, or Trail Magic, as I like to call it. Back in 2011, I was setting up camp in a ditch along Rosebud Creek Road near Forsyth, on my way toward Ashland on the Northern Cheyenne Indian Reservation. Rosebud Creek Road connects to U.S. Highway 212, which runs west to the Crow Reservation and Little Bighorn Battlefield National Monument. The road was paved so there was no dust and very little traffic.

A truck pulling a four-horse trailer rolled slowly to a stop. I didn't think much about it. Lots of people stop when I camp in a ditch next to a road. Behind me, a sign read, "Custer Camp. General [sic] Custer camped here June 22, 1876." "Move over, ghosts of Custer," I thought to myself. This ditch had plenty of grass for Essie Pearl and Hart, and

I could carry water from a nearby stock tank behind the fence on the other side of the road.

I looked up from my camp gear to see an old man leaning on hand crutches coming from around the trailer. "Now what?" I thought. I was about to meet Swede Granstrom, mountain man, outfitter, hunter, gunsmith, and jack-of-all-trades. He wore round wire-rim glasses with an aging cap on top of his headful of white hair and faceful of white beard. He was not very tall. His jean jacket and jeans were dirty and worn, and his hands had been shaped into muscular fists by a lifetime of hard work. Even though he had difficulty walking, he was a striking man—rough, tough, and even gnarly.

It did not take long before coffee poured from his beat-up Coleman thermos and vanilla creme sandwich cookies came out. We sat on his trailer bumper talking, dipping cookies into cups of hot coffee, and watching the sun set. Behind us in the horse trailer, a magnificent Fjord stallion moved about quietly. He nickered at Essie Pearl. That is why Swede stopped. He saw a Fjord on the road. There are not many of them, and Fjord enthusiasts are pulled like magnets to those who do own them. Swede and his business partner, Dottie Smith, who is just as tough as Swede, owned a herd of Fjord-Percheron cross-bred horses up Wild Horse Canyon about thirty miles southeast of Rosebud, Montana, which is about fifteen miles east of Forsyth. He was on his way home when he saw me. We became fast friends.

During the winter of 2011-2012, while I hunkered down in the little red barn north of Forsyth, I looked forward to a weekly visit with Swede. We would sit in his beat-up truck full of tools and junk, odds and ends for fixing this and that, drinking coffee and eating vanilla creme sandwich cookies. Swede admired what I did and said he wished he had done it when he was younger. He always had lots of questions, mostly about the horses.

Hart was not well suited for long riding, and I was concerned about his ability to continue. He had injured himself on our 600-mile vacation ride, and I knew he would have to retire sometime soon. Essie Pearl, a Norwegian Fjord, had all the qualities for long-distance travel.

Swede Granstrom and his Norwegian Fjords.

I had ridden with her long enough to know I wanted another Fjord and would not take any other breed out. The combination of thick, coarse hair and skin, short flat back, hooves like steel, a steadfast demeanor, and easy-to-keep weight make them superior to any other breed I've used on previous rides. Maybe this is why Swede offered me one of his horses. He just plain thought his horses were better than anything else for mountain riding and he wanted to show the world what his cross-bred horses could do. He offered me Montana Spirit, his three-year-old, untrained Fjord-Percheron mare, in exchange for advertising his mountain horses on my website.

Spirit came to me in January 2012. She had been trained to lead and load and not much else, but true to her Fjord-Percheron breeding she was willing to learn. I never trained a more eager-to-please horse. In no time, she confidently carried Claire Dog. Three months later, Claire and I and the three shaggy-coated horses braved the cold wind and headed north on a planned 2,000-mile ride in Canada.

Montana Spirit (in front) and Essie Pearl, two wonderful long-riding Fjords.

The ride up from Forsyth took us through spectacular open cattle country. There was plenty of water in the reservoirs and plenty of grass coming up, even that early in the spring. But I had my hands full with three horses. They ran off twice, and there is nothing worse than waking up and your horses are gone, and nothing more embarrassing than asking a stranger, "Um, excuse me, could you help find my horses?" I found them both times after several agonizing hours of searching. Three horses are a good deal more to handle—the logistics of leading them, what happens if one shies, how to tie up, how to stake out. Fortunately the land I was traveling through was spacious country with few cars on the roads. I deliberately chose this route for the sole purpose of training and safely introducing Montana Spirit to life on the road. I simply could not say enough for this young new start, Montana Spirit. Here she was, only three months with this tribe she found herself in, but fitting in beautifully. When I got her, she already knew how to lead and load, and she had a wonderful, gregarious personality that draws her to people. She was now riding, packing, and traveling out as the lead horse. She still had much to learn, of course—it takes years to develop a truly solid trust between horse and rider and to accustom a horse to the often challenging situations that arise when traveling across country. But Spirit was probably the best long-riding horse that I will ever take out. Her short back, thick skin, and heavy hair; her hairy feathered draft horse legs; her calm yet very alert mind; and her willingness to move forward were all skills and characteristics that I look for in a horse for long riding.

SPIRIT OF A DIFFERENT KIND

Emily McKee, a twenty-five-year-old adventurous woman from Massachusetts with whom I had connected earlier in the winter, was meeting up with us in Glasgow, Montana. Emily and I had first met at a dinner at the Gilje's Ranch. Emily had come to Forsyth for a job as a city planning assistant to work off her college debt. I loved her youthful try-anything, you-can-do-it, and sure-let's-see-what-happens attitude. She wanted to go on the long ride to Canada with me and that took a lot of courage—Emily had never ridden a horse before.

In Glasgow, Gene Hartsock graciously opened a building for us at the Valley County Fairgrounds, which he manages, so we had shelter from the unusually wet, windy, cold weather. The horses were happy in their stalls; all of us were warm, dry, and safe.

We spent a week preparing for our Canadian crossing, going over tack, food, sleeping arrangements in the tent, and so forth. There's always much to do. People often ask me, "What do you do out there, don't you get bored?" I have to smile to myself because long riding involves almost endless work, all of which needs to be done every day. Brushing horses, brushing saddle pads, washing cinches, feeding (all of us), checking hooves, packing and unpacking, finding a campsite, route-finding, and writing. Just setting up the tent and evening chores takes a full two hours; mornings are a bit less. But there is always "much to do." Add public speaking to the list—I'm frequently asked to speak at schools, senior centers, civic clubs, and such. In Glasgow, I gave a talk at the local senior center to a full house. We all enjoyed a lunch of liver and onions.

When we returned from the senior center, the situation at the fair-grounds instantly put me in a dreadful panic. I still shudder each time I think about it. Somehow a gate had been left open. I don't know whether I failed to close a gate in the maze of gates common at rodeo grounds or one was left open by a newspaper reporter who had come to take photos. I had left Spirit and Hart in one pen and Essie Pearl in another while I went into town with Emily. Now Spirit and Hart were gone! I ran to tell Gene Hartsock and he got on the phone. Sure enough, Spirit had decided to head for home down a busy two-lane highway bristling with semitrucks and afternoon traffic. We jumped in a car with Gene, who stayed on his cell phone talking with police. It seemed like the whole town was looking for the horses. "Last seen near the railroad tracks," Gene echoed. No, they were headed south on Highway 42. Oh my gosh, my heart pounded in my chest, not only for the safety of the horses, but what if someone else were injured or killed because my horses were running loose in traffic?

We sped around town, down one street after another, then south, and it seemed like forever, my mind racing with dreadful thoughts. Suddenly, there they were, just about to cross a bridge, but someone had stopped their car and was waving their arms to stop the two horses. Spirit and Hart veered off into the ditch and had nowhere to go. We drove up from behind and I jumped out and talked to them, calling their names. They nickered and I caught my two scared steeds—they were sweaty and tired from a nearly five-mile run against traffic and who knows what else they must have encountered. I rode Hart bare-back, leading Spirit back to the fairgrounds, mumbling prayers of thanks that my horses were alive and no innocent bystanders were hurt or killed. This was by far the most dangerous incident that has ever oc-curred on one of my rides. Horses running loose in traffic—it does not get any worse. The whole episode put me on edge for the rest of the ride, and for years after, young Montana Spirit was unable to face traffic and had to be led on the inside.

NORTH TO CANADA

Once my nerves recovered and we had everything in order, off we went on the first of May, we four veterans of long riding—Hart, Essie Pearl, Claire Dog, and me—and two newcomers to the long-riding adventure—Emily McKee and Montana Spirit. The weather cooperated, giving us blue skies over the rolling prairie. It took us four days to ride north to the friendly town of Opheim, Montana, population eighty-eight. The town had celebrated its centennial the year before, but boarded up storefronts and vacant lots spoke to the town's slow decline from a peak of 3,000 residents. It was once home to a U.S. Air Force radar station and was also a stop on the railroad, but the Air Force pulled out in 1979, and the railroad stopped service in 1990.

Luckily for us, the remaining residents of Opheim are remarkably friendly and welcoming. No sooner than we reached town, the weather turned truly nasty, some of the worst I have ever experienced. What could have been a long, miserable weekend turned into a comfortable three-day stay thanks to the hospitality of the Bailey family.

When the skies finally cleared, and with the horses' international papers secured thanks to the Valley Vet Clinic in Glasgow, we rode to the Canadian port of entry ten miles north of Opheim on Montana Route 24. Besides our passports, we also had all the required government documents and vaccination and health papers for the animals. Still, we had to answer a barrage of questions and then wait while the customs officer went inside to verify our papers. Local folks who live near the border had forewarned us, but we learned firsthand how much more rigorous the border crossing had become since September 11, 2001.

On a beautiful Tuesday afternoon, we arrived in the lovely community of Killdeer, Saskatchewan. We got permission to stay in the yard of the community hall. The building was full of interesting pictures from the 1940s until today and scattered with bits of local history. The next morning, a local man named Amel was generous enough to tour us around to see some of the beautiful areas southern Saskatchewan has to offer, including the communities of Wood Mountain and Rockglen. He also suggested that we detour from our planned route and go through Grasslands National Park instead. So we rode west into the vast park and made it to a beautiful scenic campground as the sun was setting.

The next morning broke cold and rainy, so we decided to stay another day. We met three park rangers who explained the history of Canada's prairies and helped us stitch together a path on back roads that would get us to the town of Swift Current about 120 miles to the northwest. Riding through Grasslands National Park was breathtaking—prairie as far as the eye could see, hints of badlands and interesting rock outcrops, and not another soul in sight. The rangers' suggested route took us to the village of Mankota where we camped at the rodeo grounds for two nights. Mankota is a lovely small ranching and farming community with a good library and an excellent restaurant, and the town park had shower facilities. Folks were friendly, quick with their smiles and handshakes. Hart and Essie were fat and sassy and moving well, and Claire Dog was clearly in her element, happy and gregarious as always.

On the road north again we were welcomed by more farm families. Emily experienced firsthand the hospitality, generosity, and instant friendships that make long riding possible. The Knox clan let us camp on their land and fed us a terrific chili for dinner and then a wonderful breakfast feast. Similarly, we were riding along when Josh Hofer from the Ponteix Hutterite Colony stopped to see who we were. We chatted and he invited us to visit the colony, which is just east of Saskatchewan Highway 628 about thirteen miles south of Ponteix. ("Highway" sounds a bit grand for this dirt and fine-gravel road. Traffic was sparse, and the horses enjoyed the road's soft, smooth surface.) As we rode into the colony, we were greeted by many curious and welcoming people. The women fed us a delicious meal of duck, soup, and wonderful canned pears. They gave us a fascinating tour. Emily had never been to a Hutterite colony and was astonished at how efficient, organized, clean, and professional the operation was, from food production to washing clothes. We were truly appreciative that they took the time (especially on a religious day) to give us a peek inside their lives and culture. They sent us away with a huge package of fresh sausage, bread, and other tasty homemade treats.

The town of Ponteix itself was a lovely community, filled with more friendly folks. Founded in 1908 by a French priest, Ponteix retains a strong sense of its French roots and First Nations culture. The Notukeu Heritage Museum on the north end of town was filled with fascinating displays of prehistoric indigenous pottery, stone tools, arrowheads and other flintknapped tools, and fossils, with tours offered in English and French. It rained while we were in Ponteix, but we enjoyed a scenic camping spot by clear-running Notukeu Creek.

The wet, cold weather continued to dog us as we rode north, so the facilities at Kinetic Exhibition Park in Swift Current were a welcome sight. The park offered camping, horse arenas, a dog-friendly play area, and new, sparkling clean showers. We settled in for a week, grateful that all of us—horses included—could be warm, dry, and safe despite the steady spring storms. I've stayed at many similar event centers and fairgrounds in the States, but this one was exceptionally nice. I was so impressed that I walked over to city hall and told the powers that be what a fine, blue-ribbon facility they had. Thank you to all of the maintenance men and the women in the office who made our stay at Kinetic Park so enjoyable!

Swift Current is full of parks and luscious greenery—very pretty. Emily and I ate at a nice café on the main downtown street. Specialty crepes with flavors from around the world kept appearing at our table, decoratively served. Mail was waiting for me at the post office, and Emily and I caught up on our emails on computers at the public library.

PARTING WAYS

Emily was a real trooper, but at Swift Current, 400 miles into our ride, she admitted defeat. She caught a bus to Saskatoon and then flew to her family home in Boston.

Back in Forsyth, we had spent two months preparing her. She had learned to ride, she knew the camping routine, and she had acquired

Emily McKee.

some road skills, but her feet were blistered, her body ached, and I probably was not an easy traveling companion. We certainly shared some good laughs and long talks. Finally she conceded, "I just didn't think it would be so extreme. Walking and riding twenty-plus miles every day, packing for two hours in the morning and unpacking two hours in the evening, the care of the horses, watching the horses, the dirt and smells, the 'out there' of life, and the seriousness of the risks and the labor involved is something I could not understand until I tried it."

I thought Emily did very well. She certainly showed the courage and spirit to try. She learned more about horses and riding and remote places than she bargained for. We parted, as friends sometimes have to do, but we stay in touch and often laugh about our crazy ride together. Today, Emily is happily married, living in San Francisco with her husband and son.

After Emily's departure, June and Darby Roy were gracious enough to invite me into their lovely home west of town. I was able to do laundry, and June kept my belly full of delicious food. The endless rain gave me time to visit with new friends. I had first met Donna Waldner and her father on a gravel road coming into Swift Current. I had flagged them down to ask for directions. Well, Donna leapt out of her old truck and to my side in a second, and we made a connection right away. She came out later that same evening with her mother and her two teen-age children when I was camped down the road a few miles. Donna and June were good friends and it was a treat to spend time with these women. They both use healing touch to help injured or sick horses. They worked on Hart, and then they worked on my old body. Both Hart and I agreed, we were feeling pretty darn good after that. Then June made us a Canadian treat called Puffed Wheat Cake, made from puffed wheat, peanut butter, butter, and sugar, and it was to die for. I worried I would gain too much weight and poor Hart would complain when I climbed into the saddle again.

Soon it was time to head back out. Donna came over and she and June waved me on with our noses facing north. The ride north from Swift Current could not have been more pleasant. Saskatchewan was premier long-riding country. Wide ditches—excuse me, *clean* wide ditches—green grass, and lots of small ponds and creeks for easy water access. The frosting was the smiling friendly folks we met along the way.

I rode back roads to Cabri, which was a fun, action-packed stop. I think I met most of the town. Lunch at the House of Heart Cafe was such good food! I met the owner, Paulette Gehl, and her mother, Eileen Hartman, who lives in Lancer, twenty miles west of Cabri. Eileen invited me to stay at her place. After more visiting in Cabri, I headed for Lancer but first stopped in Abbey where I was able to visit the school and see a 4-H exhibition. 4-H has a special place in my heart because it played an important role in my life as a young girl on a small dairy farm in Minnesota. I am always glad to see young people still learning and growing through 4-H programs. Such efforts are particularly important on the Great Plains, in both Canada and the United States, where young people often drift away from small towns for better opportunities in big cities, leaving a dwindling and aging population.

Between Cabri and Lancer, car after car of Hutterites stopped to visit with me, offering smiles and happy conversation and, of course, homemade food. It occurred to me that, as long as I was in Hutterite country, I would never starve to death.

I rode into the hamlet of Lancer late in the afternoon. Eileen Hartman's husband, Lloyd, was waiting for me. I set up camp in their backyard while Lloyd cooked up liver and onions for dinner. Eileen was not yet back from a trip to Regina, so Lloyd and I sat on their veranda and talked until dark. Now in his eighties, Lloyd had stories to tell. In 1989, he had won the World Senior Pro Team Roping Championship. I asked him how long it took him to become a good roper. He replied, "After fifty years on the rodeo circuit, it took twenty-five more to feel good at it." I thought to myself, "I wonder if it will take me that long to feel good at long riding." In the morning, as Eileen was making "pierogi," a Ukrainian pastry, we visited and she told me she had just retired from a thirty-five-year career as a schoolteacher and now was involved in the school system at the provincial level. I reflected on my sister who had also recently retired from a similar span as a teacher. Both women had devoted their lives to the education of other children. To these women, I say, "My hat is off to both of you!" (and I have a big hat).

Lloyd and Eileen's son Clayton hauled me to the Lemsford Ferry where Essie, Hart, Spirit, Claire, and I safely made our way across the South Saskatchewan River to continue north toward Kindersley. As I rode into town, several people from the nearby Springfield Colony rolled up in their cars to visit, and then it seemed like one car after another stopped to say hello.

We arrived in Kindersley with a strong southeasterly wind at our backs, a wind that grew with force and determination. The kind of wind that brings me inside. Thankfully, Kim and Melody Lamont welcomed us into their home. I went "from the ditch to the Ritz" as they put me up in a lovely enclosed gazebo, complete with a wood-fired cook stove and western decor. The horses were in separate corrals not far across the road, and I could see them from the gazebo windows.

The wind raged, but it doesn't pay to complain about the wind. If you fight it or cuss at the wind, it either blows harder or is gone in a flash and you're left with bugs and heat, praying for the wind to return. So I went visiting. I picked up a few things at the Salvation Army Thrift Shop that Kim and his dad Ron run. Kim is a man of many talents: a licensed farrier, a fine leather worker, and a welder, plus he and his dad have traveled extensively working with the provincial Fish, Wildlife and Lands agency. Melody and Kim's home was a lovely blend of creative antiques and new ideas, beautifully done to welcome visitors and also to stimulate the mind. They certainly made me feel welcome in their home, a hospitable sanctuary in a bustling, friendly town.

From Kindersley, I rode north to the busy oilfield town of Kerrobert at the junction of Highways 21, 31, and 51. The tallest structure in town is a 100-foot-tall "standpipe"-style water tower constructed to look like a coastal lighthouse with white wooden siding and a red conical roof. Built in 1914, it holds 150,000 gallons and is still in use. The last thing I needed at the moment was water, however. The season's drenching rains had followed me north, so, lured by the aroma of fresh bread, I escaped into the Kerrobert Bakery. The young couple who owns the place is on their own long ride in the ancient art of baking and providing a bright spot in town for locals and wayward equestrians alike.

INTO ALBERTA

From Kerrobert I turned west and a bit south, crossing into Alberta. I spent a night in the little outpost of Esther where the "skyline" is dominated by a red wooden grain elevator, said to be the oldest standing elevator in the province. I stayed at the home of Bill and Madge Dalton—the Dalton Gang!—a friendly bunch, and ate dinner with the branding crew at the town hall. Here was yet another group of people all wearing smiles and enjoying one another's company, people who clearly care deeply about one another and their families and friends that make up this isolated but resourceful community.

I was told time and again that I was riding through a once-in-a-lifetime spring with such spectacular luscious green and belly-deep

Alberta's oldest grain elevator at Esther.

grasses. The rains turned Alberta into paradise. I was enjoying one of my finest rides ever. This was farming and ranching country, just like the rural Minnesota of my childhood, and the Canadians I met were all delightful people.

When I rode into the hamlet of Sedalia (with just five streets), the place knocked my socks off. The Sedalia Co-op General Mercantile was a store to be proud of. First of all, the store was in the middle of empty prairie farmland and yet here you could get just about anything! They told me that fresh produce is brought in weekly, and there was a huge variety of goods—remarkable! It was like stepping back in time. The building dates from the 1920s and still has its original hardwood floors and a textured tin ceiling. The store became a co-op in 1945, at least I believe that is what Eddie Thornton told me. Eddie and his wife Heather manage the store. Eddie's father managed the store before them. Here a community has said, "Forget Wal-Mart, we want our own store," and they've made it happen. With over 200 members, the co-op

Crossing Alberta's prairies.

is an example of people pooling together to make a positive change in their lives. Sedalia also had a post office in a 100-year-old house. Postmistress Kathy said she had forty mailboxes and was open three days a week. I was camped right between the post office and the store, and the community hall was open so I had a toilet facility. Many folks stopped by to wish me safe travels.

For nearly a month, I'd been hounded by storms and rain. Evenings were filled with horrendous mosquitoes, so I covered the horses in nets and fly shields to keep them comfortable. The horizon was flat in all directions. I rose early to ride the sunrises and avoid the summer heat that would build during the day.

In Youngstown, I gave a talk at the local school. First through ninth graders were finishing up their year, and I told them that they too were on a long ride—*school*! One of the teachers, Mavis Palmer, retired that very same day after more than thirty-five years of teaching. I had to doff my hat again to another teacher who devoted half of her life to teach-

Hart and Essie in full bug attire.

ing so many children. Mavis and her husband, Murray, generously let me stay at their home as rain showers came and went. Hart, Essie, and Spirit were all doing well; we were traveling at an easy pace and taking long breaks, and grass and water were everywhere! Claire continued her role as star of the show. Really, no one wanted to talk to me, it was always Claire they wanted to visit with.

A PLAGUE OF MOSQUITOES

In the morning, we said our goodbyes and continued our path southwest, aiming for Sheerness. The Alberta prairie, liberally sprinkled with pothole ponds and winding streams, was as beautiful as the people were friendly. The weather, however, refused to be anything but wet and wild, and the hordes of mosquitoes were terrible. When we made it to Sheerness, Clifford Campbell offered shelter and we ended up staying a week. As in Youngstown, Claire was welcomed into the house and

Farrier filing a hoof before fitting a new shoe.

made herself at home on the couch. In no time, Clifford was feeding her treats and Claire was doing tricks for him and doing her nonstop talking—you'd think she had something important to say! I suppose after all the miles behind her, she did have stories to tell.

I had planned to turn southeast and head for Cypress Hills Interprovincial Park on the Alberta-Saskatchewan border south of Medicine Hat, but things didn't turn out that way. I left Sheerness heading east, and a dear friend, Janna Pekaar, drove all the way over from Seattle to meet up and deliver some supplies. Janna has traveled to meet me on every single ride I've done, but this time the visit was cut short. The mosquitoes drove us nearly mad, and Janna fled rather than risk being eaten alive. I tried to tough it out a few more days but finally surrendered, and Clifford Campbell drove over and hauled us back to his place. We spent a few days at his ranch planning out a new route and then headed west toward the Rocky Mountains and higher, hopefully drier ground. I've never experienced mosquitoes that bad!

Essie, Hart, and Spirit enjoy a snack wherever they can find it, west of Calgary.

We rode through the beautiful Hand Hills Ecological Preserve and then north to Huxley where I stayed with friends of Clifford's for nearly a week. The days were hot—too hot for riding. From Huxley, I rode south to Three Hills and then west to Water Valley where I stayed at the home of Tom Woollings on the Little Red Deer River for three days to replace some horseshoes, clean my tack, resupply food, and take a serious look at my intended route for the next 200 miles. I planned to skirt west of Calgary and then follow the Forestry Trunk Road south to Pincher Creek. From there, I would have to decide which border crossing to use on my return to the States and Montana. On top of all that, I would need a veterinarian near the border to check my horses and provide me with all the necessary paperwork for crossing the border.

INTO THE MOUNTAINS

Navigating on horseback around a big city like Calgary is always a challenge, but Leanne and Rick Kroll came to my rescue, hauling me

Kananaskis scenery.

and the horses through the Cochrane area. That included crossing a narrow highway bridge over the Bow River and the busy Trans-Canada Highway. From there, we rode south toward the mountains and into Kananaskis Country on equestrian trails and back roads.

The ride through the Kananaskis was nothing short of spectacular. Ragged, gray, monumental rock formations towered over us as we followed Highway 40 to Highwood Pass. Pat and Peggy Hickey, local ranchers out checking on their cattle, stopped to visit and then brought out sandwiches. We sat at a picnic table and ate lunch together while the horses enjoyed a break.

Where Highway 40 bends east toward Longview, I turned south on gravel road 940 and soon stumbled upon a man named Bryon Campbell and a backhoe operator, Chester, working on a closed road. They not only gave me their lunches (Claire got a sandwich too), but they directed me down a back road that was carless and as pretty and quiet as could be, embellished with mountain views I would never have had the chance to see on the main road. When the road met the Old Man River, who showed up but Bryon Campbell, this time with two cowboys, Mike and Henry, and a gentleman named Max Kolesnik from Ontario who knew all about the Long Riders' Guild. All of these men would come to my aid later in the trip, but at this point they brought much appreciated gifts of food, horse oats, and a hot turkey dinner from the kitchen of the Alberta Forestry fire station several miles up the road. Oh my gosh, was I grateful! I camped there on the Old Man River for a few days, which allowed me to re-shoe Hart and do some repairs on the tent and horse tack. I rested and I ate. We all ate—well and thoroughly. People ask me, "What do you think about all day," and my answer is "Food!" Walking and riding twenty miles a day, plus all the packing, unpacking, sleepless nights, and long days makes a person hungry.

Henry (one of the cowboys I mentioned earlier) guided me safely across fast-moving Racehorse Creek, which was almost too much for old Hart. And then Mike (the other cowboy), his girlfriend, and Darryl Campbell (Bryon's brother) met me out near the Crowsnest Highway (Canada 3) near Blairmore to haul me over Crowsnest Pass. I hesitated to let them haul me—I thought, "Boys, I'll be fine." But there was no way I could have safely ridden on that busy, high-speed highway. When they dropped me off on Corbin Road, I blew them two big thank-you kisses as they drove off.

Somewhere in the middle of all this, on August 28th, while I was camped along the Old Man River, I rendezvoused with Bob Dotson, host of NBC's *Today Show*. Actually, it was Bob who rendezvoused with me. He hiked into my camp, through bear country, sliding down shale slopes in penny loafers. Bob was very gracious, as were the film and sound crew and Bob's assistant Amanda. All were professionals, top of the line, and genuinely intrigued by what I do.

So there we were after being dropped off on the Corbin Road. We headed south, the final stretch. "We are headed home," I said to the horses and to Claire. But I still needed to connect with a veterinarian to get the documentation needed for crossing the border. For now, all I could do was ride south. Winding along the valleys just west of the Continental Divide, I ran into Sergeant Joe Caravetta with the Conservation Officers Service. Joe gave me what food he had in his cooler, but then I was on my own and soon running low on sustenance. This is a problem with riding remote back roads—there's nowhere to resupply. Luckily, as I rode into a meadow along the Flathead River, I ran into a family on a campout. The man came walking over with a big smile on his face and said, "You can't expect us not to come over and find out what you're all about when you come riding in packed like you are, with a dog riding a horse!" He introduced himself as Jon Levesque, from the nearby town of Fernie. He and his wife Aaron were just packing up, heading home after a long weekend camping, so they emptied all the food out of their camper. That was such a weight off my shoulders—Hart needed to rest, and now I could sit in one place for a few days. Then Jon said, "When you get into Fernie, call us and we'll have a place for you to stay. Also, a friend of mine is a veterinarian. . . ."

Soon the rains came again, and I was hunkered down trying to stay dry when a grader operator, driving home after the day's work, stopped to talk. His name was Harry Wilehok and he realized I needed food. I camped near the Butts Cabin that night and had a bad time of it—a bear came in and raised holy hell with the horses, but nobody got hurt. Early the next morning, in the dark and rain, came the road grader, Harry, and he brought food. I was again so grateful because it rained much of that week and I had to stay put. Thanks to Harry, I didn't go hungry. Trail angels come in all shapes and sizes, and they have a knack for showing up when you least expect them but most need them.

All of which is a roundabout way of explaining how I ended up at the home of Dr. Martin Hart and his wife Francesca in Fernie. They were kind enough to let the horses rest in a nice barn free of flies, sheltered from the sun's strong heat, contently eating all the hay they wanted. I relaxed in a hot, hot shower and cleaned off a month's worth of dirt from my skin. Then Francesca filled my belly with a delicious homemade curry soup. Even Claire was welcomed into the house by the two family dogs, Ranger and Ollie.

Unfortunately, riding back into the United States turned out to be not as easy as leaving. I arrived in Fernie one week before my papers would expire, thinking this would allow plenty of time to cross just fifty miles south at Roosville on Highway 93. I called ahead to give the border patrol a heads up before three horses, a dog, and a lady long rider rode into their sights; a courtesy call. But I was in for a big surprise. At this point, I did not understand the laws of international equestrian travel. If I had been in Canada for only a month, there would've been no problem. But I had been in Canada for nearly six months and could not return at just any old border crossing. I had to cross where a United States veterinarian was available to check my horses' health certificates. It's all very clear to me now, but then it seemed so complicated. The only two "nearby" border crossings with a vet inspector were at Kingsgate/Eastport in Idaho south of Cranbrook on Highway 95 or at Coutts/Sweet Grass on Interstate 15 in Montana a couple hundred miles away. After a series of complicated runarounds and inspections that had to be done by Canadian veterinarians, I made it to the Kingsgate/Eastport crossing, but we had to be hauled some of the way—there was simply no other way.

At Kingsgate, we stood in line, slowly nudging our way toward the border crossing, three horses, one dog riding a horse, one gal with a very big hat riding another, cars in front of us, and cars behind us. The semitrucks were coming and going on our right, some with loads of horses tightly packed coming to Canada for slaughter. As we moved slowly forward, people jumped out of their cars and pickup trucks to take photos of my two horses and Claire Dog riding. For people stuck in line, we were a welcome diversion. The horses behaved perfectly in the busy, noisy traffic and distractions. My papers had been sent ahead to the border patrol. I was a bit nervous because the panniers Essie Pearl carried were full of food, which they would confiscate if they looked inside. Once I crossed the border, I had another two weeks of mountain riding and no supplies would be available. Well, as we neared the booth, all the border patrol came out to visit and take photos of the dog and pony act. They had a good time with me.

Riding Hart, crossing from Canada into the United States.

"What does her license plate say?" one asked. Another said, "Should we take them into secondary inspection and check for noxious weeds?" "What kind of gas mileage do you get?" came another voice. All the while I am thinking, "Please don't look in my panniers." They kept us there for at least twenty minutes, all of us having a very good time of it. A long line of waiting cars grew much longer as they walked around the horses

Claire enjoyed Canada, too.

and petted Claire who is such a ham of it all, reaching out with her right front paw as if to shake hands. Finally we crossed into the United States and I waved goodbye, grateful for my first international long ride. One of the women working at the border crossing emailed later to make sure I'd made it home all right. That was so very kind of her.

I think this has been the best ride in all of my eight years of riding, certainly the easiest ride. I learned much about Canada, its government and cities, and its rural communities. There is a captivating innocence still there, a neighborliness that warmed my heart and made me feel welcomed. It is a huge, beautiful country, with a more laidback approach to life than in the States, and that suited me just fine.

CHAPTER SEVENTEEN

WEATHER OR NOT
6TH LONG RIDE

THE FOLLOWING ORIGINALLY APPEARED IN
WOMEN IN NATURE: AN ANTHOLOGY
(LOUISE GRACE PUBLISHING, 2014).

There it was again. I stopped packing and looked toward the northwest sky, listening. Yes, it was the rumble of thunder coming in over the line of jagged red cliffs bracing the north side of the Flathead River. The river was running low—the summer had been an unusually dry one. Rain would have been welcomed.

It was the late summer of 2013 and I was off schedule. Fall and winter in Montana can be tricky. This was my sixth long ride. I had no set route but had already zigzagged through much of Montana and was now headed to the small town of Boulder about thirty miles south of Helena. This "exploring Montana" ride had three goals. The first was to visit my childhood friend Paulette. Second, I wanted to add experience and training for Spirit. Third and most of all, I needed the therapy of a long ride. My faithful companion Claire was no longer with me. Plus, a dear friend who was in the throes of surviving a nasty divorce was alone for the first time and in need of companionship and also protection from her angry ex-husband. I had been working on a new and improved doggie box when the situation arose. Claire, at thirteen years old, needed more comfort and shade for her aging body. She probably could have ridden longer, but she was an octogenarian in dog years and the rides were getting harder for her. I reasoned that maybe

My long-riding companion, Claire, on an earlier trip.

it was best for Claire if I let her stay behind. And I thought I was helping a good friend.

After thirteen years of shared life with my Claire Dog, I let her live
her last years with someone else. She was lovingly cared for until the
end of her life a year and a half later. I will always wonder if I did the
right thing. She so loved long riding, both the people and the travel.
I never told my friend how much I missed Claire, how lonely and empty
the tent had become in her absence. To this day I miss my irreplaceable
companion.

I was into my morning ritual. I knelt down on one knee beside the
two large saddle packs and laced up the final black nylon strap before
loading them onto Essie Pearl's back. Already the wind was kicking
up. Overhead, the sky turned wild with disheveled clouds whipping
like the tails and manes of wild ponies running free, all stretched out
long and buoyant, decorating the sky with constant change. Another
rumble growled closer and more serious, defining my approaching
day. "Should I stay?" I said, returning my focus to three horses standing quietly, saddled and packed, their bellies full of orchard grass.
The sun flashed intermittent blasts of September heat, reminding me
of yesterday's sweltering long day of 90-degree temperatures. The
day had been an assault of flies and mosquitoes, sweaty horse backs,
and a nagging headache for me. It was a hard day's travel. I would have
welcomed a ride in the rain, but a storm with thunder and lightning,
no thank you.

I stood beside Hart, holding the bridle reins and studying the sky
and wind. "We'll ride today," I said to the horses, as if they understood.
"Chances are it will go around us. The winds are from the southwest
and we're heading due east. We'll be okay." As if the horses cared—they
would be out in the weather, sun or storm.

My boot reached for the stirrup, my hand for the saddle horn, and
I swung with ease into the saddle. "Let's go," I said. "Let's see what the
day holds for us." I sang out a slow roll call, "Essie, Hart, Spirit, let's go."
A steady rhythmical stride took hold and the team fell into a familiar
pace. Steel horseshoes struck against the hard gravel road as we headed

into a wild, blustery day of sunshine, clouds, and rain, our tails tucked from the wind, heading east, gambling on the weather.

The Mission Valley is tribal land belonging to the Confederated Salish and Kootenai Tribes of the Flathead Nation. I'd secured a permit before starting out so I could cross their lands from Hot Springs to St. Ignatius and then to Seeley Lake. The flat, fertile Mission Valley is bordered to the west by the Salish Mountains, to the south by the Reservation Divide Range, and to the east by the Mission Mountains, also known as the Flathead Alps. As I rode, admiring the view, the Sloan Bridge came into view, strapped securely across the Flathead River. It startled all four of us to a halt. We curved around on the road to meet the bridge and the horses froze in their tracks, ears fixed, standing statue still. Six wide, black, round eyes and my two blue eyes were held by the unexpectedness of the outlandish and colorful piece of art before them.

Sloan Bridge was riddled with graffiti. We were unprepared for the vivid visual this once drab bridge had become. Like a freight car, every square inch of the unpretentious cement bridge had been glorified with color, shapes, and words. It made a loud statement; the horses literally tiptoed precariously across. The bridge and art work were stunning, but my focus remained with the weather quickly unfolding around us. The river flowed carefree below us, and tall ponderosa pines swayed with gusts of wind as we were momentarily held in suspense by this structure of unique beauty. Once across the bridge, I could smell the rain before it arrived. A quick cooling of the air preceded the gently falling rain. I dismounted and pulled rain gear from the packs, wondering if I had made the wrong decision in breaking camp that morning.

MOTHER NATURE AND ME

Mother Nature never has it any other way but her way. No matter what direction you travel in, be it dirt path or paved road, she will have her way. She deals the cards, and she dictates the day, the hours, and the minutes with elements of which myth and mystery are born. No one tells her what to do. There is always weather of some kind. It is the one thing I can depend on. Never before long riding had I been so intimately connected to weather. It's an intimacy one will never know inside the shelter of four walls or the protective shell of a motor vehicle.

Being submerged in nature is the very core of what long riding is. Never before had weather so possessed me. Never before have the actions, mystery, and the challenges of weather demanded my attention as they do while long riding. It pulls me to the *now*, demanding again and again that I "pay attention."

As the daughter of dairy farmers, I saw nature's fierce grip in all facets of life. My father's constant checking of weather, the hope and prayers, the uncertainty with which these uncontrollable forces dictated to our family farm. I was fascinated by the tornadoes that ravaged the central Minnesota countryside each spring and summer. The raging winds that left mass destruction, sweeping up cows, horses, trees, and neighbors' barns terrified me. Yet I did not want to hide from it. I wanted to see it. I wanted to feel it.

STORM WARNING

A maze of straight-line, mostly gravel farm roads crisscrosses the open flats of the Mission Valley. I could clearly see the storm as we moved eastward. A soup kettle of thick gray-black clouds, likely with hail, were backed up against the fortress of mountains, building up and straining to rush into the valley. I could see mass after mass of clouds split, divide, and then spill north and south. I had only minutes to find shelter. I pulled my hat's stampede string tight, then I pulled the horses in close and shouted, "Okay, let's go!"

They knew. The horses always seemed to know. How can they not know? They are always in weather. I felt the ceiling lower and almost ducked with the feeling that my tall broad-brimmed hat would skim the nervousness above. We were riding fast, heading for a stand of tall fir trees, chased by a pack of renegade clouds.

Fences—damn the fences. There was nowhere to get in. "No Trespassing" signs, locked gates, and old rusted barbed wire fences held me to the road. It was like racing down a hallway with all the doors locked. "I need to get out of this!" I screamed in my head. Just get in somehow! I saw a loose, low spot in the fence wire and told myself, "Make it work—make it work, Bernice."

In full rain gear every move was cumbersome. The rain had started and the storm descended upon us as I held two rusty strands of barbed wire down with one foot and coaxed one horse after another to step carefully over the nasty stuff. Hart and Essie were seasoned long-riding horses, and they safely made it across the wire to stand under the fir trees. But Spirit hesitated. She balked, caught her hoof, and panicked. "Easy, easy, easy," I said, my voice hiding my pounding heart. "It's okay. Come on, you can do this." Still holding the wire with one foot, I slowly folded myself down and reached for her hoof to unlock the trouble she was in. "Okay, one more time," I said as the wind mocked my calm words. Spirit cleared the wire and we were in!

With the entire tribe now over the wire and sheltered in a grove of ancient fir trees, a sigh of relief fell from my breath. "Thank you." The branches of the trees spread out like an umbrella, forming a dry canopy beneath. Layer upon alternating layer of branches fanned out from the old-growth tree trunks, providing a natural sanctuary from the storm. The hard rains scarcely touched us. I moved from horse to horse, loosening cinch straps and removing the heavy packs while we waited. "Thank you," I said, mostly to my mother whose guardian spirit rides with me, but also to my champion long-riding horses, which were again brave and responsive. They were content standing under the trees while gusts blew and lightning cracked off to the north. I was warm, safe, and dry.

I felt like any other person that has escaped, made it through the storm, and defied the danger. I ran the risk and won. I reached into my saddlebags and pulled out a thermos of hot tea and a dented tin cup. I sipped the Earl Grey with lemon and honey. This was a cherished solitary moment, not uncommon on long rides, when nature and I were one.

What is it about weather, one of nature's many hands, that I so want to be a part of? I want it touching me, holding me in its track of infinite personalities. I want the wind crawling up my sleeves and my broad-brimmed hat resisting the sun's belittling heat. I want to lie on the earth and let the tall grasses hold me. I'm enticed by the wild invigorating and unpredictable challenge of weathering a storm, of finding myself face to face with nature's playful or unforgiving forces. It's nature that most often dictates my next move.

We were out of sight, the horses and I, as a car slowly drove by. I could hear the fast beat of windshield wipers as the rain continued in earnest. I'm not always so fortunate finding shelter like this. I've more than once found myself in a roadside ditch, exposed for all to see my folly at having been caught in a storm. Undoubtedly, I am a pitiful sight as drivers motor past in luxury, eating, drinking, with radios blaring music or warning of a storm, and chatting with passengers or talking on cell phones. And there I am: a pitiful sight indeed, but unwilling to trade places.

Nature has me wrapped in her arms with no immediate escape. She fills me with vitality and nourishment, and offers me mounting challenges. It is the secret to being alive. It's just too easy the other way. I find this life as a long rider interesting, intimate, and engaging. It's no-nonsense, cut-to-the-chase living; direct, persistent, and yet reliable— I always know the sun will rise and the sun will set.

I chuckle at the notion that long riding is about freedom. Actually, I come and go as nature dictates, not freely as I please. I wait for subsiding rain showers; I wait for calmer winds, for snow to melt. I ride the desert in the winter, the mountains in the summer. I cannot ride in sweltering heat or violent storms. My tent is set up according to wind direction or the sun's heat. This storm would have held much less meaning to a person sensibly secured in a building or motor vehicle. But I simply must face the fears, doubts, criticisms, and the weaknesses that keep many people from ever daring to go on the adventure that is tantalizing them. I must be in it, engaged in all that this life is.

I don't want escape from civilization with the idealized notion that nature holds all the answers. When I look down at the pen and paper I journal on, when I reach for the high-tech nylon tent and camping gear I use or the lightweight pack saddle I use, I realize that all of these things have evolved from civilizations where people with ideas and notions and visions have come together to form even more ideas and notions and things like headlamps and small propane burners. I do not delude myself that I'm "leaving it all behind." Unless one has the knowledge and experience of primitive living skills, it's impossible to leave behind everything that's not of its original casting and live "naturally." My rides are infinitely easier because of these modern conveniences I carry. I'm not trying to "go back to nature," as many people seem to think. I just want to go along with her and learn all she has to teach me as I make my pilgrimage on her earth.

Beneath the sheltering fir trees, a daddy longleg spider crawled up my rain gear, looking for warmth I suppose. "Sorry, you can't rest here, I must go," I whispered, directing it back down my leg to earth.

This would have been a good place to camp, but there was no water. The horses had me up and moving as the clouds faded into gentle pinks and lavenders as afternoon slid into evening.

The horses began an anxious let's-get-started jig. I readjusted packs, tightened cinches, and handed out a third of an apple to each of their eager lips before walking them out single-file across the fence. This time all three calmly walked over the barbed wire. I repaired the fence before mounting, then turned in my saddle to say "thank you" as I always do for the gift of safety.

I narrowed my attention, focusing on finding a suitable campsite. On our race for shelter, I had noticed a couple of possibilities near the Crow Dam a mile or so back. Late in the day, it would be better to retrace steps than to move forward on unfamiliar ground. A side road dropped into a deep canyon, but a steel gate blocked access and again there were those damn fences. A man smoking a cigarette stood leaning against a beat-up old car parked near the gate. I approached cautiously and asked if he knew of somewhere I could camp for the night. "Hell, just go in through here," he said while pointing to an opening in the fence. "No one will bother you—they can't get in."

I accepted my good fortune with a smile, nodded with my big hat, and thanked him. The road twisted and circled down into a narrow canyon. Everything was damp and musky smelling. The sky lost its remaining light in less than an hour. I had little time to think about the dropping temperature or if this would be a safe place to spend the night. Before a complete blanket of darkness covered us, I made a quick check of the area we would camp in, familiarizing myself with the surrounding area.

Where could I access the creek for water? Where would I tie the horses? Where was the best grass? The tent would go where? All these questions ran through my mind, the same whenever I select a home for the night.

Fog slowly settled in, and the smell of rotting fall leaves enhanced the cold, wet, moonless night as Crow Creek, filled with fresh rains, entertained me with a joyous evening music. A fire would've been nice, but building one in such soggy weather was more work than setting up my warm dry tent. Hart, Essie, and Spirit ate with no-nonsense eagerness as I secured them with hobbles and twenty-five-foot picket lines and then covered their backs with warm flannel sheets. My eyes adjusted to the dimming light by the time I completed setting up camp and crawled inside my cave-like tent for a savory supper. "Rice and beans and dandelion greens," I sang softly, already nibbling on nuts and cheese and anything else I could get my hands on. "Claire, I miss you." I thought out loud. "I miss you."

"How are my horses?" I shouted out, listening for the jingling and jangling of handmade Romanian gypsy bells that were snapped to each horse's halter. If they were troubled in any way—tangled in the rope or not happy in some way—they would whinny back or the bells would ring wildly. All was peaceful.

Inside my tent, three lit candles serve to heat and light the small space easily. The night's tranquility and sobering darkness embraced me as I stripped down and changed into clean night wear. The stainless steel pot of supper boiled on my single propane burner. I wore a headlamp over my cap when I stepped outside to water and check on the horses.

As a child, a dark room terrified me. I would never, ever step into

My cozy home on the trail.

a dark room without first sliding my hand along the wall searching for the light switch or pushing my little sister in before me. I had horrifying, suffocating nightmares that sent me running barefoot, mouthing a silent scream, down the dimly lit stairs to my parents' bedroom in tears. What happened to that fear I do not know. It fell from my saddle somewhere along the trail. How could I be out here like this without the fear that once bound and gagged me as a child? Did I simply outgrow it?

Where and how did I come to embrace the solitary nights so alone and unprotected? With my horse, of course. It's no mystery; it was my horse.

One o'clock in the morning, I opened the tent flap and stepped into a breathlessly still sheet of blackness to make one last check on the horses. Essie Pearl and Montana Spirit were lying down. Hart stood near the creek. I lay across Spirit's warm back and looked at the dazzling array of dancing stars, thinking with satisfaction that we had not traveled very far but we'd made it through the day. I thought again how days

Camp in the evening.

and nights had merged, no longer broken by 9 A.M. to 5 P.M. routines. Sometimes when on a long ride, I have had to sleep during the day and eat at night. It's a life of accepting changes.

Spirit got up. I petted her and calmed her, then gave attention to Essie Pearl and Hart before calling it a day. Nature's arms were wrapped securely around us. I crawled back into my tent and slept the deep sleep of the contented.

HERE I BELONG

These years of long riding have provided a platform to discover my core strengths: resilience, self-confidence, physical well-being, and, like my family before me, a thirst for firsthand experiences and knowledge. It was never my intention to ride out and find this woman I have now become; it just happened. A window opened and I simply climbed through. I remember the first ride in 2005 and ask myself once again, how will I ever go back to what is considered a normal life? I am now in my own skin. By taking these precarious steps closer to nature—to the weather, the land, the water, the animals, and the feeling that I am a part of it all—I have found contentment and happiness, and it is here I belong.

COAST-TO-COAST INTERNATIONAL RIDE — 7TH LONG RIDE

APRIL 2014 TO JUNE 2016

8,000 MILES

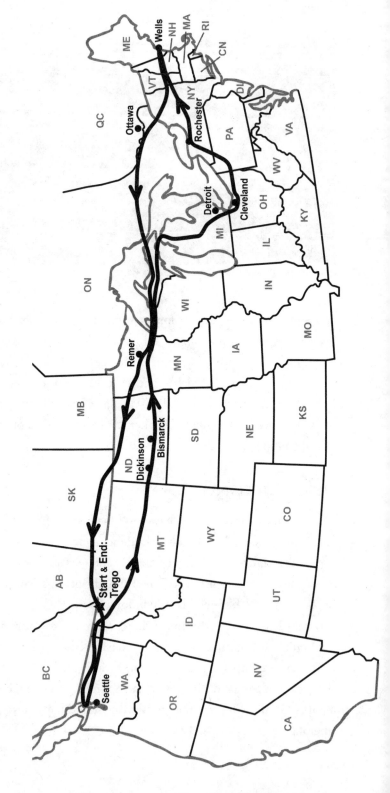

CHAPTER EIGHTEEN

SEA TO SHINING SEA

Spring again in Montana. Essie Pearl, Montana Spirit, and I were wrapped in winds pressing us eastward, pushing against our backs, determined to make us miserable. It whipped the horses' long manes and tails and threatened to undermine our journey, but we were sailing, sailing for the East Coast, Maine, and the Atlantic Ocean. Like a ship's sail, the wind only blew momentum into our steps. We were three weeks into an ambitious 8,000-mile, two-and-a-half-year, round-trip coast-to-coast ride, and settling into a daily routine of travel.

I don't actually remember when or how the idea of a round-trip coast-to-coast long ride came about. It was likely a culmination of thoughts and events. I do remember tracing a thick black line on a map marking a coast-to-coast route and being thoroughly enticed by the notion. I had ridden 20,000 miles through the Southwest, the Northwest, the Plains, the Bible Belt, and the Midwest, but what about the Northeast? What were the people like there? What would it be like to ride across the continent from the Pacific Ocean to the Atlantic Ocean and explore the East?

One thing that amplified my desire to know more about the places and people in the East was my profound interest in women's rights history and my own family's lineage of women who worked for the movement. "But it's so far," I told myself. "I can't ride that far!" I thought that the only way I could do the trip was if I trailered the horses across the midwestern states, but I couldn't afford the cost of hauling me and

the horses 2,000 miles and that stopped me. Still, I never turned loose of the idea. Then one day, I said to myself, "Bernice, if this is what you want to do and where you want to ride, then you better get going." And so I did. I got going!

Three months into the ride, I received an email from the Long Riders' Guild. CuChullaine O'Reilly wrote to say no one had ridden a continuous coast-to-coast round-trip across the United States before. "Umm," I thought, "The pressure is on." Eight thousand miles and two and a half years in the saddle is a heck of a long ride even for a rider with my experience. I started out knowing I would be attempting something no one else had done before.

SUFFRAGETTES AND LADY LONG RIDERS

The year I headed for the Northeast and the Atlantic Ocean was 2014, which just happened to be the hundredth anniversary of women's right to vote in Montana. I decided to add a bit of color to this ride by highlighting those women who brought us the right to vote. So, with postcards from the Montana Historical Society proclaiming, "Women's History Matters—Celebrating 100 years of women's hard fought struggle for the right to vote," I rode east, pulled by the vision of Susan B. Anthony, Elizabeth Cady Stanton, and Matilda Joslyn Gage. I would visit their homes and gravesites and pay homage to those who brought me not only the right and freedom to vote but who inspired the courage to ride my horse alone across two great countries—Canada and the United States of America.

This ride proved to be an epic journey. It was not exceedingly hard or terribly dangerous as had been the case in previous rides. But it was the most interesting ride I have undertaken. What fed my interest was history. The history of the West is a mere child compared to the timeline of historical events in the East. I traveled through the Northeast as my ancestors once had, 100 to 300 years ago. Our nation's historical places and sites came to life for me. I heard the sound of steel horseshoes resonate on cobblestones as I rode down narrow roads bordered by 250-year-old crumbling and moss-covered stone walls. I overnighted in 250-year-old barns. The ornate architecture in towns oozed with reminders of historical events. Riding the Northeast of the United States is to be living in history.

THE LONG RIDE EAST

Montana

We headed east from Fortine, Montana, in April 2014. The land in eastern Montana opens to a panoramic view of the prairie. I always think of Willa Cather and her books about the Nebraska prairie she loved so much when I see this country. I love the expanse and how the eye rests calmly upon the undisturbed horizon. It's all wind and sky, wheat, cattle, and an occasional grain elevator reaching for the blue sky.

As I rode eastward across Montana's dirt roads that bordered vast fields of new green grasses, I was witness to newborn calves dropping from their mothers' Black Angus bellies. The offspring were wet and wanting to live even as a bitter, unrestrained westerly wind quickly dried their birth-damp hides. In my mind I called out to them, "No time to waste. You are in the now, here on this planet of wind, sun, green grass, herds, teats, milk, fences, ranches, men, separation, slaughter, and finally meat for someone's table."

North Dakota

One month out, I met up with Terri Thiel from the Dickinson, North Dakota, Convention and Visitors Bureau. Terri and I met in 2010 as I came into Dickinson, North Dakota, pressing hard into cold westerly winds as I headed home from my 6,000-mile fourth ride. Terri and others from the visitors bureau had helped enormously by calling ahead and arranging for places for me to camp and have feed for the horses. It was good to see friends along my way. North Dakota gets a bad rap as being flat and boring, but it is one of my favorite places to ride. It's neither boring nor all flat. The amazing vastness is filled with remarkable

Salem Sue welcomes us to New Salem, North Dakota.

vistas, flowering prairies and grasslands, interesting historical landmarks, and friendly—go out of their way to help a stranger—people.

A couple days later, the folks working at the Morton County fairgrounds in New Salem greeted a weary traveler when I came in late, shadowed by New Salem Sue's udder. Salem Sue, also known as the World's Largest Holstein Cow, is a gigantic fiberglass sculpture sitting on School Hill near Interstate 94 at exit 127S. Sue can be seen from a long way off. Salem Sue was built in 1974 and cost $40,000. The New Salem Lions Club sponsored the project in honor of the local dairy farming industry. The statue stands thirty-eight feet high and is fifty feet long. I laughed as I watched a herd of Red Angus bulls in a pasture west of Sue. I wondered if those bulls ever got a hankering to go up that steep hill and visit that cow.

I had decided to ride through North Dakota instead of South Dakota on this trip because it gave me the chance to visit with friends from my 2010 ride whom I thought I would never have an opportunity to see again. One of these was Faye Sanders, in New Salem. Terri Thiel had connected me with Faye on my 2010 ride, so we had some catching up to do. Faye treated me to lunch at the local café and introduced me to many of her friends and neighbors. That sense of community—*my* community of friends scattered across the country and across the years—really helps dispel any twinges of loneliness that might otherwise creep up during a long ride.

Minnesota

Riding through Minnesota offered a great opportunity to visit with my family and enjoy reminiscing about my childhood days there. I've been to my homeland several times on my various long rides and have shared many of my childhood stories throughout this book. On this ride, my family gathered for a week's visit in Remer. I was also overjoyed by a surprise visit from five of my Elk River High School friends from McGregor, Minnesota. I had not seen four of them since graduating. We spent some quality time laughing about things we did as teenagers, and we pondered, not very seriously, about how we managed to survive those fun, reckless years.

I took the Soo Line Trail north to Lawler. The Soo Line is an All-Terrain Vehicle (ATV) trail that follows an abandoned railroad grade with sweeping curves through dense hardwood forests and the beautiful northern Minnesota landscape. I have ridden ATV trails before, but these Midwest trails are not at all like those I have ridden in the past. These trails are like small, well-maintained roads, kept spotless with no litter whatsoever. They are well marked and the ATV riders were courteous. Off and on, I had been riding ATV trails since leaving Remer. They were all beautiful, with shade trees, water, grass, and straight flat grades, and the bridges thus far have all been horse safe. Oh, yes, I must mention there are mosquitoes. I didn't expect such grand ATV roads here in Minnesota and in Wisconsin. I'm told they are very popular, and the states, in collaboration with snowmobile and ATV enthusiasts spend a good deal of money to provide these recreational trails. I followed the Tri-County Corridor, also an ATV trail that runs along the bottom of Lake Superior from Duluth, Minnesota, to Ashland, Wisconsin.

Wisconsin

Iron River, Wisconsin, has no stoplights, is the self-proclaimed "Blueberry Capital of the World," and is what I call a "Blue Ribbon Community." It is one of those towns where everyone is friendly—truly everyone you meet is friendly. In my book, a town earns a blue ribbon not only because of that obvious friendliness but also thanks to underlying community pride, a tolerance for others, and clean and pretty streets. But there is more to being a Blue Ribbon Community. Such towns also have a post office, library, laundry, senior center, grocery store, and parks all centrally located for easy accessibility. I felt welcomed the minute I rode into Iron River. Thank you, Iron River, you're a lovely place!

I rode in from the west, from Brule, on the Tri-County Corridor Trail, another abandoned railbed. It must have been about noon when I rode up to the chamber of commerce building. Out walked a very enthusiastic and friendly Geri Dresen. That's when it started. I began meeting people who were look-a-likes, sound-a-likes, people who could have been twins of my friends in Montana. I felt very much at home. In no time, Scot Eisenhauer, the friendly chief of police, found me a place to camp next to the Iron River Community Center. At every street corner, people stopped and talked to me with interest and surprise.

Iron River is not a large town. It was really hard to tell what size the towns were in these northwoods. Everything was tucked in and around trees, tall grasses, ponds, and lawns. Hidden from view were houses that peered out from behind oak, pine, poplar, and maple trees. The Iron River Community Center was not at all like the little community center in Trego, Montana. The Iron River Community Center was more like a convention center.

Essie and Spirit were on a picket line, filling their already big, round bellies with more luscious Wisconsin grass. I set up home outside the building on a large lawn. I carried a pooper scooper to keep everything clean. The community center management had thoughtfully left the door unlocked so that I could use the bathroom facilities and I was very appreciative.

Iron River was a major stop for me on my sea-to-sea cross-continent journey. Boxes with horseshoes were being shipped in, and I would ship out boxes of equipment I no longer needed. I also took time to wash, repair, and adjust saddle and pack gear; update my website; and find maps for crossing Michigan. I stripped off as much packing weight as I possibly could. From here we would travel light and hopefully quickly. I aimed to dance across Michigan, lightly.

When we crossed the Wisconsin-Michigan border, I was walking, leading Essie Pearl and Montana Spirit. Quite by accident, Essie Pearl stepped on one of my spurs, making me stumble and fall. I cracked a finger bone and dislocated my wrist. At least I think that is what happened. My right hand swelled up. I didn't want to alarm anyone and surely didn't want to ride into Michigan as the Lady Long Rider with an obvious injury. As soon as I could find a large glove, I covered the swollen hand. After a week of regular soaking in cold water, the swelling subsided.

Michigan

Michigan is beautiful country. It has the longest freshwater coastline in the world, and over half the state is forested and dotted with more than 100 parks. On my journey through the state, I learned about "Yoopers," the name given to those living in the Upper Peninsula (you'll understand the nickname if you pronounce "U.P." out loud), and the "Trolls" who live in the lower half of the state. I ate pasties, a pastry filled with meat and vegetables, which were once made for the miners. And I was bitten by Michigan's famous nasty blackflies. During my travels through the state I saw lots of both Michigan's state bird—the robin—

and the state reptile—the painted turtle. Michigan is a good state for long riding. It has lots of grass, water, and friendly people who seem to find an equestrian traveler interesting.

To get from the Upper Peninsula to Michigan's mitten-shaped mainland, we had to cross the Mackinac Bridge, a five-mile span over the Straits of Mackinac between Lake Michigan and Lake Huron. (If you're not a local, you might be surprised to learn that "Mackinac" is pronounced "Mackinaw.") The bridge allows motorized traffic only, so we loaded Essie Pearl and Spirit into a trailer and Jerry Eden, a project manager on a nearby powerline construction project, drove us across the busy bridge. The authorities even gave us a vehicle escort. Once we were safely on the south end of the bridge, I unloaded the horses and headed south on the North Central State Trail, another wonderful rails-to-trails conversion.

On August 1, we were in the middle of northern Michigan, approaching the Camp Grayling Joint Maneuver Training Center. It's the largest U.S. National Guard training facility in the country. It was founded in 1913 on an initial grant of land from Grayling lumber baron Rasmus Hanson to the State of Michigan for military training and now spans 147,000 acres in three counties. Much of the acreage is accessible to the public for hunting, fishing, snowmobiling, and other recreational uses when military training is not taking place. As it happened, while I was in the area, Camp Grayling was in session, training thousands of military personnel from National Guard units in Michigan, Indiana, Illinois, and Ohio, as well as regular Army Reserve units. A military zone stood in my path. Sign after sign read "Road Closed," or "Do Not Enter—Military Maneuvers," or even more daunting, "Keep Out—Tank Crossing." Roads that my map indicated I could ride on were now off limits to me. I would have to ride around the installation, and the road would take me through freeway and city traffic. A plane flew overhead; I could hear guns and large booms from the direction of the base. "This must be what war sounds like," I thought. My horses were nervous. They jumped from a loud boom and a machine gun's ratta tat tat.

I rode until darkness finally pulled me to a stop. Fortunately, the gunfire had also stopped. We made camp in a wide ditch behind a clump of trees. The horses were tethered on long picket lines attached to the spindly trunks of small willows. In addition to the halters and bells they usually wore while tethered, I put bed sheets on both horses to protect them from the mosquitoes.

At 8 A.M. the next morning, the sun already threatened us with heat. While I broke camp, a woman walked toward me. She appeared to be dressed like a police officer or maybe she was military police. I bent down to reach for one of my travel cards in my pack remembering how once, while crossing North Dakota, I did this and the police officer walking toward me pulled his gun on me, thinking I was reaching for a gun. I had dropped to my knees then, disbelief racing through me more than fear. I actually felt hurt that he would think of me as threatening. Since then, I've been told by numerous officers, "Just stand still with your hands on your thighs until you have made verbal contact. Then you can reach for a card." I don't object to being investigated by the police or a forest service ranger or a homeowner who stops to check out what I am doing and why I am doing it. It's important that they know what is going on in their territory, and sometimes I need help and at least someone knows where I am.

The woman with a bouncing ponytail looking like an official of some sort was still a ways off, so I quickly pulled a card from my pack and stood quietly waiting for her, my hands visible. Shortly, Officer Gail Foguth from Crawford County Animal Control stood before me in a crisp blue short-sleeve shirt, dark blue trousers, and the usual assortment of items found on the belts of law officers. "I had a few calls this morning—horses loose in the ditch," she said with a smile. I handed her my card, told her my story, and explained my route dilemma. I apologized for making her come out unnecessarily, but she seemed genuinely interested in my story. I could tell this woman was a problem solver. "Okay," she said. "You're going to ride up to this house about three miles from here. I'm going to meet you there and the woman who lives there is going to escort you on a trail that will take you safely away from the military activity, and you won't have to go through the city of Grayling."

I love women like this—just tell me what to do, get it done; let's not mess around with small talk.

As I trotted into the designated driveway, the homeowner, Beth, and Officer Gail were waiting for me next to a beautiful white farmhouse and horse facility. We didn't waste much time, but somehow there was time enough for them to fill my saddlebags with food. Beth had her big sorrel horse saddled and ready to go. I rode Essie and packed Spirit. I followed behind Beth on a dirt path weaving through cool shade trees until a four-wheeler road appeared. "Okay," she said, "This is it, just follow this road and you'll end up on the other side of the military zone." And away she rode.

I rode a few miles but could not pass up the tempting waters of the cold creek running under a bridge. Tree branches along the road were the only thing remotely useful as a hitching post. I tied up the horses, stripped down, and jumped into the creek. I wasn't there long, just long enough to cool down, wash up, and wiggle my clothes back on over wet skin—only seconds before a car rolled slowly by. I returned an innocent smile.

Dirt roads, probably four-wheeler roads, took off right and left. There were lots of them, and after a while I wasn't sure which road to take so I flagged down a car. I do this often to ask for help or directions. Asking for help is always harder for me than giving help, but out of sheer necessity I will muster the courage to stand at an intersection, looking very much like a homeless person, holding my map in one hand and signaling with the other. One car drove by, leaving me in lingering dust. There was a long wait, then another car drove by without stopping. A clean, newer-model beige Chevy Suburban appeared around the corner with three women and a young boy. I could see that they were middle-aged women who were going to ignore me. I stepped out a bit further, pointing to my map, mouthing "I need help." I could see the woman driving hesitate then change her mind and roll to a stop. I could tell they weren't quite sure what to make of me. I had slept in a ditch the night before and was dirty despite my dip in the creek and I was holding two horses by the reins. I could see them say something to one another before the passenger window rolled down. The women were clean and nicely dressed, with colored nails and salon haircuts. The contrast between me and them would make anyone stare. "I'm terribly sorry to trouble you ladies, but could you tell me where I am?" I asked while holding my map for them to look at and pointing at places on the map. "Am I here or here?" They weren't sure either, but they said, "We have a GPS, let's try that." While they busied themselves with their GPS computer, a UPS truck approached from behind. "It's a UPS truck, they'll know where I am," I said, dashing around, dropping the reins leaving the horses to grass and flagging the driver down. "No, sorry, I just know how to get to my deliveries," the driver said. "I really don't know any of the road names. I'm just filling in." I couldn't believe my ears; UPS drivers always know where they are.

From the time it took me to run the UPS guy down and return to my patiently waiting road ladies, something had transpired. I could tell immediately—the look on their faces had changed. They were staring at me, intently staring at me. "Is there something the matter?" I asked, standing with one foot on the steprail of the Suburban, one elbow resting on the open window and my hat pushed back. There was a long period of silence, then the woman in the passenger seat spoke. "Are you the woman who rode her horse from the North Pole to the South Pole and back?" she asked. "Well no, I don't believe I am that person," I answered slowly. "Do you have a dog?" asked the other woman. "Were you on the *Today Show*?" the third wanted to know. "Oh, you must mean the story Bob Dotson did about me?" I answered, then went on to explain, "In 2012, Bob Dotson from the *Today Show* arranged for an interview as I traveled across Canada, near Pincher Creek in British Columbia. They aired the story this fall." I recalled that by 2012, I had traveled 18,000 miles by horseback. For his television viewers, Bob showed a globe and said, "If you were to travel from the North Pole to the South Pole and back to the equator, that's how far 18,000 miles is." The ladies somehow confused his illustration and thought I had ridden from the North Pole to the South Pole.

The woman sitting in the passenger seat with neat black hair stopped talking, then slowly said, "Yes, we saw you on the *Today Show*. You are the woman who rides around on a horse with her dog aren't you?" The three of them looked at each other and were very quiet for a minute, then one of them said, "We call you the crazy lady." "Understandably so!" I thought. With a look of disbelief in her eyes, she continued, "We were talking about you over the campfire last night. We heard a branch snap behind us and we said, 'What do you think the crazy lady would do?'" They laughed. "We talk about you all the time when we get scared or something happens like last night and we say, 'I wonder what that crazy lady would do.'"

Isn't life wonderful in its serendipity? While I lay in a ditch not far from them, they sat around a campfire talking about me: a crazy woman traveling alone with her horses and a dog.

The ladies, vacationing at a summer home, had gone into town and were heading back when I stopped them. Out of the car they came with screams and smiles and laughter, and we had a short but very lively meeting. They took photographs. We did a selfie. I explained how I had left Claire Dog at home on this ride. The horses were not the least bit interested in the chaos happening behind them. They continued eating, reins dragging on the ground, as the entire episode unfolded with laughter. I obtained little information about the women or the young man who sat in the back seat, looking baffled by the entire scene. I mentioned that I would be stopping at the Rosebush Library in a few days to use the computer, and this elicited more joyous screams because, lo and behold, Carolyn, the woman in the passenger seat, worked there!

Before I stepped into the saddle, we collectively surmised I should continue on the current road. I would find out soon enough if it was the right road. I squeezed Essie into a trot. "Crazy lady!" I thought and smiled as Essie and Spirit and I moved south with hearty waves and wide smiles lingering behind us.

The next part of our journey to the Northeast would take us through a tangle of major population centers and traffic that would put both me and the horses (and the drivers) in these cities at risk. I chose to have us hauled from Detroit and through Toledo and Cleveland, Ohio.

Ohio

The haul from Detroit went quickly. We sailed the ocean of traffic that makes up Toledo and Cleveland in Clyde Miles's big truck and horse trailer. Clyde is a professional hauler and hauls racetrack horses. It was a smooth three-hour ride that would have taken me a full month, which I did not have the time for, nor the desire to attempt navigating the urban maze. The horses and I were dropped off east of Cleveland behind a convenience store in the tiny town of Burton. This had not been a prearranged drop. I had no idea where I would land when I loaded the horses in Clyde's trailer earlier that day. It was simply good fortune that an empty lot figured into the picture. Fortunately, I had the sense to pack a half bale of hay for the horses, as there was very little grass on the empty lot behind the store.

Two young police officers stopped by later that night. Someone had reported horses loose. After sorting things out, I went back to bed under a nearly full moon. I had chosen not to use my tent. I must admit it did feel like a discombobulating leap from Michigan to Ohio. It's just 150 miles or so, but the change is apparent. The landscape is suddenly thick, dense, and lush with vegetation. The maple and oak trees stand taller. The gardens are works of art, as are the lawns and historical homes.

Pennsylvania

I innocently entered Pennsylvania from the west in early morning. The traffic was already heavy. The traffic being Amish buggies, I found myself among other horse travelers and it was the oddest feeling. It's never happened before. The Amish use fast, sleek Hackney ponies or Saddlebreds or Thoroughbred horses not successful on the racetrack. The sight and sound of steel horseshoes striking pavement and the whiz of carriage wheels on their heels driven by men with beards and straw hats was like stepping back in time. I simply stopped and stared. I had to. It was like being in a dream—powerful and surreal. Lined up beside Wal-Mart were thirty buggies with horses tied to hitching posts. There were more buggies outside Burger King and

212 Lady Long Rider

Essie Pearl and Montana Spirit share a hitching rail with Amish horses.

another row at the laundry. There were horses and buggies everywhere.

After regaining my composure, I maneuvered through northwestern Pennsylvania with a sense of excitement filling my days. I had wanted to ride this part of the country for years, and I soon realized there was so much to see and not nearly enough time to fully enjoy it all. I had to keep pushing toward the Atlantic or I'd be stopped by winter. Still, it was thrilling to be riding like a ghost from the past, along streets that have held some of our nation's most important historical moments.

I have never had so many people stopping by for a visit as I did in Pennsylvania. The curious young and old stopped to chat. I admit we are an odd sight: two Fjord horses packed and traveling with a lady wearing a big hat. "You came from where?" asked an astonished elderly man. "Oh my goodness, how in the world did you do it?" a young woman asked while shaking her head at the prospect. I shared my story and they shared their stories, and so it went every day on the trail.

On all of my rides, not a day goes by when I don't feel like I am the luckiest woman in the world. But please don't misunderstand me. There is nothing easy about long riding. It's overly romanticized, hard on me, and requires above-and-beyond care for my hard-working horses. We work at it just like anyone works at a job. I practice and apply hard-won skills, load up on attentiveness, and fill the gaps with caution. Putting it another way, I have to be constantly alert and careful in everything I do. The work is hard and the risks and dangers are many every day that I ride. But it's what I do, and I'm lucky and happy to be doing it.

Here in Pennsylvania, I was occupied with the heat, the mosquitoes, the wood ticks, and the humidity all piling up. But I had ridden through the hardest part of summer. Deerflies and pesky blackflies were not quite as bad. There was a bit more open space and the roads were quieter. The horses were holding up better than I was. We were packed light: Essie carried only 75 to 80 pounds, and Spirit carried nearly 200 pounds—the weight of me and extra gear. I walked at least ten miles a day, so I wasn't on her back as much as people might think. I have said many times that fatigue is my greatest enemy on long rides. I must be up by 3 A.M. and in the saddle by 5 A.M. Over the long haul, it wears me down. So as I rode through summer, I trotted the horses in the early morning, chased by a red ball of heat until we gave in and found shade for the afternoon.

In the Pennsylvania countryside, there was no want for food. As I traveled, I stopped at farms with "Eggs for Sale" signs, and the Amish, Hutterites, and Mennonites all sold produce. In my saddlebags, I carried dandelion greens, nettles, and lambsquarters for my evening meals. A week earlier, I passed an abandoned home whose garden still had stalks of rhubarb and strawberries flourishing. I cooked the strawberries, apples, and rhubarb with salt and honey. Yum, it was delicious!

Spirit and Essie had a cornucopia of grasses they grazed from as we traveled. I let them eat and walk. As traveling horses, my Fjords have learned to eat and walk, sometimes even run and snatch a bite. Spirit and Essie were in magnificent condition. They looked good and moved well, with eager steps.

Each ride is ruled by the changing seasons. Fall is the best time for travel but never lasts long enough. I had another 800 miles to go this year, and the weather was already turning cooler. From Pennsylvania, I planned to head north to New York's historical sites and the homes and gravesites of three of the most prominent women's rights leaders of the nineteenth and twentieth centuries: Elizabeth Cady Stanton's home in Seneca Falls, Susan B. Anthony's home and grave in Rochester, and Matilda Joslyn Gage's home and monument in Fayetteville. I was excited to finally stand on such hallowed ground.

New York State

Motorists on New York's busy roads were courteous and moved over or slowed down even though I was a nuisance to them. State roads were free of litter, and the creeks and most rivers were surprisingly clear.

Giant silos loomed behind a building that did not look like much as I rode east on Humphrey Road about seven miles northeast of Salamanca, New York. I could not make out what the funky structure's purpose could possibly be from where it sat just in front of a dairy farm. It appeared to be part of the dairy farm, but there was a line of cars stretched out in front. Then I saw the sign on the wall near the door that read "Sandy's Bakery." What in the world was a bakery doing out here in the middle of nowhere? I could not believe it! I slowly dismounted Essie Pearl as I watched people walk out the door holding new, perfectly white boxes stacked in their steady hands. As I tied my horses to the dumpster off the left side of the building, I took a deep breath of the scent of freshly baked bread wafting through the air. A bakery! How unexpected. How delightful.

The small green building was nothing fancy. I found out later it was once a tool shed. When I opened the door, a line of people stood patiently waiting to be served by the one and only Sandy Rust. It was as if I stepped inside a busy downtown bakery, but there was no downtown and some of these folks had driven many miles to satisfy their sweet tooths. I squeezed my way in past three elderly men sitting at a round table with coffee and sweets. Every week, they come twelve miles for

Sandy's twice-a-week extravaganza. The vast assortment of baked goods and the number of people who kept coming in and lining up made my head spin. I stepped to the side. I couldn't make up my mind what to buy, so I visited, stared, and drank a cup of self-serve coffee waiting for the opportunity to talk with the owner.

Here I was, in a bakery, literally in the middle of the countryside, and people were lined up, coming and going as Sandy served them from behind the counter surrounded by two days of baked goods. She had baked everything herself, from jelly-filled bismarcks, glazed doughnuts, thick molasses cookies, and brownies, to big chunky cinnamon rolls drenched in white frosting, buns, and loaves of bread. Sandy said she bakes for two days and sells for two days. That's it. I noticed her fill a white box with a dozen gooey cinnamon rolls, then reach with her tongs and add a few more for no extra charge. She said with a smile, "Might as well fill the box." Everyone seemed to know each other, talking morning talk. Not long ago, she served up an all-you-can-eat breakfast buffet. "But I had to cut back," she told me. "I'm heading for retirement. It's been thirty-five years, or something like that. That's long enough."

Sandy is legendary in this part of the country. She is unassuming and tattooed many times over. She has five children and fourteen grandchildren. "I got started because I just wasn't seeing my children enough when they were growing up," she said. "So I started a home business." Fortitude and resilience, I thought. Every week, she sells out all her breads and pastries. I'd say she's been on a long ride with her one-of-a-kind bakery business. She reluctantly let me take her photo with the encouragement of her loyal customers. Between customers, she slipped out from behind the glass counter for a look at my noble steeds, now nickering, telling me, "Time's up, time to get moving."

Both Essie and Spirit eagerly accepted doughnuts. Two brothers, locals who had been coming to Sandy's for years, kept me from paying for my bread and gooey roll now packed in my saddle bags. I swung into the saddle and waved goodbye to the moment of sweetness and smiles. Stops like these are always an unexpected but welcome surprise that etches a smile across your face for the rest of the day. These are brief moments of sweetness, where you just know you have been someplace special and tasted something special.

Canaseraga, New York

New York's number one export is farm products. We tend to think of New York state as New York City, with high-rise buildings, high fashion, and Wall Street. I am here to tell you it's not like that at all. In one week, I had seen more small dairy farms in the New York countryside than I have in any other state in all my years of riding. I measure a dairy farm by the way it smells. A good dairy farm smells sweet, not offensive. A few miles west of Canaseraga, I walked up the hill to visit Golden Windows Dairy on Shawmut Acres. I took a long, deep, familiar breath of sweet corn silage. I knew I was walking into a good dairy. I wanted to interview Chelsea Bouffard, a gal in her mid-twenties who earlier in life came to a figurative fork in the road and made a turn from a major in art and education to dairy farmer.

Chelsea began milking for Harv and Sue Lacy when she was fourteen years old. Harv is her mentor and now her business partner. He will phase out in a few years, retire, and pass the small farm on to Chelsea. None of his children were interested in farming. But Chelsea sure was, and after eleven years of working on the farm she felt a keen devotion to it, to the life, to the cows, and to the satisfaction at the end of the day. The farm has been in the Lacy family for three generations. Harv's grandfather milked thirty head. Today, Chelsea and Harv milk seventy cows, mostly long-legged, black-and-white Holsteins, with an eight-station milking parlor. Eight cows at a time come inside, are milked, and then lumber out to feed. Harv and Chelsea stand in the pit. The cows' udders are at shoulder height. The milking machines swing over and under with ease and are placed separately on each teat. Not anything like my father's dairy barn where the entire herd walked in single file, their bags swinging side to side with milk dripping out the teats. Knowing its place, each cow stood in stanchions eating feed raised in my father's fields and ground at the nearby mill. My father's Holsteins rested on fresh straw and were

Harv Lacy and Chelsea Bouffard, Golden Windows Dairy.

milked by a machine that my father moved from cow to cow. Needless to say, it was more labor intensive than the dairy farms of today.

Each cow at Golden Windows gives on average eighty pounds of milk a day, an amount unheard of in my father's day. Golden Windows cows graze on grass! Not all dairies do this. I'm all for it; my Dad always had the cows on grass. On most big dairies, the cows never have the pleasure of grazing. In my humble opinion, a herd of cows stays healthier when they have access to green pastures and exercise. It seems cruel to deny them the pleasure of grazing.

Chelsea says she doesn't favor conglomerate factory farming. "I could protest all I wanted," she says. "But this is one way I could do something about it." She wants a well-run, small dairy farm, plain and simple, and soon she will make all of the decisions: which heifers to keep, which will be sent to market, choice of breeding stock, daily feeding rations, to buy or not to buy a new piece of expensive machinery, or if an older cow must be let go. A farmer is met with a fistful of decisions every day.

Chelsea is trained in how to artificially inseminate a cow, which gives her a broader choice of breeding. She also scouts for the Western New York Crop Management Association. In that position, she tells farmers what's going on in their fields if they're having problems. For example, she can identify pest problems or if a crop is growing slow because of a soil deficiency, and she can offer expert advice.

At Golden Windows, two other girls help with the milking, which takes place twice a day—6 A.M. and 6 P.M. Mornings begin at 4:30 A.M. I noticed that when Chelsea called the cows in from the pasture, she used a lighter, high-pitched "Come Bessie." My dad used to call out deep and low and so did Harv, saying, "Come Boss, Come Boss." Evening milking ends about 8 P.M. Dairy farming is long days and hard, dirty, poopy work. Muck boots are a must.

Each day, 4,800 pounds of milk pour from this herd. The milk truck had just pulled up as I was leaving. We visited as milk machines were sterilized and walkways were washed down. My senses were bombarded with childhood memories, all of it so familiar to me. I have noticed over the years that more and more women are working as ranchers or farmers. I have read articles detailing the changes that these brave women are incorporating into the business. I think we are naturals at it. I was delighted to see this energetic young woman stepping into a position unavailable to me at her age. Farming is not easy—never has been, never will be.

The next time you pull a carton of milk from your refrigerator, remember it's been a long haul from a cow's udder to the container you now pour it from so conveniently. Remember every once in a while that there may be a hard-working young woman in muck boots, washing a cow's udder, asking that cow for another load of precious milk that will eventually find its way to your table, your glass, your lips.

Genesee Valley

Somehow I ended up riding into the Genesee Valley. This is real horse country. There may be more horses here than in Montana. The oldest hunt club in the United States continues to operate in this picturesque valley. I saw women and men wearing traditional English riding attire, posting up and down in their English saddles as they kept stride on tall, sleek Thoroughbreds while hounds dashed about their fine-boned legs. Tradition holds true here, except they no longer use live animals for the hunt. As I passed through the valley looking at the steeplechase field, the hunt club, and homes made of stones surrounded by stone walls, I felt like a character in the novel *National Velvet*. The air was saturated with history, and the people of New York are proud of the legacies that stay alive through the stories they share.

I was enjoying my ride through New York. It was so much more than I expected. I thought they'd take one look at my big hat, fat Fjord ponies, and western riding gear and laugh.

Laura Lane and Lisa Burns from the Livingston County Chamber of Commerce had heard about my arrival and came out from Dansville to meet me at the Hoag residence where I was staying. They graciously brought a beautifully arrayed welcome basket. After getting acquainted and hearing my story, they passed me on to Joanne Crossman. Joanne is a retired U.S. Department of Agriculture loan officer, a beekeeper, community activist, sheepherder, wool spinner, and all around shaker and mover. Joanne and her husband Bruce made arrangements for me to enjoy a two-day stopover at the Caledonia Fairgrounds. When I arrived, Bob Hilderbrant, manager of the fairgrounds, stopped by to ask if I needed anything, as did many other people. Joanne also arranged a local New York wine and cheese party at the fairgrounds. I wrote in my journal: "I was beginning to feel like a celebrity even though I know very well that I am just a lonesome Long Rider, covered in trail dirt and tired much of the time."

Rochester, New York

At 9 A.M. Essie, Spirit, and I were being hauled from the Caledonia Fairgrounds into Rochester, New York, by Sergeant Gary Cicoria, from the Livingston County Mounted Patrol. Our first stop was at the Mount

Susan B. Anthony wrote: "Men, their rights, and nothing more; women, their rights, and nothing less. The older I get, the greater power I seem to have to help the world; I am like a snowball—the further I am rolled the more I gain."
COURTESY OF LEO ROTH, ROCHESTER DEMOCRAT & CHRONICLE

Hope Cemetery where I paid tribute to Susan B. Anthony and Frederick Douglass at their gravesites.

From Mount Hope, Sergeant Cicoria hauled us across town for our tour of the Susan B. Anthony home. Two more officers (whose names, sadly, I did not write down) from the Rochester Mounted Police Patrol joined the festivities.

We arrived at 1:15 P.M. and were greeted by Deborah Hughes, the executive director of the home. Once again we rode into a neighborhood setting where significant historic events took place—Rochester was the center of multiple reform movements, including abolitionism and women's rights. I imagined women in long dark skirts walking briskly toward the Anthony home with news for Susan and her staff. A team of horses and carriage wait outside her door as she prepares herself for yet another speech. The hustle and bustle, the seriousness of their intentions in attaining the right of women to vote, happened here where I now stood.

If you are ever in Rochester, please see the Susan B. Anthony House. It has been restored and is filled with sentiments left behind from a time when women, with great determination, had begun to open doors previously closed to them. It is inspiring!

My visits to the Susan B. Anthony home and gravesite were covered by the local press. I spoke briefly at Anthony's gravesite, and Leo Roth kindly captured some of what I said for the *Democrat & Chronicle*:

In the past week I have met the Mayor of Caledonia. I have spoken with the Master of the Hunt from the Genesee Valley Hunt Club. I've been interviewed by a half dozen news reporters. I've visited with a young teenager who is captain of the soccer team and I have spoken with a farmer managing a dairy herd. They all have one thing in common. They are all women. And like me, who has ridden across the country—alone—a single woman, we are walking through doors unlocked by this courageous self-determined woman, Susan B. Anthony. She was the glue that held women together long enough for the radical idea of emancipation for not simply the right to vote, but the right to self-govern themselves, to take hold, to sink into the minds of millions until, finally, there was no turning back.

I have ridden here from the northwest corner of Montana where we commemorate the 100th anniversary of women's right to vote. I am here to pay homage, remembering to say "Thank you." Please let us not forget these "brave beyond words" women and the men who supported the novel idea of liberty for all.

What do you say about a woman who devoted her life to unlocking doors you now freely walk through? What do you say about the woman who cleared what was once a pitiful path to become a freeway I now travel on. I could not even believe I was here! Simply being in the home of this remarkable woman, Susan B. Anthony, who did not live to enjoy the fruits of her labor, humbled and moved me.

We take for granted our current lives where almost any woman can have a career if she applies herself. We take for granted that a woman can choose whether or not she will marry, whether or not she'll have children, or how many. Women live considerably different lives now because of women like Anthony and their pursuit of liberty. During the mid-1800s, the only occupations generally open to a woman were as seamstress, cook, maidservant, governess, and prostitute. If she married, and most did, out of love or necessity, everything she owned, inherited, and earned automatically belonged to her husband. A married woman could not make contracts, keep or control her own wages or any rents, transfer property, sell property, or bring a lawsuit against another person. A woman who remained single met with social disapproval and pity. She could not have children or cohabit with a man; the social penalties were simply too high. Yes, there were some, especially in the West, who ignored the social consequences and went their own way. Most paid a terrible price.

It was in this atmosphere that a handful of educated women, brave beyond words, courageous and determined, set out to bring equality and emancipation to women. Beginning in the mid-1800s, women organized, petitioned, and picketed to win the right to vote, but it took decades to accomplish their purpose. Generations of women's suffrage supporters lectured, wrote, marched, and lobbied to achieve what many Americans at the time considered a radical departure from the Constitution. Even today, women continue to advocate for full equality.

CHAPTER NINETEEN

HISTORY, HERITAGE, AND HOOF PRINTS

Riding the Northeast region of America is inspiring. History resounds throughout this part of the country; it leaps at you from Federalist-style colonial homes and mossy stone walls. It whispers to you from enchanting cupolas, narrow twisting country roads, and weathered gray barns. There is an obvious high regard for our heritage here. How could it not be so? After all, the concept of democracy took shape here: the foundation was set, the lines drawn, the pot stirred, and the cake baked. What surprised and delighted me is how much of the physical evidence of our nation's founding history has been preserved and how great the attempt has been to retain the natural beauty of the countryside, including small farms. Living in a 200-year-old home is not uncommon. I have witnessed a high level of citizenship and a concern for the welfare of community and not just the individual. Generally, the people here are very tolerant and diverse and there's a great effort to find a common good for all.

We had ridden through Pennsylvania and New York and were on our way to Maine to put toe and hoof into the Atlantic. Essie Pearl and Montana Spirit were in excellent condition despite having traveled nearly 2,000 miles in the past four months. That's about 500 miles a month or 125 miles a week. But the conditions had been right—lots of grass, water, and good dirt roads. Miles like that can be done only in cool spring or fall weather. I also kept the packs very light, going without so as not to burden my two girls with luxury items, like extra goodies for me.

This was the first ride I did without my beloved Claire Dog. I missed her companionship. It was unlike any ride I've previously ridden in other ways. I trotted a good deal, then got off and walked. Every ten miles or two hours I pulled the gear off the horses. I let them cool down, washed their backs, and thoroughly brushed both horses and pads. I traveled thirty miles a day. Spirit was now for the most part my ride horse and Essie packed unless I was in traffic or a tight spot where I needed Essie's steadfast mind calmly leading us. I was so proud of these two. We were, all three of us, bound together by miles of travel and experiences. When one disappeared behind a bush for a minute, a kind of panic would set in, a head popped up, until a worried whinny brought the horses back together. I've never taken out a finer team of horses.

A GLORIOUS NORTHEAST FALL

As we journeyed north, a thick layer of dew greeted us each morning. Fog lifted slowly to reveal a display of color that I don't have adequate words to describe. I had never seen the Northeast in its glorious fall attire; rusty reds, gentle golds, pale pinks billow out like fluff. It was as if a head of broccoli had been painted by Picasso. I quite happily joined the stream of "leaf peepers" who travel many miles to examine the magnificent fall foliage of the Northeast. In two weeks, during Columbus Day weekend, this brilliant season would reach its colorful height and I'd be heading back from the Atlantic coast.

SEPTEMBER IN VERMONT

The home of Dick and Mina Turner in Plymouth, Vermont, is one of those bubbly, lively, revolving-door households where you cannot help but be devoured by family. It's brothers and sisters, grandchildren, neighbors, nieces and nephews, more friends and food, dogs, and talk, and everything that reminds us of how fortunate we are. Kelly Sieman, from New Jersey, is a part of this delicious family salad. She's my East Coast connection, making arrangements for stops, helping with routing, and making sure my boxes arrive and are sent on for pick up later.

Fall riding through New England.

I couldn't have gotten this far without her help! We met nearly twenty years ago when, as a young woman, she worked at the Glacier Institute in Glacier National Park, Montana. She noticed my ad in the paper offering riding lessons. After two or three lessons, I said, "Listen, why don't you just come out and ride, you don't need lessons." We've been friends ever since. I spent a week with Kelly and the Turners preparing for my Atlantic Ocean landing. I'll leave most of my gear here to travel light, spend a few days at the ocean, and return through this incredibly beautiful and hospitable country of Vermont.

OCTOBER IN MAINE

The seacoast village of Wells, Maine, turned out to be an excellent choice for my Atlantic landing. With Kelly's help, we chose quiet roads leading into town. New England drivers were very courteous, and I did my best to stay off the road, riding on the shoulder. Still, I was another distraction to the people driving along with other thoughts on their minds, simply trying to get to their destinations. As always, mixing horses and traffic was risky—for the drivers and for me.

I am deeply grateful for the help the Wells Chamber of Commerce extended to me. Eleanor Vadenais, executive director, helped arrange newspaper interviews, camping spaces, and a visit to the nearby Rachel Carson National Wildlife Refuge.

I rode into Wells feeling lost, dirty, and tired. The main street of town buzzed with activity. Many people stopped me with questions: "Who are you? Where'd ya come from? Where did you get that hat?" I rode one mile north before realizing it was the wrong direction. I turned the horses around and crossed U.S. Highway 1, a four-lane highway. I did not see the monster ahead. Essie, who I was riding, suddenly shied into traffic. We were nearly hit. Essie froze. Her four hoofs were planted wide in a refusal to move as she stared at a green dinosaur standing innocently in front of a storefront. Cars swerved around the horses and horns honked, but thankfully no one was hurt.

"Never ride into a town during late afternoon, Bernice," I said, reprimanding myself for the mistake I made by surrounding us with rush hour traffic. "Easy, easy, you're okay," I said, coaxing Essie back in line. I brag about my horse's road skills being as good as any police horse, but I can only ask so much of them and I had pushed too far. Even my own nerves were wearing thin, and fatigue had dulled my attentiveness. I maneuvered down the street mindful of what just almost happened and looking for hope. I looked ahead and saw a person, off from the sidewalk, jumping up and down waving arms, nearly obstructing traffic. Good, I thought. A local official has come out to greet me. Hope rose from the ashes. But as I drew closer I could see it was not a stranger, it was my good friends Cathy Schloeder and her husband Mike from Fortine, Montana. My goodness, how could this be? I knew they were in Maine vacationing, but I had no idea just where. We had talked about meeting up in Maine, but that we actually connected was nothing short of miraculous. Best of all, it was on this day of all days when I most needed a hearty, familiar hug from back home. I screamed, picked up a trot, and jumped down from the saddle before Essie came to a stop outside Moore's Hardware. I hugged them both again and again. Trail Magic! This was Trail Magic.

Mike and Cathy carried with them a carload of encouragement, smiles, love, and hugs. They represented friends in Montana who right now did not seem as far away. I so needed those hugs and smiles and familiar voices that day. Cathy was so sure she would find me, she had purchased a lobster roll for me. It had been a trying day and then suddenly all became bright and cheerful.

Moore's Hardware, whose place of business the three of us had so rudely interrupted on a sunny Thursday afternoon, offered a place where I could camp for the night. A full moon presented itself as I ate the food Cathy and Mike left in my saddle bags. I had a perfect, quiet campsite. What a wonderful chaotic day, I thought. Did I really make it all the way from the northwest corner of Montana to the Atlantic Ocean? And who greets me when I arrive? Friends from back home. Now that really is Trail Magic!

Mike and Cathy had other obligations, but our visit, although not long, certainly filled my empty tank. Before they drove away, Eleanor from the Wells Chamber of Commerce arrived and worked her magic. Not only had she made arrangements for me to visit the Rachel Carson National Wildlife Refuge, she had also secured my next three nights nearby at Riverhurst Farm, a noted equine boarding facility close to the Atlantic Ocean.

Essie and Spirit enjoyed a much-deserved rest at Riverhurst Farm. Pete and Elaine King have managed the facility since 1998. It's old-world quaint and totally charming. The barn is over 200 years old; it provided a safe haven for soldiers during the War of 1812. It was once a dairy barn but now provides motel space for equine guests. The farm has a soft, gentle feel to it. A short distance away is the Rachael Carson National Wildlife Refuge, and a quarter mile from Riverhurst Farm is Parson's Beach on the Atlantic Ocean. The ocean's constant roll lulls us to sleep at night. It's a sound this inlander rarely hears. The rhythmic roll and splash of the ocean water is our reward for so many miles and

Essie Pearl and Montana Spirit enjoy an evening at Parson's Beach, Maine.

months of arduous travel and near sleepless nights. It's a gentle, soothing voice that says, "I am the Atlantic. You made it!"

When I began this journey in April, my goal was the Atlantic Ocean, but I had not conceived of a satisfying point on the East Coast where I could land. Landing at the Rachel Carson National Wildlife Refuge had been Kelly Sieman's suggestion. It was the perfect place, and how fitting to pay homage to yet another woman who also wrote a new chapter into our history: Rachel Carson. I found a fitting description of Carson's legacy in the refuge archives.

Facing ridicule and formidable opposition, as did other women, she persevered and today her legacy lives on. To her as to all those women who significantly altered the course of history by demanding liberty and equality, she was an individual committed to changing society's attitude toward the environment. Rachel Louise Carson was an American marine biologist and conservationist whose book *Silent Spring* and other writings are credited with advancing the global environmental movement. Rachel Carson, writer, scientist, and ecologist, grew up simply in the

Dear Bernice,

Often times those who strive to enrich the lives of others never take the time to realize the tremendous long-term positive impact they create. Your journey will serve as a tiny seed, the true results of which may not be fully known for many years. Perhaps a child you meet will one day tell her grandchild about the woman on a horse who changed her life via a magical journey? Thus the Guild's support mirrors your own actions and acknowledges the purity of your mission. Likewise, the Long Riders flag represents all of us who protect, preserve and promote the ancient art of equestrian travel. Protect its message. Carry it with pride and ride well Long Rider.

CuChullaine
September 1st, 2014
Toucy, France

rural river town of Springdale, Pennsylvania. Her mother bequeathed to her a lifelong love of nature and the living world that Rachel expressed first as a writer and later as a student of marine biology. She was hired by the U.S. Bureau of Fisheries to write radio scripts during the Depression of the 1930s. She supplemented her income writing feature articles on natural history for the *Baltimore Sun*. She began a fifteen-year career in the federal service as a scientist and editor in 1936 and rose to become editor-in-chief of all publications for the U.S. Fish and Wildlife Service. Disturbed by the profligate use of synthetic chemical pesticides after World War II, Carson reluctantly changed her focus in order to warn the public about the long-term effects of misusing pesticides (specifically DDT). In *Silent Spring* (1962) she challenged the practices of agricultural scientists and the government, and called for a change in the way humankind viewed the natural world.

Eleanor Vadenais accompanied me on a quiet, leisurely stroll along a shaded trail through the refuge. The horses remained behind, saddles

At Rachel Carson National Wildlife Refuge with the Long Riders' Guild flag.

and packs off their strong backs, attended by a group of workers from the wildlife refuge.

CARRYING THE LONG RIDERS' GUILD FLAG

The Long Riders' Guild had granted me the honor of carrying the Guild's flag on my 8,000-mile journey. We displayed the flag at the Rachel Carson National Wildlife Refuge.

SHORES OF THE ATLANTIC

For months I had felt like a rolling stone slowly turning, making my way to the sea.

Now, here I was on the shores of the Atlantic. I was unable to proceed any farther east, at least not carried onward by sturdy equine legs. But my imagination continued outward beyond where hoofprints cannot be made, pulled by receding waves where my thoughts could swim in the uninterrupted space of ocean waters. "Remember this," I said to myself as I rode along Parson's Beach. "Savor this; taste the salt air, see the brightness in your brave mares' eyes, hear the seagulls, the slapping waves, and children's voices." Riding bareback, I felt Essie's warm sweat against my legs. My horses danced across soft sand with the wind blowing through their long black-and-white manes. I knew I would never forget these partners, teachers, comrades—Essie and Spirit—who taught me by example, resurrecting me on days with the belief that, yes, we would make it. Each day their strength and willpower, innate and natural as breathing, carried me over obstacles I could not have managed alone, silencing my voice of doubt. I was humbled by their trust in me.

Neither one of these horses had ever heard ocean sounds before. How must the roar of the ocean and the bigness of it all have felt to them? I was moved to tears at the sight of the ocean, at the sight of my two Fjord mares that so bravely walked and endured the miles with me and were now stepping into foamy Atlantic Ocean waves that raced over their sturdy black hoofs. Many of the people I meet ask about my horses' health and well-being. As they should. The horses are the true champions of these rides.

Unlike the flat horizon line of North Dakota or Nebraska, on the beach my eyes gazed across an unobstructed horizon that I cannot travel to with my horses. It's like this in life. If you intend on moving forward, you can only go so far until you're forced to leave something behind, shed nonessentials, reconfigure, or change directions or you just go no further. Wendell Berry once said, ". . . when you no longer know which way to go, you have begun your real journey. If the mind is not baffled it's not employed. The impeded stream is the one that sings."

I wished Claire Dog were here with me. Her four white paws would have run and pranced circles around us. She would have barked and grabbed at waves and stolen the show. I thought about her every day.

Deep in my heart I wanted to share my joy of reaching the Atlantic Ocean with my mother, a woman who loved traveling and appreciated undaunted female determination. And I also thought about those who

A rare respite.

shoved doubt down my throat, saying, "You'll never make it, you're nuts." But then I looked back at the enormous strides I'd made and the hundreds of generous, supportive hands, encouraging voices, and sincere words that helped bring me and my horses to this point.

WESTWARD HO TO THE PACIFIC OCEAN

We camped at Riverhurst Farm for three days, visiting with dozens of people, taking mini tours of the surrounding towns, and doing interviews. We left in the morning, headed back to New York. The plan was to winter in Fort Edward and then proceed to the Pacific Ocean.

On our return trip west, our eyes would be shaded from the morning sun as we faced the westward sky each morning. I realized it would seem odd to have the sun resting on my left shoulder as I rode west throughout the day and not on my right shoulder as it has been for the seven months during the trip eastward. The return trip felt daunting when I scanned my maps, plotting the next move. The word "impossible" blots my mind when I think of the miles we just traveled and the miles ahead of us to reach the Pacific Ocean. "Bernice, you rode here, but can you make it to the Pacific Ocean and back home?" I asked myself. Of course we made it back west to the shores of the Pacific Ocean, arriving at Bay View Park north of Seattle in Washington state on June 17, 2016, and then back home to Montana.

I think of the words at the end of Thomas Wolfe's book, *You Can't Go Home Again*: "To lose the earth you know for greater knowing; to lose the life you have, for greater life; to leave the friends you loved, for greater loving; to find a land more kind than home, more large than earth." Maybe this answers why I long ride—for the search and the rendering of "greater knowing." Maybe it's just that simple!

After I completed these 8,000 miles through Montana, North Dakota, Minnesota, Wisconsin, the Northeast, and back again, I learned that I had ridden squarely through the lives of my grandmother, her sisters, many suffragettes, and other lady long riders. Their stories are worthy of a book of their own. To honor them and tell their stories, I plan to write another book, with the working title, *Mothers, Aunts, Suffragettes, and Lady Long Riders.*

CHAPTER TWENTY

FAREWELL OLD FRIENDS

ESSIE PEARL

March 2001 – September 17, 2016

In October 2016, *This American Life* presented a story about a Japanese phone booth that a man placed on a windy hill overlooking the beach near the town of Otsuchi. It was an old-fashioned folding door kind and had a non-working rotary phone. The phone was there so people could call their beloved and dearly missed family members and friends that were taken by the 2011 tsunami. I listened to the radio program as Japanese widows and widowers came, called their beloveds, and left. It was very moving. They had found a way of staying connected to the deceased, a place to talk and shed tears. Such a good idea—call them up and talk. If I could do that, I would call Essie and tell her, "I am so sorry Essie, I could not save you. I am so, so sorry. It will take a long time before I stop calling your name to come, I miss you terribly."

Shortly after we returned from the seventh long ride, Essie became lame. Somewhere in our travels, Essie Pearl had contracted the parasite that causes equine protozoal myeloencephalitis (EPM). At first, the veterinarian diagnosed that she was just lame and probably would recover, and then Essie lost control of her body. A blood test revealed she had advanced EPM. We had to mercifully put her down. The disease is caused by a parasite hosted by barn cats and wildlife such as opossums and believed to be passed on to horses through feed contaminated

Essie Pearl.

with feces. It causes generalized weakness and lameness and alters brain function, eventually causing death. EPM is treatable if caught early enough, but even with treatment irreversible damage to the nervous system is possible. Recently, new drugs show promise in treating the disease, but such medicines weren't available for Essie.

Traveling with her always felt like traveling with something ancient. She was different, her look, her gaze, her attitude like a wise old impatient woman. She reminded me of pictures of the cave drawings in France. She was my first pack horse and my first Norwegian Fjord. We traveled 21,000 miles together. It also takes a lot of miles and years developing the skills Essie had acquired. Damn she was good. Whether pack or lead horse, she had it down. She knew what to do. She preferred being in front next to me. Her favorite traveling position had Claire leading the troupe, me at her left side walking with her, and Spirit, packing, at her right rear. When we were lined up the way she liked, there came over her a look of pure contentment. Everything was just as it should be; her ears were forward, alert, interested. We were doing it right!

Her picket and rope skills were astonishing, and her traffic skills were second to none. Nine years we traveled together. She was easy to pad and pack, and she treated her most precious cargo, Claire Dog, with great care. She was an "easy keeper." But my, oh my, she could be cantankerous, downright vicious, when it came to food. She had her own ways of doing things and made it known that they were to be done that way. Essie swam in both the Pacific and Atlantic Oceans and three of the Great Lakes and crossed Death Valley (Mojave Desert) and the Sonoran Desert. She made two Canadian trips and traveled from Texas to Calgary. She crossed the United States twice, the Rocky Mountains nine times, and the Cascade Range four. I like to think it beat a long, slow, uninteresting life as a pasture potato.

Essie Pearl, you beautiful girl! To me you shall remain a champion, the greatest long-riding horse that ever lived! "Thank you" will never be enough.

Claire and Essie Pearl.

CLAIRE DOG

Winter 1999 – Summer 2015

Those of us who have loved dogs can share lengthy heartfelt stories about that one exceptional dog whose life with us was like no other. For me, that would be Claire. Add to that the fact that we rode or walked more than 20,000 adventurous miles together. She loved people. She loved their touch and she was a sensational hit wherever we went. I depended on her for protection, leadership, warnings, and companionship, which she gave unconditionally. She had an exceptionally interesting life and died peacefully in the summer of 2015 at the age of sixteen.

In 2011 when Claire was twelve years old, with a little help from me she wrote her memoirs for *Fido Magazine*. Excerpts from some of her dog tales are retold here.

I am asked many times by my friends, who think I am somewhat of a celebrity, what it's like to be a long-riding dog? They want to know how

Claire Dog.

I ever made it across Death Valley and what I did when we crossed the Rocky Mountains and saw the grizzly bear. They want to know how I saved Bernice from the wild black stallion. My friends get all excited when I tell them how I growled, showed my teeth, raised the hair on my back straight up, and barked out my fiercest guard dog bark, warning, "Unexpected intruder drawing near!" They think I'm the luckiest dog in the world and so do I, but I say, "Well yes, but it is not all fun and excitement. I have a great deal of responsibility. I must always be on guard. I can never chase after cats or wild animals. I must always be cordial with other dogs even if I don't like them. I get tired and sometimes I get hungry. So you see it is not easy to be a long-riding dog," I insist.

As a younger dog, I walked with Bernice most of the day. But at the mature age of twelve I ride most of the twenty or so miles we travel in a day. The doggie box has a flat platform in each corner where I stand balanced and comfortable. The center is thickly padded and offers a soft bed I sink into when we stop. We stop often as people whom Bernice refers to as "the curious and interested" turn their heads with long stares until they stop inquiring of this odd and unique sight . . . which is me! I can no longer jump effortlessly onto the back of Essie Pearl as I once could, but Bernice and I have a routine that goes like this: I trot around on the right side of Essie where Bernice stands on my left and says, "Okay, are you ready?" I prepare to launch myself upward, and as I begin leaping, Bernice quickly wraps her hands and arms under my belly and behind and lifts me with one smooth swoop into the box. I can also rise to the occasion by standing on a boulder or a picnic table. Essie Pearl will considerately lend a hoof by carefully edging herself within a few inches of the table, allowing me to easily hop on. Essie Pearl waits until I have turned around and settled in before she starts walking. After all, we are good friends and that's what friends do. When we stop for a rest in the afternoon, I'm expected to wait patiently for Bernice to lift me down. She insists the impact of jumping down is much too hard on my aging legs and shoulders.

For an afternoon snack, Bernice reaches for the maroon saddle packs and pulls out crackers or nuts or seeds or an apple she cuts into four pieces and passes around to our impatient mouths. Any little pieces the horses drop I quick as a click snatch up. When late afternoon shadows grow long, Bernice begins searching for a campsite where we'll spend the night. Once a campfire is going, the tent is set up and the campsite arranged; once the horses are brushed, rubbed down, and have their hungry muzzles buried in longstem meadow grasses, then Bernice turns to me with a brush. Whether I like it or not, each night I have my neck and hips massaged, my legs stretched, and my paw pads rubbed down with zinc-oxide ointment. Sometimes I take an aspirin. Bernice and I share a meal of rice and beans, vegetables, and maybe eggs or cheese or raw meat for me. When I'm finished, I roll over and over in the cool grass feeling full and content.

As the cold blanket of night spreads over our "home," the horses are brought near us. Bernice and I wrap ourselves together in the sleeping bag. I can hear the horses outside lie down next to our tent. In the distance, coyotes raise their voices in evening song. The smell of lingering campfire smoke fades into the calm of the night. I rest, dreamy with thoughts; I am the luckiest dog in the world.

I truly believe that Claire loved her life as a long-riding dog. She seemed happiest when we were on the trail. I also believe that I am the luckiest woman in the world to have had Claire Dog as my companion. There is no adequate way to convey how much I loved her and how much I know she loved me and how much I miss her. She was an exceptional dog living an exceptional life. Farewell old friend, until we meet again!

When you sink into depression and uncertainty
it is to open your eyes to your humanity,
and to remind you of how far you have to go.
—CAROL SWIEDLER, *LETTERS FROM THE COSMOS*

"Reentry," as I refer to it, stands out as the hardest part of my journeys. Reentry comes at the end of a ride when I fold up my tent, put the horses in my corral, and return to the busy and social existence that most people would consider normal living. I have felt stifled every time I've reached this part. It was even more apparent when I completed my 8,000-mile epic journey in 2016. I suppose it is understandable. I moved from horse to car, from four miles an hour to seventy miles an hour, from uncertainty to security. In contrast, when I'm *out there*, the edge is sharper, the attentiveness is higher, and there's no time to be dull, no time to dismiss your surroundings. The immediacy of life is thrust down your throat, and if you lack the discipline to push back the instinct of flight, you'll choke on your own fears. It's the exposure to nature and the submersion in living I love, and I dislike ending these adventures even for short periods. I don't know what to do with myself; I seem to be overwhelmed by "stuff" when I stop.

"I sure wish I could do what you are doing," or "I'd give anything to just get on a horse, ride off, and forget about it all like you're doing." Those words have been spoken to me literally hundreds of times. "Do you really?" I ask them. "Would you really like giving up that family of yours, the comfort of friends you say hello to everyday, that income or that home and community holding you together?" It is easy to glamorize the adventure and the glorious look of being care-free, but it comes with a price. I know!

When I completed my seventh long ride, the agonizing loss of Essie Pearl and Claire Dog was compounded by a devastating betrayal by a person I had once considered a sincere and trusted friend. I also had the feeling I was no longer a valued part of my community. All of this plunged me into a deep personal crisis. I had been traveling down a path, sure of its outcome and confident I was indeed heading in the right direction for my life and for who I was. Then suddenly it all seemed to fail me. My confidence and my will to go on disappeared overnight. I felt I was standing on a precipice looking for a way around the fragmented scene I came home to. It felt like my bones had all been broken, that I had lost more than my beloved horse and dog and trusted friend. Weeks of solitary, sobering days left me wondering if I would ever know happiness again.

On my second ride (in 2006-2007), a journalist interviewed me for a magazine story. She asked me how long I thought I would long ride. I flippantly replied, "I would ride until it had changed me completely." What I did not realize then was the price I would pay for my passion for long riding. I had been gone long enough and changed enough that I lost my place in my community; I no longer fit. Thomas Wolfe was right. It's quite natural and it's true: if you go away long enough, home will change as surely as you will and *you can't go home again*. Just as I had changed, the community I had ridden from twelve years earlier had also changed in my absence. I tried renewing a worn-out view that no longer existed, and it hurt deeply that it was lost to me.

And so I ask again, what matters? What makes me feel alive, what makes me feel like me? I look around at others and for some it is children, grandchildren, a glorious garden, painting, weaving, a home, a lover, writing. It's something that sparks a flame within and makes the heart beat stronger and eyes shine brighter. "How will I go back to a normal life," I asked myself on the first ride, and here I am asking it again when I returned from my seventh ride. But now I know the answer.

I know I'll never be satisfied to live a neat, safe, ordinary life. I seem to now fit well in my solitary life, but I know too that a solitary life

Community interaction.

without a sense of belonging, without a sense of community, is barren and lonely. Then it dawned on me—like the old cliché—a bolt out of the blue. I was not without community and I needn't feel lonely. I am a humble and very grateful part of a great community of people spread far and wide—the community of people that I have met long riding. I smile, thinking of the faces and the communities woven into my rides. I have ridden home with saddle bags loaded heavy with friendships all over the country. These friendships came easily with a smile, something said or done or some out-of-the-blue connection, and we would agree, "Seems like I've known you all my life." Our far and wide community and friendships continue "keeping in touch" today.

LIFE ON THE TRAIL

It's one thing going out for a short three-month, 1,000-mile ride. It's another thing going out for twelve consecutive years and 28,000 miles. All

PHOTO COURTESY OF LYDIA HOPPER.

those miles trailing behind me continue rushing over me, surrounding me with stacks of journals lying about like old horseshoes. I stare at the piles of maps, torn and faded, and photos, newspapers, magazines, and memorabilia, trinkets, good luck charms, pocket-size New Testament books, a silver belt buckle. What will I do with it all? But then I say that about the flood of memories in my head . . . what will I do with them? Wrap them around my heart, that's what!

We live for the most part in our minds, planning, remembering, hoping for, and wishing for this or that. We recoil from fear and vulnerability, and we cling instead to certainty. When asked, "But aren't you afraid?" I think of something legendary mountain climber Reinhold Messner said when he spoke of meeting mountains, "I expose myself, I accept the natural powers as the rulers of my world. . . . There's no more human rulers if I'm out there. . . . I think that courage is only the other half of fear. . . . If I am well prepared and if I'm living a long time in my visions . . . climbing . . . there is no danger anymore the danger is gone but the concentration is absolute. . . . . There's just pure nature in myself and the nature outside."

In other words, you stop thinking and become in the present. Maybe that's the mistake I make in reentry—I start thinking again and relatively unimportant issues bark at me like mad dogs.

Yesterday I received an email from a young man asking for information regarding his future long-riding plans. I receive similar letters often. But this one had my head shaking. No previous horse experience, not much money, but plenty of get up and go. He already had a horse and was looking for another. I replied, "Please do not repeat the same mistakes I did. Do not put others at risk by being unprepared. Do not set forth without extensive knowledge of equine health and vet care. Know each step of your well-researched route and do your first ride in relatively empty, open country where the mistakes you are bound to make will resolve themselves without endangering others! You'll know your horse is ready for a long ride when it stands for a semitruck racing by at seventy miles per hour and close enough that you can reach out and touch it. Long riding is not a pleasure ride. There is much to fear and yet no place for fear. Fill your days of long riding with skill, attentiveness, and caution. Slow down, be in the present of every minute, and be grateful at the end of each day."

Today the difficulty of equestrian travel is not nearly as great as it was during the first years and miles I've written about in this book. It seems I shed a lot of lonely tears back then. I take enormous pride in the care and comfort I now offer my traveling companions. Situations requiring special effort have repeated themselves enough times that I no longer worry with preconceived notions about what lies around the next corner. I no longer find myself wondering why I long ride. I know! Most importantly, I no longer take for granted this country I live in and the freedoms we enjoy. As I said during that *Today Show* interview with Bob Dotson, there's something thrilling about turning around in the saddle and looking back at a ribbon of highway. I wish that you could just come and see what I see. You'd think differently about our country. We really are good, generous people, people who can and do pull together for one another.

In the winter of 2006, as I prepared for my second ride, I heard the following read on a television documentary about the iconic ballet dancer Marta Becket who founded the Amargosa Theater in Death Valley, which I visited in 2007 on my second ride. The words held my attention then and still do today.

> *It begins with a distant notion, a plaintive whisper of the heart. It comes in the flash of an epiphany or through a deeper unexplained longing that it has always been present. It is the recognition of conception, the understanding that a new idea has been born. It is embracing the dream-scape that is imagination and having the courage to go there.*
>
> *For those who accept a life of self-exploration through willful acts of creation, the journey offers the ecstasy of all that is possible, along with the agony of unattainable perfection.*
>
> *It is a solitary road into the unknown self and offers no destination but a journey. But for those who follow, it does lead somewhere and such a life will never be uninteresting.*

Happy trails,
Bernice Ende

P.S. The first page of my website states: "There are many reasons why I ride, here are four: to encourage female leadership, to discover, learn, and grow. If something sounds good to you, don't let your fears stop you from latching on to that compelling notion of going and doing. Dust your heart off and hitch your wagon to something greater than you. I do hope with all my heart that my rides will impart encouragement to those longing to reach beyond their fears for more.

In 2017, Harvard archivist Heather Mumford invited Bernice to give a speech about her great aunt, Linda James Benitt, who was the first woman to graduate from the Harvard T.H. Chan School (then the Harvard-MIT School for Health Officers). In response to a notice of the Harvard invitation, CuChullaine O'Reilly of the International Long Riders' Guild sent a letter to Harvard. The following is an excerpt of that letter.

Dear Heather,

We would request that someone provide info and images after Bernice has concluded her speech at your facility, whereupon we shall publish a summary on the LRG (Long Riders' Guild) News page.

Meanwhile, I believe it may help those at Harvard to understand the equestrian side of this unique story and situation. With members in forty-six countries, every major equestrian explorer alive today belongs to the Guild, including Hadji Shamsuddin of Afghanistan, who recently rode a thousand miles through that war zone, Jean-Louis Gouraud of France, who rode 3,000 miles from Paris to Moscow, Tim Cope of Australia, who rode 6,000 miles from Mongolia to Hungary, Claudia Gottet of Switzerland, who rode 8,000 miles from Arabia to the Alps, Adnan Azzam of Syria, who rode 10,000 miles from Madrid to Mecca, and Vladimir Fissenko of Russia, who rode 19,000 miles from Patagonia to Alaska.

Though we are used to dealing with remarkable individuals at the Guild, Bernice achieved a special place in Long Rider history. Bernice Ende's singular journey into equestrian travel history began in 2005 when she rode from her home to New Mexico. In the subsequent years she made numerous other trips across

Linda James Benitt at the ranch in Blackleaf, Montana, 1915.

the United States and Canada, which resulted in her riding more than 25,000 miles.

Yet, equestrian travel is not a competitive event. Counting miles is akin to watching the odometer spin endlessly on an automobile's dashboard. What set Bernice apart was that she carried a message of historical significance, one that had been passed down by female champions from the past.

In 2016, Bernice became the first person to ride "ocean to ocean" across the United States in both directions on the same journey. Bernice's journey is listed in the Guild's Hall of Records.

Not only was this journey of geographic importance, Bernice used the opportunity to inform the public about the vital role played in society and politics by suffragettes and Lady Long Riders such as herself.

Because this journey was deemed to be so unique, Bernice is among the few equestrian explorers to have carried the Guild flag on an international expedition.

When the journey began, the story jumped the Atlantic and was shared in *Randonee a Cheval*, France's premier equestrian magazine.

Thus, the inspirational example set by Linda James Benitt has spread beyond Harvard and is now urging others to follow their dreams, like Bernice did. And that is a concept which is not restricted to one age, campus, or country.

BIBLIOGRAPHY

Beker, Ana. *The Courage to Ride: One Woman's 17,000-Mile Mounted Odyssey from Argentina to Canada.* The Long Riders' Guild Press, 2001.

Bridger, William. *The Way of Transition.* Da Capo Press. Boston, 2000.

Christiansen, Rubert, Sephanie Vonrerscits, Beth Brophy. *The Complete Book of Aunts.* Hachette Book Group, France, 2007.

Hendrickson, Paul. "Savoring Pie Town." *Smithsonian Magazine.* New York, February, 2005.

O'Reilly, CuChullaine., Colonel John Blashford-Snell. *The Horse Travel Handbook.* The Long Riders' Guild Press, 2015.

O'Reilly, CuChullaine. *The Encyclopedia of Equestrian Exploration. Vols. 1, 2, 3.* The Long Riders' Guild Press, 2016.

Tschiffely, Aimé. *Tschiffley's Ride: 10,000 Miles in the Saddle.* Skyhorse Publishing, New York, 2013.

Weiser, Kathy. "Legends of Kansas, Nicodemus-A Black Pioneer Town." www.legendsofamerica.com/ks-nicodemus. June 2015.

Wilkins, Mesannie. *Last of the Saddle Tramps: One Woman's Seven Thousand Mile Equestrian Odyssey.* The Long Riders' Guild Press, 2001.

ABOUT THE AUTHOR

PHOTO COURTESY OF LYDIA HOPPER.

As a fearless young girl on her parents' Minnesota dairy farm, Bernice Ende loved to gallop bareback through pastures and cornfields. Today, at a slightly more sedate pace, she has become Lady Long Rider, with more than 29,000 miles in the saddle, criss-crossing the United States, Canada, and in 2018, southern France.

Readers can follow Bernice's travels through her blog at www.endeofthetrail.com. Between long rides, Bernice makes her home in Trego, Montana.